1974

power,
law,
and
society

power, law,

a study of
the will to power
and
the will to law

edgar bodenheimer

and society

crane, russak & company, inc.

new york

Published in the United States by
Crane, Russak & Company Inc.
52 Vanderbilt Avenue, New York, N.Y. 10017

Library of Congress Catalogue Card Number 73-81049

International Standard Book Number 0-8448-0215-8

Printed in the United States of America

PREFACE

In periods of great turmoil, human political and social institutions are subjected to severe stresses and strains. Although these institutions may have worked with a reasonable degree of smoothness and adequacy in normal times, their operation is apt to become disturbed by the effects of a prolonged crisis situation. This state of affairs may easily produce, in the minds of observers of the social scene, a somewhat distorted picture of the functions served by such institutions.

In many countries of the contemporary world, including the United States, it is particularly the institution of law which has become the target of sceptical attitudes and corrosive doubts.[1] The suspicion is expressed today by many persons critical of their society, especially among the young, that the law is a creation of powerful groups in the social order to promote their special interests and self-serving aims to the detriment of broader societal concerns.[2] Is is this phenomenon of widespread antipathy to the law which has provided the motivation for the preparation of the present study. That there is much reason for dissatisfaction with many important facets of contemporary law and legal processes, few will deny. The extent and tone of some of the present-day criticism raises the more fundamental question, however, whether there is justification for carrying this dissatisfaction to the point of a full-scale assault on the institution as such.

In exploring this subject, considerable use will be made of an approach which has been introduced by a movement in modern thought known as "philosophical anthropology". Among the matters which are of particular interest to this branch of research is the discovery of ties between man's natural equipment and his cultural works. Philosophical anthropology, among other things, seeks to investigate and clarify the relations which exist between the biological and psychological components of man's nature

---

[1] See *infra* Sec. 1.

[2] For an expression of this viewpoint which is representative of the reactions of certain groups among law students today see Zona Sage, *Hastings Law News*, Vol. II, No. 10, p. 8 (1971). Broadly-phrased anti-law statements by various authors (which must be distinguished from specific criticisms of defects and abuses of contemporary legal processes) are found in *Law Against the People*, ed. R. Lefcourt (New York, 1971), pp. 3, 68, 79-80, 181-182, 337-338, 345-346.

and the accomplishments of his mind which give meaning and content to civilization. Among the cultural products of man must be counted the law. Philosophical anthropology directs its attention to the connections that can be discerned between the institution of law on the one hand and the common traits and basic needs of human beings on the other.[3]

The general orientation of philosophical anthropology is a holistic one. It conceives of its subject matter in a broad sense as "the science of man", and the scope of its inquiry encompasses all layers of the human personality. Its method of investigation is an interdisciplinary one, in that it seeks to correlate and integrate the findings of the specialized sciences in an effort to gain a picture of man as a whole.

Life-long teaching and research in the border areas between law and related disciplines gives me the courage which a lawyer needs in undertaking side trips into psychology, sociology, and philosophy. The excursion into theoretical physics found in the third section was subjected to thorough surveillance by my son, Peter H. Bodenheimer, Associate Professor of Astrophysics at the University of California, Santa Cruz. I am also greatly indebted to Professor Max Kaser, a leading authority on Roman Law at the University of Hamburg, Germahy, who kindly consented to review the section entitled "The Strong and the Weak in Ancient Roman Law", and who recommended a number of revisions designed to bring the presentation into conformity with the latest state of historical research. My special gratitude goes to my wife, Brigitte M. Bodenheimer, who read the manuscript carefully and made many valuable suggestions for changes and additions.

I acknowledge with sincere thanks a grant from the National Endowment for the Humanities which supported the preparation of this work.

EDGAR BODENHEIMER
Davis, California   Professor of Law
April, 1972   University of California, Davis

---

[3] For a detailed discussion of the objectives of philosophical anthropology and its uses for jurisprudential inquiry see Edgar Bodenheimer, "Philosophical Anthropology and the Law," 59 *California Law Review* 653 (1971). The significance of philosophical anthropology for an analysis of the natural-law problem is successfully demonstrated by Alfred Verdross, *Statisches und Dynamisches Naturrecht* (Freiburg, 1971), pp. 73-91.

CONTENTS

CHAPTER I

THE ANTHROPOLOGICAL ROOTS OF THE LAW

SECTION 1
The Spectre of Legal Nihilism

A phenomenon has made its appearance throughout the reaches of Western civilization which is beginning to penetrate into the consciousness of the people: the spectre of legal nihilism. The outstanding characteristic of this phenomenon is an erosion of the belief in law as a beneficial institution of societal organization. There are many today, especially in the rising generation that will shape the future of this planet, who view the norms and restraints of the law as undue fetters upon human self-realization. Such discontent with legal limit-setting is sometimes fed by a deep-seated conviction that no group in society has any legitimate authority to make binding rules for any other group of human beings.[1]

For many centuries, law was looked upon in Western civilization as a basic requirement of human survival and coexistence. Mankind has witnessed the organization of clans, of tribes, of city states, and of nations as far back as human history is known. All of these social units developed systems of rules and regulations as bulwarks against fratricidal force and untamed greed for the spoils of this earth. While there have been tumultuous periods in human history when (for good reasons or not) naked power and violence have burst the bounds of legal ordering, mankind has always found it necessary to rebuild its walls, in different shape perhaps, but impelled by the necessity of giving structure and form to the social edifice.

Today we have many prophets. Some of them, impatient with the wisdom of the ages, are intent upon proclaiming something new and unheard of for the sake of sheer novelty. We need not stop to consider them. But there is one man, the great philosopher Friedrich Nietzsche, who appeared on the scene like a meteor, tore into long-held beliefs, shook up

---

[1] References to legal nihilism are found in René Marcic, *Rechtsphilosophie: Eine Einführung* (Freiburg, 1969), pp. 16-17, 24-26, 83. For a preliminary survey see Edgar Bodenheimer, "Antilaw Sentiments and Their Philosophical Foundations," 46 *Indiana Law Journal* 175 (1971). Sceptical views towards law not touched upon in this introductory section are discussed *infra* Sec. 15.

our consciousness, and attempted to transform all of our fundamental values with an unequalled power of poetic expression. His powerful voice, which was heard throughout the civilized world, cannot and should not be ignored.

Nietzsche relentlessly exposed much that was shallow, hypocritical, and spurious in Western culture.[2] He often analyzed the conscious and unconscious motivations of men with great psychological trenchancy. But he was also the prophet of nihilism, a state of consciousness whose imminent advent he greeted as a sign of human rebirth. What he expected from nihilism, which he called "the uncanniest of all guests",[3] was a devaluation of the highest values cherished in Western civilization and a radical break with the age-old distinction between good and evil.

The transvaluation of values advocated by Nietzsche included the institution of law. Throughout its history, law had been used to impart a relative stability and continuity to the arrangements of life; it had also served the task of curbing the struggle for power among men. Nietzsche's super-dynamic philosophy was opposed to stabilizing structures and limitations on power. He saw the world as a turbulent sea of incessant, chaotic change and human life as a pitiless contest for power. He conceded to law some value as a temporary expedient but denied it a right of existence as a pervasive agency of social control. By promoting security of the conditions of life and furthering equality by checks upon power, the law in his opinion placed undue restraints upon an ever-expanding life-force. He condemned, in particular, any attempt of the law to give protection to the weaker members of society at the expense of the stronger as an unhealthy interference with natural and beneficial facts of reality.[4]

A psychoanalytic interpretation of Nietzsche's work might link his philosophy to his personal history. Nietzsche led an ascetic life which, because of his passionate disposition, may have been responsible for the state of hypertension in which he produced his writings.[5] The chaotic dynamism of his world view might be said to reflect his own state of unabated, feverish restlessness which terminated in mental breakdown. Such causal and psychological explanations do not, however, do justice to a great man's ideas, nor do they diminish the unique product of his superior mind.

---

[2] This aspect of Nietzsche's teaching is elaborated in Walter Kaufmann, *Nietzsche,* 3rd ed. (New York, 1968). Kaufmann's general interpretation of Nietzsche differs in some significant respects from the approach offered in the present book.

[3] Friedrich Nietzsche, *The Will to Power,* ed. W. Kaufmann (New York, 1968), p. 7.

[4] For a detailed discussion of Nietzsche's view of the law see *infra* Secs. 2 and 6.

[5] For a vivid portrait of Nietzsche's personality see Stefan Zweig, *Master Builders,* transl. E. and C. Paul (New York, 1939), pp. 441-530.

Seminal ideas cannot be adequately evaluated by unmasking their hidden springs. In dealing with them, it must be asked whether they are sound in their premises, desirable in their objectives, and acceptable in their pragmatic consequences. This approach is called for with particular urgency in the case of Nietzsche, because the impact of his teaching on the minds of men in the twentieth century has been strong and incisive. There are probably many who have never heard his name but nevertheless have experienced the influence of his philosophy.

Since Nietzsche was a fountainhead of authority supporting the growth of legal nihilism, his thoughts on law and society form a logical starting point for a reassessment of legal ordering in terms of its social benefits. Is it true that law is an inhibiting force which represses healthy human self-assertion and self-realization? Does the institution perhaps have enduring roots in the psyche of human beings? In the light of the historical record, has law performed a primarily beneficial or deleterious role in human affairs? And finally, can we survive without law?

In discussing such questions, the social scientist and legal philosopher faces serious problems of methodology.[6] The difficulty stems from the fact that the causal-descriptive method used in the natural sciences, which is often deemed to be the scientific method *per se,* has only a restricted usefulness in the area of such an inquiry. The law is not a pure fact of physical and psychological reality which can be explained fully by means of an analytic description of cause-effect relations. It is, to a considerable extent, a purposeful creation of the human mind.[7] Comprehension and elucidation of value-oriented aims in legal control are therefore required: the meaning and significance of legal arrangements and legal institutions for human social life must be brought to light. Law needs to be understood not only in terms of its genetic origins but also in reference to its intended function.

---

[6]On the methodological problems involved see Edmund Husserl, *Phänomenologische Psychologie* (The Hague, 1962), pp. 7-11; F. J. J. Buytendijk, "Husserl's Phenomenology and Its Significance for Contemporary Psychology," in *Readings in Existential Phenomenology,* ed. N. Lawrence and D. O'Connor (Englewood Cliffs, N. J., 1967), pp. 354-357; Franz Brentano, *The Origin of Our Knowledge of Right and Wrong,* ed. O. Kraus (New York, 1969), pp. 13-20.

[7]See Mario Lins, *The Philosophy of Law: Its Epistemological Problems* (Rio de Janeiro, 1971), p. 22: "It cannot be denied that law has a contextual basis, formed from the historico-social factors that condition it, but on the other hand we cannot ignore the fact that man is not a wholly passive element. Within limits, he can operate on this basis. Thus law is not preformed, perfect and finished, but flows from human intervention on the real context."

Investigations of this kind should, of course, be supported by a maximum amount of empirical evidence. But more is called for than a mere presentation of facts, data and findings. The factual material requires evaluation in terms of the goal values inherent in social control through law. Of particular relevance in this connection is the historical record of legal evolution. This record is always ambiguous to a certain extent, because we have only partial and sometimes conflicting pictures of what happened at a particular time. It is true for this and other reasons that a synopsis of multicausational developments and complex, tangled interconnections is bound to be an amalgam of objective explication and subjective interpretation.[8] The ultimate test of verification will be the attainment of maximum consensus among observers who have investigated the subject from different angles and through the prism of various disciplines.

The ensuing study will consider the meanings of law in the context of its existential foundations in human nature. For reasons outlined in this introductory section, the starting point of the inquiry will be the philosophy of Friedrich Nietzsche.

SECTION 2
Nietzsche on Power and Law

The "innermost essence of being", the "final fact to which we can penetrate", "the ultimate ground....of all change" is, according to Nietzsche, the will to power.[1] Contrary to a strong contemporary trend towards a

---

[8]On the effects of multiple causation upon research see Abraham H. Maslow, *Motivation and Personality,* 2d ed. (New York, 1970), pp. 299-302; Ludwig von Bertalanffy, *Robots, Men and Minds* (New York, 1967), pp. 57-59.

Note on Nietzsche Citations. Page number citations are followed by references (in parentheses) to the number of the aphorism in which the cited statement appears. These aphorism numbers are (with a few exceptions perhaps) the same in all Nietzsche editions. References to the complete German edition (Musarion edition) indicate that the cited statement cannot be found in the English translations of Nietzsche's works. (Translations of quotations from the German edition are mine.)

[1]Friedrich Nietzsche, *The Will to Power,* ed. W. Kaufmann (New York, 1968) [hereinafter referred to as *The Will to Power*], pp 364, 369 (Nos. 685, 693); Nietzsche, *Gesammelte Werke,* Musarion ed. (Munich, 1920-1929), Vol. XIV, p. 287.

multicausational description of reality, Nietzsche seeks to explain the basic phenomena of this world in terms of one single, all-pervasive principle.[2]

Since "power" is not a self-defining term but, on the contrary, a concept displaying itself in numerous colors, its meaning in the framework of Nietzsche's philosophy must be elucidated.

Power, in Nietzsche's way of thinking, includes brute force and domination but is by no means synonymous with them. It encompasses all fundamental physical processes in nature and human life, all forms of impulse activation and ego-enhancement, sexual conquest, the acquisition of wealth or political influence, the ability of intellectual or charismatic leaders to capture the minds of others by the force of their ideas, the sway which great artists exercise over the emotions of their admirers. The impact of power may thus be experienced in all realms of existence, including the physical, psychological, political, intellectual, aesthetic, and religious spheres.

There are, according to Nietzsche, some manifestations of the will to power which appear in a deceptive garb and therefore have not been recognized by philosophers or psychologists for what they really are. The endeavor of the scientist to know the truth about his subject is at bottom an avenue to the gaining of inner or outer power through "mastery" of his discipline. Even the philosopher who presses forward to discover the ultimate causes of things does this, at least unconsciously, for the love of power. The charitable acts undertaken by the philanthropist, supposedly from motives of generosity, receive their stimulus from self-regarding impulses of ego-gratification. The faithful servant who tries to make himself indispensable to his master strives in this way to gain power over the master by rendering him dependent on his services. To the ascetic saint, self-inflicted torture or persecution by others are ways and means of power-enhancement, even though he may subjectively experience them as sufferings to be borne for the sake of religious truth. Even morality, in Nietzsche's view, is linked to power, since it is a device employed by the weak and poorly-endowed to force their valuations upon the superior

---

[2] Jaspers, although critical of this "dogmatic" element in Nietzsche's metaphysics, believes that the monolithic character of the will-to-power theory is to some extent offset by the Nietzschean doctrine of eternal recurrence. Karl Jaspers, *Nietzsche*, transl. C. F. Wallraf and F. J. Schmitz (Tucson, 1965), pp. 293-295, 308, 316-318. The view that there is no fundamental contrast between these two primary ideas in Nietzsche's philosophy is developed *infra* Sec. 3.

classes and thereby to blunt their domination.[3]

It is not only in the life and activities of the human race that Nietzsche finds the ubiquitous working of the will to power; he believes that *all* organic functions can be traced back to its presence. The trees in the jungle, he says, are fighting a struggle for power. The same observation holds true for the animal world. Even the inorganic world must be described as a collocation of "dynamic quanta" standing in a "relation of tension to all other dynamic quanta".[4] The basic particles of nature, he asserted, are not inert little lumps. They are sources of powerful energy, operating by way of mutual attraction and repulsion and quite apt to annihilate each other. The so-called "laws of nature" are to Nietzsche merely formulas for power phenomena.[5] Thus conceived, the entire world, in its organic and inorganic forms, reveals itself as a playfield of power processes — and "nothing besides".[6]

Since Nietzsche finds the will to power in every appearance of this world, the question arises as to whether this basic concept becomes so broad, so all-encompassing to his scheme of thought that it loses its meaning, its distinctiveness as a tool of philosophical interpretation. Is there any unifying bond which holds together all the innumerable transformations, elaborations, specializations of the primary force in Nietzsche's morphology of power? Surprisingly enough, the answer to this question must be in the affirmative.

In the words of Karl Jaspers, the will to power as conceived by Nietzsche "does not give rise to an eternally static realm of forms but transmutes all forms within the flux of incessant becoming".[7] Nietzsche denies any "being" in the sense of a stable equilibrium. Nothing remains

---

[3] Nietszche, "Beyond Good and Evil", in *Basic Writings of Nietzsche*, ed. W. Kaufmann (New York, 1968) [hereinafter referred to as *Basic Writings*], pp. 205-206 (No. 9); Nietzsche, "The Genealogy of Morals," *id.*, pp. 552-554, 571-572 (3rd essay, Nos. 11, 18); Nietzsche, "Thus Spake Zarathustra", in *Complete Works*, ed. O. Levy (London, 1909-1911) [hereinafter referred to as *Complete Works*], pp. 134, 136; Nietzsche. *The Will to Power*, pp. 156, 216, 290, 314, 407 (Nos. 274, 400, 534, 583, 776); Nietzsche, *Gesammelte Werke*, Vol. XIV, p. 283, Vol. XV, pp. 414-415.

[4] Nietzsche, *The Will to Power*, p. 339 (No. 635).

[5] The phrase "law of nature" is declared by Nietzsche to be a "word of superstition". See Nietzsche, *Gesammelte Werke*, Vol. IX, p. 18, Vol. XVI, p. 57.

[6] Nietzsche, *The Will to Power*, p. 550 (No. 1067). The will to power in nature is analyzed by Nietzsche in a special chapter of the same work. *Id.*, pp. 332-341 (Nos. 618-639). See also *Gesammelte Werke*, Vol. XVI, p. 76.

[7] Jaspers, *supra* n. 2, p. 313.

the same, perseveres in a state of rest, exhibits constancy. Perspectives are shifting all the time, so that it is impossible to find any lasting, immutable truths.[8] Nietzsche compares life with a snake, an animal which rolls forth in endless wriggles and convolutions, which coils up deceptively only to leap forward in the next moment in order to strike. Brief illusory flashes of gold sometimes appear on its belly — a symbol of the transiency which is the fate of everything which exists.[9] The faultily constructed mind of human beings, however, is unwilling to recognize the impermanency of things: it finds satisfaction in thinking of eternal substances, stable structures, and absolute values. Nietzsche suggests that this unwillingness may have its explanation in the very structure of our thinking, which cannot dispense with reifications of passing phenomena, with conceptual constructions of fixed units, with categorizations of "things" exhibiting permanent characteristics.[10]

The perpetual flux produced by the struggle of dynamic quanta in the inorganic or organic world is not, according to our philosopher, directed toward a cosmic goal or divine purpose. It is without any objectively discernible sense and direction. Any meaning that is imparted to the process in the context of human activities is subjectively imposed by individuals or groups. Furthermore, the great spectacle does not roll off to a happy finale. There exists, according to Nietzsche, no Hegelian absolute spirit which leads the world, and especially the human race, to higher and higher forms of evolution. If man should develop into superman, this would be a consequence of intelligent human breeding, planning, and training, and not the realization of a predestined goal of nature. All that is observable in the operations of nature is, according to Nietzsche, a pure *process*. The essential feature of this process is the activation of power through the *overcoming of resistance*.

This notion provides us with a major clue to an understanding of Nietzsche's philosophy. Already in inorganic nature we notice, according to him, the inertial resistance offered by bodies at rest to the impact of force. A similar phenomenon occurs in the clash of units of matter: the stronger unit overwhelms the weaker one which attempts to withstand its assault. "Every specific body strives to become master over all space and to extend

---

[8] Nietzsche, "Human, All-Too-Human", in *Complete Works*, Vol. VI, p. 15 (No. 2).

[9] Nietzsche, *The Will to Power*, p. 310 (No. 577).

[10] *Id.*, pp. 280-281 (Nos. 517-520). See also *Gesammelte Werke*, Vol. XI, p. 163: "That which endures exists only by virtue of our coarse organs of perception."

its force (its will to power): and to thrust back all that resists its extension."[11]

It is in organic life, and especially in the life of human beings, that the principle of "overcoming" reaches its fullest momentum. Nietzsche describes life as a contest for power in which the adversaries are endowed with unequal strength.[12] In this spectacle of perpetual combat, power can manifest and prove itself only through the mastering of resistance. The will to power seeks out that which opposes it: it strives to appropriate, annex, conquer, and overwhelm. "Life is not the adaptation of inner circumstances to outer ones, but will to power which, working from within, incorporates and subdues more and more of that which is 'outside'."[13]

According to Nietzsche, it is from growth of power, from moving beyond one's present self to a stronger, enhanced self, from adding to one's capabilities as well as to one's possessions, that the greatest satisfactions are experienced by human beings. The indispensable condition of such growth is discontent with conditions as they are: dissatisfaction is to Nietzsche the great stimulus to life. It is not the essence of life to seek pleasure and to avoid pain—he listed Bentham in his catalogue of "impossibles". Men live by meeting challenges, he said; what human beings want more than anything else is to gain a plus of power, an advanced position on the great competitive battlefield. Every step forward on this road, every triumph and victory, presupposes a painful effort, a jump across barriers. "The obstacle is the stimulus of this will to power."[14] True happiness consists in the feeling that power is increasing, that resistance has been overcome. The fittest members of the human race strive for insecurity, not for security or contentedness; they seek out danger, risk and the hard life; they build their cities on the slopes of active volcanoes and send their ships into uncharted seas.

Nietzsche apparently did not believe (although his comments on the point are somewhat ambiguous and not wholly consistent) that the universal operation of the power principle could be corrected by human efforts to tone down the struggle for power by artificial restraints of a moral character. He was convinced that he was describing inevitabilities,

---

[11] Nietzsche, *The Will to Power*, p. 340 (No. 636).

[12] *Id.*, p. 342 (No. 642).

[13] *Id.*, p. 361 (No. 681).

[14] *Id.*, p. 373 (No. 702). See also the whole chapter entitled "Man", *id.*, pp. 347-366 (Nos. 659-687).

inexorable dynamic phenomena which were impervious to effective control. "A certain force cannot be anything other than this certain force...It can react to a quantum of resisting force only according to the measure of its strength; — event and necessary event is a *tautology*."[15] Although he declared that this absolute necessity was not a determinism *ruling* events, he meant by this statement merely to deny purposeful direction of the course of things by a supreme power towards a preordained goal. The necessity he spoke of was an *immanent* necessity, caused by the very properties of the dynamic quanta whose lawless whirl accounted for the movements of the universe. Every power quantum, he thought, at each moment acts out the ultimate consequences of its nature and strength. "Calculability exists precisely because things are unable to be other than they are."[16]

Nietzsche's assumption of a necessity which was not brought forth by purposeful supreme direction but by the intrinsic structure and energy content possessed by the elementary units of nature led him to a denial of any transcendent world of ideas and ideals. According to Heidegger, a dualistic belief in "two worlds" has dominated the thinking of the Western World for two thousand years under the influence of Plato's metaphysics and Christian theology.[17] The Platonic-Christian view assumes that there is a transcendental world of truth, goodness, justice, and love, of which the actual world in which we live is only a feeble copy. Since human beings have some *a priori* knowledge of the "true" world, this knowledge, although it is imperfect, enables them to make an effort to live up to the ideal postulates of the higher sphere of reality, *i.e.* to bring about (within the limits of human capacities) the reign of goodness, justice, beauty and love on earth.

Nietzsche vehemently rejected the dualism inherent in this distinction between a perfect world of pure values and an imperfect world of sense perceptions. To him the latter world was the *only* true and existing world. Nietzsche therefore deemed it necessary to launch a frontal attack on the cult of ideals and, even more pervasively, on the "ought" element in human thinking, especially in ethical theory. "All idealism is mendaciousness in the face of what is necessary."[18] Life in its concrete

---

[15] *Id.*, p. 341 (No. 639).

[16] *Id.*, p. 337 (No. 634). See also *id.*, p. 297 (No. 552).

[17] Martin Heidegger, *Nietzsche* (Pfullingen, 1961), Vol. I, pp. 87, 180-181, 231-242; Vol. II, pp. 22-23, 33-34.

[18] Nietzsche, "Ecce Homo", in *Basic Writings*, p. 714.

existential manifestations was to him a value in itself, regardless of its conformity or nonconformity with moral postulates.

The degree of value inherent in the life of an individual was determined by the amount of power possessed by him, and not by greater or lesser approximation to the ideal of ethical good.[19] It bears emphasis in this connection that Nietzsche's "superman" was not conceived by him as a model for humanistic self-perfection, but as the incarnation of the pure will to power, producing a magnificent animal with unimpaired instincts which lives out its vitality fully according to the degree of its strength. A human being as he *ought* to be, *i.e.* an individual orienting himself through belief in ethical values toward higher and perhaps more spiritual forms of existence, sounded to Nietzsche as absurd as "a tree as it ought to be".[20] He strongly denied that he was interested in "improving" mankind: "No new idols are erected by me....*Overthrowing idols* (my word for 'ideals') — that comes closer to being part of my craft."[21]

This fundamental Nietzschean credo has consequences of utmost significance for Nietzsche's thinking about law. According to a view which has been widely and persistently held throughout the ages, law in its most important characteristic is a congeries of precepts for private and official conduct. These precepts form guideposts for human action which may or may not be observed in a concrete situation by the addressees of the law. This conception injects an *ideal* element into the interpretation of legal phenomena. Law is a standard of action which is in a certain sense transcendental: in the sense, namely, that it does not simply mirror or describe the actual, empirical behavior of men. Law is traditionally viewed as an "ought", demanding of men that they conform their conduct to a certain set of postulates.[22]

Nietzsche's rejection of Platonic dualism induced him to ignore or at least play down the conception of law as an aggregate of "oughts". Law is to him above everything else a term which describes certain conditions or interrelationships arising out of the struggle for power between human beings or groups of human beings. In this struggle situations will inevitably occur in which two (or more) holders of power discover that they have

---

[19] Nietzsche, *The Will to Power*, p. 37 (No. 55).

[20] Nietzsche, "The Will to Power", in *Complete Works*, Vol. XIV, p. 266 (No. 332).

[21] Nietzsche, "Ecce Homo", in *Basic Writings*, pp. 673-674. See also Nietzsche, *The Will to Power*, p. 50 (No. 80).

[22] This aspect of law is emphasized by Hans Kelsen, *Pure Theory of Law*, transl. M. Knight (Berkeley, 1967), pp. 4-10.

attained an equality of strength. Each of them realizes that he might not be able to overwhelm, subjugate, dominate the other and in this way control his actions. Then, "where there is no clearly recognizable supremacy, and where a conflict would be useless and would injure both sides, there arises the thought of coming to an understanding and settling the opposing claims."[23] Law, thus conceived, is a trade or barter based on the assumption of an approximately equalized power position. The adjustment resulting from the stalemate is, however, a merely temporary one. As soon as one of the parties improves his position and becomes definitely superior to the other, the bargain based on equality of strength will in all likelihood be scrapped, to be replaced by an implementation of the newly-gained superiority. Law as a compact between equals gives way to subordination or subjection.

In what manner does this concept of law actualize itself in the context of the relation between a Government and its subjects? Governments frequently grant "rights" to those over whom they exercise sovereign power, although the ruling authority finds itself clearly in a position of supremacy. How does Nietzsche fit this unquestionable fact into his theory of law?

Here again Nietzsche thinks in terms of preservation and stabilization of power relations. He is aware that no ruling power can maintain itself for long without paying some attention to the feelings of the citizens or subjects. It must secure their cooperation; it must enlist their loyalty; it must sometimes muster their enthusiasm and fighting strength in a struggle with another sovereign State. A concession of rights is often the most prudent and effective way to bind the people closely to their Government. There exists, however, according to Nietzsche no absolute obligation on the part of the ruling authorities to maintain or respect these rights indefinitely. In certain situations, the Government or dominant group may consider it safe, expedient or justifiable to ride roughshod over previously conceded rights: "When we have become a great deal more powerful, the rights of others cease for us, at least in the form in which we have so far conceded them."[24]

There is, of course, implicit in this conception a disapprobation of the view that the fundamental rights of individuals are "inalienable", that they

---

[23] Nietzsche, "Human, All-Too-Human", in *Complete Works*, Vol. VI, p. 90 (No. 92). Nietzsche adds the thought that the origin of justice must be found in the egoistic reflection, "Why should I injure myself and perhaps not attain my aim after all?" *Id.*, pp. 90-91 (No. 92).

[24] Nietzsche, "The Dawn", in *Basic Writings*, p. 170 (No. 112).

belong to a person by virtue of the fact that he is a human being endowed with freedom, dignity and self-determination. There also cannot be found in Nietzsche any trace of the belief that there exists a connection between recognition of human rights and a notion of justice divorced from the actual state of the positive law. It is true that the word "justice" is sometimes used by Nietzsche in his discussion of the functions of law; but he makes it clear that to him justice is a derivative and not a primary value. "To speak of just or unjust *in itself* is quite senseless; *in itself,* of course, no injury, assault, exploitation, destruction can be 'unjust', since life operates *essentially,* that is in its basic functions, through injury, assault, exploitation, destruction and simply cannot be thought of at all without this character."[25] The terms "just" and "unjust" therefore gain meaning for Nietzsche only after a certain form of law has been instituted. They do not describe manifestations of an independent sense of justice, *i.e.* spontaneous, original reactions of human beings to a noxious act, but refer to value judgments which are produced by infractions of the positive law in force in a particular place at a particular time.

That the institution of law is downgraded in this view as a beneficial agency of social control requires no elaborate proof. Nietzsche, in his frankness and freedom from hypocritical palliation of what he considers to be unvarnished realism, assigns a highly secondary role to the law. "From the highest biological standpoint, legal conditions can never be other than *exceptional conditions,* since they constitute a partial restriction of the will of life, which is bent upon power, and are subordinate to its total goal as a single means: namely, as a means of creating *greater* units of power."[26] Where law reigns, Nietzsche holds, brakes are placed upon the untrammelled exercise of power in the form of rules which bind the power holder to a certain course of conduct. To Nietzsche, however, life is display, activation, exercise of power. This essentially disorderly process should not be unduly channeled and dammed up by the imposition of strict, inviolable principles of action. "In order to satisfy the will to power, every absolute precept should be eliminated."[27] Nietzsche is for the most part opposed to rules, whether these be of a moral or legal character. They do not fit into his conception of life as an essentially chaotic swirl of encounters between power-complexes.

---

[25] Nietzsche, "Genealogy of Morals," in *Basic Writings,* p. 512 (2d essay, No. 11). See also Nietzsche, "Beyond Good and Evil," *id.,* pp. 393-394 (No. 259), where he characterizes exploitation as a "basic organic function" and a "primordial fact of all history".

[26] Nietzsche, "Genealogy of Morals", in *Basic Writings,* p. 512 (2d essay, No. 11).

[27] Nietzsche, *Gesammelte Werke,* Vol. XIV, p. 228.

Law therefore is relegated by Nietzsche to the task of securing temporary states of equilibrium and neutralization, which are merely preparatory to the occurrence of new dynamic events in the seesaw of eternal struggle. The rule of law conceived as a principal regulatory device in the organization of human affairs would be an undue contraction of a life-force which expresses itself through constant attempts to augment its power. "A legal order thought of as sovereign and universal, not as a means in the struggle between power-complexes but as a means of *preventing* all struggle in general — perhaps after the communistic *cliché* of Dühring that every will must consider every other will its equal — would be a principle *hostile to life*, an agent of the dissolution and destruction of man, an attempt to assassinate the future of man, a sign of weariness, a secret path to nothingness."[28]

This last quotation hints at another reason why Nietzsche is generally antagonistic to the institution of law. Nietzsche perceives a certain tendency in the law to regard every will as equal to every other will. The very fact that law speaks in abstractly formulated rules implies a proclivity to generalize, *i.e.* to apply the precept equally to persons, groups, or situations which, in the very nature of things, will in many respects be unequal. This notion of "equal justice under law", a justice administered without respect of persons, violates in the eyes of Nietzsche the principle of individuation which, because of the highly uneven distribution of power among men, makes inequality the true "law" of life. "The doctrine of equality! But there is no more deadly poison than this; for it *seems* to proceed from the very lips of justice, whereas in reality it draws the curtain down on all justice."[29] Over and over again Nietzsche proclaimed his conviction that a grant of equal rights to all men and women would constitute an extreme form of injustice. Since life only thrives "at the expense of other life",[30] since it demands "appropriation, injury, overpowering of what is alien and weaker, suppression, hardness, imposition of one's own forms, incorporation and at least, at its mildest, exploitation",[31] law used on a wide scale as an equalizing force, as a protective shield of the weak against oppression by the strong, must necessarily be viewed by Nietzsche as an "agent of the dissolution and destruction of man, an

---

[28] Nietzsche, *supra* n. 26, p. 512.

[29] Nietzsche, "The Twilight of the Idols", in *Complete Works*, Vol. XVI, pp. 108-109.

[30] Nietzsche, *The Will to Power*, p. 199 (No. 369).

[31] Nietzsche, "Beyond Good and Evil", in *Basic Writings*, p. 393 (No. 259).

attempt to assassinate the future of man, a sign of weariness, a secret path to nothingness".[32]

Nietzsche's low estimate of the law is related to his unsympathetic attitude toward the State. If the State is too well organized and too much committed to the politics of welfare, he argued, it induces people to value comfort highly and thus to shun "the liberation of the individual through struggle".[33] The general security, in his opinion, was paid for too dearly by setting up the elaborate legal machinery of the Leviathan. Furthermore, this machinery was used too often for the purpose of aiding and abetting the conspiracy of the weak against the strong, with the effect that human mediocrity was promoted by governmental policies.[34] "There, where the State ceaseth — there only commenceth the man who is not superfluous."[35]

SECTION 3
Weaknesses of Nietzsche's Basic Position

Nietzsche's approach to the problem of power and law stands in close rapport not only with his sociology and psychology but also with his philosophy of nature. In this respect he is the heir of a long tradition in intellectual history which has not been interrupted even by the modern turn to positivism and empiricism in social science method. Since man is a product of nature, the totality of our picture of nature as a whole tends to make an imprint on our conception of man's own peculiar constitution and the activities which flow from it.

Nobody, for example, is in a position to understand the Aristotelian view of man as a society-builder without a firm grasp of Aristotle's teleological picture of nature, according to which everything that exists strives to attain its most perform form. Medieval Thomism derives a hierarchical theory of human social organization from the basic assumption of a gradated scale of objectively existing and immutable values culminating

---

[32] *Supra* n. 28.

[33] Nietzsche, *Gesammelte Werke*, Vol. VI, p. 216.

[34] Nietzsche, *The Will to Power*, p. 383 (No. 718); Nietzsche, *Gesammelte Werke*, Vol. VI, pp. 31, 68, 381; Walter Kaufmann, *Nietzsche*, 3rd ed. (New York, 1968), pp. 162-167.

[35] Nietzsche, "Thus Spake Zarathustra", in *Complete Works*, Vol. XI, p. 57.

in the holiness of a Supreme Being. The Kantian philosophy was an ingenious attempt to reconcile the determinism inherent in Newtonian physics with a social philosophy premised on the recognition of human free will and autonomy. Hegel viewed the human endeavor as the unfolding of a historical and dialectical process in which reason slowly but steadily moves upwards towards higher and higher forms of realization. Modern empirical and analytic philosophy is based on a general metaphysical assumption which pervades positivistic thinking in all branches of science: that only the investigation of concrete sense data which are immediately given in our experience can provide us with certainty and truth, while theories which go beyond the observation of facts and try to synthesize observed phenomena into a connected view of the total scheme of things are fictional products of imagination or speculation. It was shown by a famous scientist that this premise itself is the outflow of a connected view of the world which interprets "reality" as a mere assemblage of observed facts and deems the mind inferior to the senses as an instrumentality of cognition.[1]

In the case of Nietzsche, the relation between his cosmology and his theory of man in his interaction with other men is particularly conspicuous. A critique of his philosophy of nature must therefore be offered as an integral prelude to an evaluation of his social philosophy.

Nietzsche views the world as a huge powerhouse in which everything therein contained is in a state of incessant motion. An uncountable number of dynamic quanta are in interplay with each other through attraction, repulsion or direct impact. The world is one of "becoming", not of "being". The notion of the atom, conceived as an immutable, durable, indivisible unit of matter, is declared by him to be a pure invention.[2] The world is a "monster of energy", a sea of stormy, onrushing forces, eternally changing, eternally flooding back and forth.[3] Even the existence of "laws of nature", imparting a certain regularity and invariability to the various movements, was denied by Nietzsche, as we have seen. To him the entire process was one of struggle between elements of unequal power: "Things do not behave regularly, according to a *rule*....The degree of resistance and the degree of superior power—this is the question in every event."[4] Predictability of future occurrences in this view depends entirely on proper estimates of the relative strength of contending forces.

---

[1] Max Planck, *Where Is Science Going* (New York, 1932), pp. 68-98.
[2] Nietzsche, *The Will to Power*, ed. W. Kaufmann (New York, 1968), p. 334 (No. 624). See also *id.*, p. 339 (No. 636), where the atom is called a "subjective fiction", and p. 360 (No. 715), where the existence of durable ultimate units is denied.
[3] *Id.*, pp. 549-550 (No. 1067).
[4] *Id.*, p. 337 (No. 634).

An informed student of Nietzsche's philosophy might interpose the objection at this point that the preceding account has overdrawn the dynamic elements in his conception of nature. He might point out that, side by side with the doctrine of the supremacy of the will to power, there stands a second basic thesis which Nietzsche deemed to be of equally fundamental importance: the doctrine of the eternal recurrence of the same. This doctrine, the argument might continue, contains a severe limitation on the view that the world is nothing but an endless process of "becoming". It assumes that there is a cyclical repetitive element in everything that happens, in the movements of nature as well as in the history of the human race. This might point to a Nietzschean conviction that, although things change constantly, they remain in a certain sense the same. It might mean that individuals with highly similar features, characteristics, and qualities appear on this earth from time to time. Historical situations strongly resembling one another may arise in different ages and different countries. Forms of society and social organization deemed long extinct may make an unexpected comeback somewhere on the global scene. The whole universe might go through alternating motions of expansion and contraction, with a return to a former state from which a new cyclical development might start.

Some philosophers and literary scholars have had great difficulty in fitting Nietzsche's doctrine of eternal recurrence into the general framework of his philosophy of dynamism. They have attempted to slight the importance of this doctrine[5] or to explain it away as a mysterious by-product of the period of life immediately preceding Nietzsche's mental collapse.[6] Martin Heidegger, on the other hand, declared — in consonance with Nietzsche's own appraisal — that without this doctrine Nietzsche's teaching would resemble a tree without roots.[7] Although what concerns us here is chiefly an exposition and discussion of Nietzsche's views on the relation between power and law, a brief excursion into "eternal recurrence" is necessary in order to place Nietzsche's thoughts into their proper perspective.

Although Nietzsche believed that, in the dynamic interactions of energy units in inanimate and animate nature, everything was in a state of "becoming", of constant flux, this did not signify to him that new,

---

[5] Karl Jaspers, *Nietzsche*, transl. C. F. Wallraf and F. J. Schmitz (Tucson, 1965), pp. 352-367.

[6] Ernst Bertram, *Nietzsche* (Berlin, 1918), p. 12.

[7] Martin Heidegger, *Nietzsche* (Pfullingen, 1961), Vol. I, p. 256.

spontaneous creation was going on all the time. Two theories firmly entrenched in nineteenth-century physics shaped Nietzsche's thinking on this problem: the principle of conservation of energy and the belief that, in terms of the time dimension, there was no beginning and no end to the universe. If there is no spontaneous creation of new energy, the total amount of available cosmic energy remains the same. This means that the number of permutations, combinations, and states which the existing quanta of energy distributed throughout the universe can enter into must necessarily be limited. Since the whole play of forces has gone on from infinity, identical situations, changes and relationships between matter and energy units must have occurred uncountable times, and will occur over and over again in a future which has no terminal point. "Everything has existed innumerable times, because the total reciprocal relationship of all forces repeats itself again and again."[8] There is a perpetual dynamic activity in the world, but the number of concrete manifestations or resultants of this activity is limited.

The denial by Nietzsche of any final goal, or direction towards a final goal, of the cosmic movements — which was mentioned in the preceding section — is a second important ingredient of his doctrine of eternal recurrence. "We deny end goals: if existence had one it would have to have been reached."[9] Why does Nietzsche make this last and rather startling statement? Because he assumed that in a world which, on the one hand, has existed from infinity but, on the other hand, operates with a finite amount of energy, everything that is possible must already have occurred many times. The reaching of a final goal, such as the arrival of the Kingdom of God, is unthinkable without belief in the creation of new levels of energy which can serve to improve the existing state of things and raise it to a higher state of perfection. Such belief in foreordained progress Nietzsche considered incompatible with the structure of physical reality. He also deemed it irreconcilable with the denial of God, which was an integral part of his philosophy. If there is no Supreme Being directing and helping the world along an upwards road, the only possible alternative that appeared tenable to him was the assumption of a cyclical process of the universe.[10]

Nietzsche's doctrine of the eternal recurrence of equal things, which has

---

[8] Nietzsche, *Gesammelte Werke*, Musarion ed. (Munich, 1920-1929), Vol. XIV, p. 172.

[9] Nietzsche, *The Will to Power*, p. 36 (No. 55).

[10] The foregoing account of the doctrine of eternal recurrence is based on the following sources: Nietzsche, *The Will to Power*, pp. 544-550 (Nos. 1053-1067); Nietzsche, *Gesammelte Werke*, Vol. XIV, pp. 172-183.

a strong metaphysical tinge, contains an important qualification of Nietzsche's thesis that our world, in which power exerts and unfolds itself in multifarious forms, is a world of dynamic change. The doctrine of recurrence is not, however, fundamentally at odds with this view since it is not based on the hypothesis that anything ever comes to a standstill. Nietzsche once compared the world with a sea which rushes on in periods of tide and floods back in periods of ebb, with an infinite repetition of this cycle.[11] There is no stability in any of its inanimate or animate creations; there is only, over long periods of time, a return of previous events.

There is no doubt that Nietzsche, in his philosophy of nature, anticipated certain developments in twentieth-century physics which were only very faintly foreseeable in the natural sciences of his day. Due to discoveries made in the areas of quantum physics, thermodynamics, electromagnetic fields, nuclear theory, and others, the universe appears to us today as a less stable place than it presented itself to the perception of earlier generations. For instance, the view widely held in the past that the ultimate particles of nature are indestructible can no longer be maintained. Protons and electrons may disintegrate as a result of natural interferences, such as exposure to high-energy cosmic rays. Neutrons will be apt to decay into protons and electrons when freed from the atom. Basic particles can through human interference be transformed into qualitatively different ones.

Furthermore, the former belief in the existence of inexorable causal laws imparting a maximum of consistency, regularity and "lawful" behavior to all processes of nature has been upset by the discoveries of quantum physics. Under the present state of microphysical research, the notion of an all-pervasive causality which leaves no room for contingency and chance fluctuations in nature cannot be supported by experimental facts. Although leading contemporary physicists do not deny the presence of necessary causal interconnections, they seem to regard indeterminacy and chance as a second side of many physical events. This means that microphysics today reckons with the occurrence of random disturbances which may be viewed as loopholes in nature's uniformity and regularity. These findings appear to be incompatible with the assumption that nature is wholly planful and exclusively law-determined.[12]

---

[11] Nietzsche, *The Will to Power*, p. 550 (No. 1067).

[12] On the unstable aspects of matter and the impact of chance see, among others, Max Born, *The Restless Universe*, 2d ed., transl. W. M. Deans (New York, 1951); David Bohm, *Causality and Chance in Modern Physics* (New York, 1957); Hermann Weyl, *The Open World* (New Haven, 1932); Jacob Bronowski, *The Common Sense of Science* (London, 1951).

Although Nietzsche's philosophy of nature has certain points of contact with the world view of modern physics, his picture of nature as a whirlpool of chaotic power pressures is highly overdrawn.[13] Nature presents many phenomena which demonstrate features of relative constancy, regularity, and uniformity.

First of all, although nothing in nature ever appears to come to a complete standstill, there are objects and conditions which, in comparison with the most dynamic, turbulent and explosive occurrences, are characterized by some measure of stability. Even though a mountain composed of granite stone steadily undergoes slow transformations through the impact of solar heat, rain, wind, and other causes of erosion, these are hardly visible to the human eye, except perhaps over extremely long periods of time. Old paintings of the Matterhorn, for instance, do not disclose any shape different from that revealed on modern photographs. A petrified forest will last for indefinitely long periods of time. The landscape on the moon, although altered in spots by new craters opened up through the bombardment of meteorites, has largely remained the same over thousands or ten-thousands of years. Very ancient monuments of art carved into rock have withstood the test of time surprisingly well. The Egyptian pyramids, although subjected to processes of gradual disintegration, have retained their general form and appearance.

Nietzsche once remarked that every tree changes every single second. There is some truth in this statement. And yet, a 4,000-year old redwood tree in a California forest possesses sufficient attributes of permanence to warrant a linguistic characterization which distinguishes it from a butterfly whose metamorphoses include several seasonal forms. By the same token, the difference between an enduring piece of matter and a momentary flash of lightning is simply too great to be disregarded. There are quantitative differentiations in the rates of movement and change which take on the character of qualitative distinctions in the description of natural phenomena. Compared with a hurricane, a mountain peak may be said to be stable.

Even objects in motion frequently behave in a constant and orderly manner. The movements of the planets around the sun are characterized by great regularity of pattern; small alterations in orbit occur only over extremely long periods of time. There is a gravitational constant, called "G", which controls certain relationships between gravitational force and

---

[13] A different metaphor is used by Nietzsche in "Thus Spake Zarathustra", in *Complete Works*, ed. O. Levy (London 1909-1911), Vol. XI, p. 266. Nietzsche speaks there of nature as a "wheel" rolling on forever (even though over long periods of time the wheel returns to the same places in its cyclical path).

the moving masses affected by it. It has also been experimentally verified that the velocity of light in a vacuum is always the same.[14]

According to contemporary physical theory, the range of instability even in the microcosmic processes is not nearly as extensive as had sometimes been assumed under the first impressions created by the discoveries of the twentieth century. There are, to be sure, factors of inconstancy and occurrences of a chaotic nature. Photons interacting with matter are sometimes absorbed and reemitted with changes in direction and energy. Particles in a gaseous substance will undergo all kinds of random motions and fluctuations at a certain temperature. But there are also substantial areas and configurations which present evidence of great stability. Even though atoms may alter their identity through collision with units of extremely high energy, even though they may disintegrate as a result of radioactivity, such events cannot be generalized into permanent or pervasive attributes of the atomic structure. "Not all nuclei are explosive," says Born, "otherwise matter could not continue to exist."[15] Under normal circumstances, protons, electrons and atoms are entities which are basically stable. Their transformations and alterations for the most part take place under artificial conditions of human intervention.

The relation between stability and instability, continuity and change in nature, especially organic nature, is one of complex interaction. The process lends itself to incomplete direct observation only and cannot easily be described. The ancient redwood tree in the California forest, after having become a full-grown tree, will continue adding very slowly to its height and putting on a new ring to its trunk each year. It will nonetheless be identifiable as "the same tree" not only by its location but also by its general appearance, its colors, the shape of its branches. The bulk of the cells in the human body (though not all of them, as for instance the brain cells) come and go in an on-going process of replacement. In spite of these frequent alterations in the substance of man's physiological makeup, he retains a "self" which persists in many essential respects from early childhood to old age and enables us, significantly enough, to speak of a human *being*. Man "is" and "becomes" at the same time, exhibiting identities as well as differences in the various stages of his life.

The phenomena of unity and continuity, in the face of an ever-changing animate and inanimate world, stem from the fact that most changes are not

---

[14] It might also be noted that the electric charge and the rest mass in an electron is constant under normal circumstances, as well as the proportionality between frequency of radiation and associated energy (Planck's constant "h").

[15] Born, *supra* n. 12, p. 234.

total, "wholesale" and sudden, but gradual and partial. Therefore they leave intact at least the core of the substance of a thing. This becomes particularly obvious in inorganic nature, where the modifications taking place in an object are so slow and minute that they will not be noticed by the human eye even over long periods of time. The changes that are immediately visible are the discontinuous, abrupt, explosive changes and those which, although they occur gradually (like the caterpillar-butterfly metamorphosis), transform their object radically.

The conclusion to be drawn from these observations is that we may speak of stability in a relative (not absolute) sense when the rate of change affecting a thing is extremely slow, and that we may use the concept of continuity when the identity of an object is preserved in spite of modifications in its component parts. Nietzsche, in his overdynamic account of nature, gave insufficient consideration to these phenomena.

The second basic shortcoming in Nietzsche's view of the universe was his denial of natural laws. We dwell in an essentially inhospitable and untidy world, he thought, expressing this conviction in the form of the statement that "the world is not an organism at all, but chaos".[16] What appears to our perception as laws of physical nature he considered, as we have seen, as necessities rooted in the vagaries of the distribution of power.[17]

There are few, if any, natural scientists today who would be ready to endorse Nietzsche's position. "The external world of reality is governed by a system of laws", said Max Planck, an outstanding modern physicist.[18] To be sure, the exact nature of these laws is not free from controversy. Some physicists believe that the uniformities observable in the microscopic and macroscopic sphere are genuinely causal laws, although the operation of these laws is punctured by occasional chance events which make certainty of prediction impossible in certain respects. In this view, "the necessity of causal relationships is always limited and conditioned by contingencies arising outside the context in which the laws in question operate".[19] Other scientists suspect the prevalence of arbitrariness and randomness in the individual behavior of microphysical objects but maintain that regularities permitting a high

---

[16] Nietzsche, *The Will to Power*, p. 379 (No. 711).

[17] Nietzsche, "The Joyful Wisdom", in *Complete Works*, Vol. X, p. 152 (No. 109).

[18] Planck, *supra* n. 1, p. 22.

[19] Bohm, *supra* n. 12, p. 29. Bohm is one of the chief protagonists of this view. Louis de Broglie, *The Revolution in Physics*, transl. R. W. Niemeyer (New York, 1953), pp. 216-217, 220-238, inclines in the same direction. See also Max Born, *Natural Philosophy of Cause and Chance* (Oxford, 1949), p. 3. A belief in strict physical causality, excluding the notion of chance, was maintained by Planck, *supra* n. 1, pp. 100, 143; cf. also Albert Einstein, *Out of My Later Years* (New York, 1950), pp. 91-93.

degree of accuracy in prediction arises from the concurrent action of very large aggregates of physical entities. While in this view most natural laws assume the character of statistical probability laws, it is conceded that on the level of ordinary human activity these statistical laws approximate or equal the effects of truly causal laws.[20]

There is no need for taking sides in the controversy regarding the existence of strict causality for purposes of the present argument. There is found, according to both views, "a certain stability of the characteristic modes of macroscopic behavior".[21] The incidence of this stability and regularity makes it possible to predict the orbit of satellites with complete accuracy and to send men to the moon with the help of computers whose programming is predicated on the assumption of essentially invariable, universal laws which are applicable to stellar bodies and their relations in space. The determinateness with which such laws operate is enhanced by the fact that chance fluctuations existing at the microcosmic level tend to cancel each other out whenever huge aggregates of particles are involved.

Nietzsche's thesis that "the general character of the world....is for all eternity chaos"[22] does not, therefore, hold up as a tenable scientific proposition. We must in its place accept the statement of Max Born, a leading twentieth-century physicist, that "amid the flight of phenomena stands the immutable pole of law".[23] Because of the existence of law, we find a great deal of orderliness in most of the large-scale processes of the cosmos. We also find states of rest and equilibrium in nature, although the term "rest" may in some contexts mean no more than relative constancy in comparison with changes taking place with great velocity and momentum.

Nietzsche's cosmic philosophy strongly affected his conception of man. In the world as he saw it, the will to power embodied in the ultimate particles of nature was also stored up in man's biological system. The supposed absence of law in the movements of nature translated itself in his mind into the chaotic dynamism and far-reaching lawlessness of perpetual human struggle. Man-made law was not in his opinion rooted in any. deep-seated psychological traits of the human race but solely in the expediencies of power relations which, from time to time, press for consoli-

---

[20] Richard von Mises, *Probability, Statistics, and Truth,* 2d ed., transl. H. Geiringer (London, 1957), pp. 66-103; Werner Heisenberg, *Physics and Philosophy* (New York, 1958), p. 145; Niels Bohr, *Atomic Theory and the Description of Nature* (New York, 1934), p. 4.

[21] Bohm, *supra* n. 12, p. 51.

[22] Nietzsche, *supra* n. 17, p. 152 (No. 109).

[23] Born, *supra* n. 12, p. 278.

dation or stabilization. The use of law for the primary purpose of taming the aggressive impulses of men was deemed by Nietzsche a misuse of the institution. It was therefore logical for him to reach the conclusion that legal arrangements between men, groups of men and States should be confined to exceptional situations.[24]

Nietzsche's views on these fundamental problems have not remained pure paper theories but, as was pointed out in the introductory section, have influenced the thinking of the present generation. It therefore behooves those interested in the fate of the law to reflect on his provocative ideas and to refute them if they are found to be mistaken, misleading or dangerous. This endeavor calls for an inquiry into the question whether the will to power, as asserted by Nietzsche, is the dominant force in human nature. It also requires a response to Nietzsche's attempt to downgrade the role of law in human affairs. The question must be asked whether the institution of law has its roots in certain biological and psychic traits of men, whether there is a "will to law" anchored in the structure of human nature. The remaining sections of this chapter will be devoted to a discussion of these subjects.

SECTION 4
Human Nature and the Will to Power

For Nietzsche, human nature and the will to power were almost identical concepts. This follows necessarily from his basic assumption that the desire to acquire, maintain and increase power forms the mainspring of human action. Although he conceived the term "power" in a broad sense which would include the most diverse manifestations of human effort, he nevertheless viewed individual and social psychology from a unitary perspective by relating practically all phenomena of personal and collective life to the dynamics of the power impulse. The "spontaneous, aggressive, expansive, form-giving forces that give new interpretations and directions" were for him tantamount to life itself.[1]

We have already seen that the Nietzschean will to power does not exhaust its significance in the desire of human beings to exercise dominion over their fellowmen but comprises all forms of ego-enhancement which

---

[24] See *supra* Sec. 2, n. 26.

[1] Nietzsche, "Genealogy of Morals", in *Basic Writings of Nietzsche*, ed. W. Kaufmann (New York, 1968), p. 515 (2d essay, No. 12).

involve the overcoming of resistance.[2] The power impulse therefore includes the human desire to grow and develop one's capabilities.[3] Nietzsche made it clear, however, that he wished to see the drive for self-perfection interpreted as a wholly egocentric striving. Personal fulfillment was not to be attained through social concern, involving a determination to contribute to the improvement of the social whole. Individual growth, in his opinion, served the purposes of an "aggressive and defensive egoism".[4] When it approached the state of self-perfection, it turned into an "extraordinary expansion of the feeling of power, riches, necessary overflowing of all limits".[5] What, then, is the ultimate aim of this process of intense self-actualization? Nietzsche's often-repeated statement that the wielding of power entails appropriation, subjugation and exploitation leaves little doubt where the answer must be sought, and Nietzsche himself expressly linked self-perfection to the will to rule and dominate. "Perfecting consists in the production of the most powerful individuals, who will use the great mass of people as their tools."[6] While it need not be assumed that this statement summarizes Nietzsche's power philosophy in all of its ramifications, it shows that in Nietzsche's view a close tie exists between self-realization and the desire to be superior over others.

It is at this point that Alfred Adler parted company with Nietzsche. He went along with this philosopher part of the way by taking the position that a striving for perfection and power accompanied each individual throughout his life, beginning in early childhood in the shape of an innate disposition. "The key to the entire social process is to be found in the fact that persons are always striving to find a situation in which they can excel."[7] We all pursue some goal through the attainment of which we feel strong, satisfied and complete. The "impetus from minus to plus", the "urge from below to above", the "great upward drive" is never absent; it is something without which life is unthinkable.[8] Adler also expressed a

---

[2] See *supra* Sec. 2.

[3] Nietzsche, *Gesammelte Werke,* Musarion ed. (Munich, 1920-1929), Vol. XIV, pp. 110, 364; Vol. XVI, p. 404; Nietzsche, *The Will to Power,* ed. W. Kaufmann (New York, 1968), p. 386 (No. 728); Martin Heidegger, *Nietzsche* (Pfullingen, 1961), Vol. II, p. 271.

[4] Nietzsche, *The Will to Power,* p. 386 (No. 728).

[5] *Id.,* p. 422 (No. 801).

[6] *Id.,* p. 349 (No. 660). An excellent critique of Nietzsche's position is found in Martin Buber, *Between Man and Man,* transl. R. G. Smith (New York, 1965), pp. 148-156.

[7] Alfred Adler, *The Science of Living* (New York, 1929), p. 74.

[8] *The Individual Psychology of Alfred Adler,* ed. H. L. and R. R. Ansbacher (New York, 1956) [hereinafter referred to as Adler, Individual Psychology], pp. 103-104.

Nietzschean thought when he declared that "the fundamental law of life...is that of overcoming".[9]

The difference between Nietzsche and Adler must be sought in the latter's theory of "social interest", which is thoroughly at odds with Nietzsche's credo. Nietzsche, as we have seen, was interested in the self-centered, self-sufficient individual ready to enlarge his power at the expense of others, if necessary. He glorified the lonely genius and showed an aristocratic unconcern for the fate of the common man.

Adler, on the other hand, preached the reduction of the urge for personal power and the development of a strong sense of communal solidarity. He emphasized the need for empathy and mutual understanding, and he admonished men to cooperate with their fellowmen in working for the common aims of their society. When social interest is throttled, he maintained, neurosis, psychosis, crime and suicide will make their sure appearance on the scene.[10]

How it is possible, in Adler's view, to reconcile the impulse for self-realization and excellence with the development of social interest? More specifically, are there any psychological ingredients in human nature which will make it possible to turn self-enhancement into collaborative activity without doing violence to basic human drives?

In Adler's thinking, the reconciliation of individual self-actualization with self-transcendence based on interest in others does not raise any serious psychological obstacles. Adler was convinced that egoistic as well as altruistic instincts are inborn in man, and that his nature is plastic enough to permit a channeling of ego-development into socially valuable directions. If this endeavor is not met with success, Adler believed, pathological disturbances will be the inevitable consequence of the failure. Social feeling will become perverted into noxious forms of self-aggrandizement, and concern for the common welfare will be supplanted by self-bounded, antisocial activity. Every effort must therefore be made to instill socially constructive attitudes in man. "Every human being strives for significance, but people always make mistakes if they do not see that their whole significance must consist in their contribution to the lives of others."[11] In more recent times, Viktor Frankl has stressed the need of human beings to

---

[9] Adler, *Social Interest*, transl. J. Linton and R. Vaughan (New York, 1964), p. 71.

[10] Adler, *Individual Psychology*, pp. 112-113, 126-162. See particularly the statement on p. 114: "The views of Individual Psychology demand the unconditional reduction of striving for power and the development of social interest." See also Adler, *Superiority and Social Interest*, ed. H. L. and R. R. Ansbacher (New York, 1964), pp. 34-40, 253-256. For a further discussion of this problem see *infra* Sec. 18.

[11] Adler, *Individual Psychology*, p. 156.

find a meaning in life through self-transcendence and commitment to a worthwhile cause.[12]

Sigmund Freud not only opposed Adler's views on self-perfection but also questioned the biological premises of the latter's theory of social interest. With respect to self-perfection, he was doubtful in particular whether this drive was part of each man's natural and innate equipment.

> "I do not believe in the existence of such an inner impulse, and I see no way of preserving this pleasing illusion. The development of man up to now does not seem to me to need any explanation differing from that of animal development, and the restless striving towards further perfection which may be observed in a minority of human beings is easily explicable as the result of that repression of instinct upon which what is most valuable in human culture is built."[13]

In contrast to the forward orientation of human nature stressed by Adler, Freud placed great emphasis — especially in his later works — upon the regressive side of man's instinctual life, his longing for repetition of earlier gratifying experiences. He actually spoke of a "compulsion" to repeat the events of childhood, without limiting the phenomenon to cases of psychically sick persons.

> "At this point, the idea is forced upon us that we have stumbled on the trace of a general and hitherto not clearly recognized — or at least not expressly emphasized — characteristic of instinct, perhaps of all organic life. According to this, *an instinct would be a tendency innate in living organic matter impelling it towards the reinstatement of an earlier condition,* one which it had to abandon under the influence of external disturbing forces — a kind of organic elasticity, or, to put it in another way, the manifestation of inertia in organic life."[14]

The innate organic impulses of man were thus construed by Freud as essentially conservative drives toward the restoration of antecedent states of satisfaction. We shall find this idea helpful later when we turn to a more detailed exploration of the anthropological roots of the law.

---

[12] See Viktor E. Frankl, *Man's Search for Meaning* (New York, 1963), pp. 154-155, 164-175; Frankl, *The Will to Meaning* (New York, 1969), pp. 31-49. A full account and sympathetic evaluation of Frankl's psychological doctrine (known as "logotherapy") is given by Joseph B. Fabry, *The Pursuit of Meaning* (Boston, 1968).

[13] Sigmund Freud, "Beyond the Pleasure Principle", in *The Major Works of Sigmund Freud,* ed. R. M. Hutchins (Chicago, 1952) [hereinafter referred to as *Major Works*], p. 654.

[14] *Id.,* p. 651.

Freud's conclusion is closely connected with his conviction that the desire to avoid, reduce or abate tension is one of the chief motor forces of the human psychic apparatus.[15] If this is true, then the human organism has a tendency towards stability rather than change. It seeks to maintain or to restore an equilibrium of the nervous system by repeating acts or procedures which past experience has shown to be capable of allaying inner tension and excitation.

Freud did not take the position that *all* human instincts or impulses have an exclusively backward-oriented character. He exempted the instinct of self-preservation, which may actuate an individual to cope inventively with new and perhaps unprecedented situations. He also made an extensive exception for the sexual instinct, which as a vehicle for the affirmation and renewal of life often runs counter to the trend of the other instincts. Freud asserted, however, that in various respects the sexual impulses are "conservative" in the same sense as the others are, because they tend to reproduce earlier states of satisfaction of the living substance.[16]

How does Freud in his theory of organic life account for the fact that many human beings, apart from the few examples mentioned by him, have a general ability to be innovative and resourceful, to embark on new ventures, and to achieve progress in many fields of human endeavor? He answered the question by maintaining that the results of advancement and development must be attributed to the operation of "external, disturbing, and distracting influences".[17] Among the most powerful of these influences he counted the culturally-imposed restraints on instinctual gratification. A repressed instinct which is blocked in returning to a primary experience of satisfaction will seek modes of substituted or sublimated fulfillment. "The path in the other direction, back to complete satisfaction, is as a rule barred by the resistances that maintain the repressions, and thus there remains nothing for it but to proceed in the other, still unobstructed direction, that of development, without, however, any prospect of being able to bring the process to a conclusion or to attain the goal."[18]

Progress and innovation are thus ascribed by Freud primarily to the effects of repression and sublimation, and the drive for self-perfection leading to cultural achievements is largely restricted by him to those individuals whose possibilities for complete libido-satisfaction have been frustrated in some fashion. The contrast of this conservative and pessimistic

---

[15] *Id.*, pp. 639-640.

[16] *Id.*, p. 653. See also Freud, "The Ego and the Id", in *Major Works*, pp. 708-709.

[17] Freud, "Beyond the Pleasure Principle", in *Major Works*, p. 652.

[18] *Id.*, p. 654.

version of cultural anthropology with Adler's sanguine belief in the forward march of civilization through self-actualization for the common good is obvious and striking. Freud held that, for the most part, human beings will move ahead on the road of life only in the event that the direction backwards is blocked, while Adler took the opposite position.

Freud also did not see eye to eye with Adler on the question of man's social nature. He was fully persuaded that man's aggressive and pugnacious traits were strongly and decisively preponderant over his altruistic and cooperative potentialities. He quoted with approval Hobbes's famous *homo homini lupus* statement:[19] Men are fond of hurting one another, they like to dominate and exploit their fellowmen, to steal their wives and possessions, and to humiliate them. Since civilized society is perpetually threatened with disintegration through this primary hostility of men towards each other, it will do everything in its power to erect barriers against socially injurious forms of human conduct. Freud thought, however, that this endeavor by organized society to check enmity, distrust and combativeness through the imposition of ethical injunctions (reinforced perhaps by legal prohibitions) had not met with a great deal of striking success in the history of the human race.[20] Since he was convinced — in contrast to Adler — that ethical demands are contrary to certain ineradicable components of human nature, he could harbor no great hopes for the effective realization of large-scale political experiments to improve relations between human beings and groups of human beings. In his view, a greater socialization and domestication of the creature called man could be achieved only at the cost of severely repressive means and stringent super-ego controls which, because they were at war with normal instinctual gratifications, would pose serious dangers to the continued existence of civilization.[21]

The questions raised by Nietzsche, Adler and Freud have important implications for a discussion of the psychological roots of the law. If human life is an essentially chaotic, limit-rejecting, ever-dynamic drive for personal expansion, why have human beings, instead of restricting law to

---

[19] Freud, "Civilization and Its Discontents", in *Major Works,* p. 787. "Man is to man a wolf" is the English translation of this Latin phrase.

[20] *Id.,* p. 787.

[21] It is not easy to reconcile Freud's insistence on man's endemically pugnacious nature with his observations concerning the regressive and inertial character of a large part of man's impulse structure. The most adequate explanation is probably that he deemed both components, although they contradict each other to some extent, present in man's makeup. For some thoughtful comments on Freud's conception of human nature see Ronald V. Sampson, *The Psychology of Power* (New York, 1966), pp. 20-44.

"exceptional conditions" as Nietzsche demanded, erected legal systems aiming at order and power control whenever they have formed social associations? Furthermore, if men are endemically aggressive and hostile toward each other, as Freud seemed to have assumed, where do we find the source of innate dispositions making men inclined to accept strong bridles upon their belligerent impulses? Why would they wish to do violence to their own nature? Unless there is built into this nature some solid base of support for cooperative attitudes and "social interest", as Adler taught, it is not easy to see why law as a universal institution has played such a prominent role in the history of human societies.

There is much reason to believe that Nietzsche overrated the dynamic and expansion-seeking forces in human nature. It is, of course, true that the urge to improve and enhance one's self (as distinguished from the biological fact of growth) is present in every normal and healthy human being. It is already noticeable in the child to the extent that it seeks new experiences and demonstrates its desire for the acquisition of knowledge. It becomes more conspicuous and diversified in the adolescent and mature phases of life when the individual endeavors to broaden his spheres of activity, to cope with difficulties and obstacles, and to develop his peculiar capacities. In performing the tasks of his life, a person is not necessarily anxious to maintain a stable and constant psychic equilibrium: he is usually willing to suffer tensions and undergo stresses for prolonged periods of time.[22]

It is also true that the desire for growth and self-actualization, whatever particular form and direction it may take, often encounters resistance in the instinctual structure of human beings. Although Freud was perhaps prone to overaccentuate this facet of psychic reality, there can be little doubt that human nature has an inertial and regressive side. The wish to be active, innovative and creative is opposed, in all but a small minority of men, by the desire to economize energy. The organism has a tendency to "retain old patterns on the principle of inertia".[23] The appetite for new ventures is checked to some extent by the propensity to repeat former experiences which have proved to be satisfactory. It must also be realized

---

[22] That the human organism has a self-actualizing potentiality which is different from its conserving and homeostatic tendencies was stressed by Abraham H. Maslow, *Motivation and Personality,* 2d ed. (New York, 1970), pp. 36, 78; Maslow, *Toward a Psychology of Being,* 2d ed. (Princeton, 1968), pp. 29-31; Kurt Goldstein, *Human Nature in the Light of Psychopathology* (Cambridge, Mass., 1951), pp. 111-112. Goldstein expressed the view that the tendency to discharge tension, if it becomes predominant, is the expression of a defective organism. *Id.,* pp. 140-141.

[23] Franz Alexander, *Fundamentals of Psychoanalysis* (New York, 1948), p. 39.

that there are definite limits to human capacity to bear tensions and excitation: at some point or other, the determination to achieve a tension-less state will break through with strong force.

In some individuals, vigorous activity, daring, and unrelenting effort constitute the principal characteristics of their personality makeup. In others, habitual, routine ways of doing things and the saving of energy are preferred to venturesome acts and unaccustomed modes of living; the old horizons remain fixed and full attainment of the person's potentialities may be impeded. Apart from such differences in personality structure, the tug of war between productivity and sloth presents in general an ever-present danger of stalemate and incomplete performance. In the words of Franz Alexander: "There is a psychological urge toward growth and reproduction and a strongly opposing tendency, the basic inertia of the living substance — the tendency to the preservation of an established equilibrium"[24]

Nietzsche was convinced that the drive for ego-enhancement and increase of power was closely allied with the will to dominate others. That there are individuals anxious to exercise power over their fellowmen cannot be questioned. That this drive is a primary and natural force in every man is, however, a highly doubtful assumption. Many human beings seem to be perfectly able and willing to treat others as their equals. Nietzsche's statement that "life itself is *essentially* appropriation, injury, overpowering of what is alien and weaker, suppression, hardness, imposition of one's own forms, incorporation and at least, at its mildest, exploitation"[25] cannot be substantiated and verified by looking at the social scene around us. In civilized societies — and also probably to a far-reaching extent in less civilized ones[26] — most men seem to be capable of taming the desire (if present in their character) to overpower, dominate and oppress their fellow-men. It is true that the twentieth century has taught us that some remnants of the bestial elements in man's nature may always remain

---

[24] Alexander, *Our Age of Unreason* (Philadelphia, 1942), p. 210.

[25] Nietzsche, "Beyond Good and Evil", in *Basic Writings*, p. 393 (No. 259). Nietzsche adds that "refraining mutually from injury, violence, and exploitation and placing one's will on a par with that of someone else" may under certain conditions become a tenet of good manners but cannot be accepted as the fundamental principle of society without causing society to decay and disintegrate. *Ibid.* See also Nietzsche, "Genealogy of Morals", in *Basic Writings*, p. 512 (2d essay, No. 11), where it is again asserted that life operates in its basic functions "through injury, assault, exploitation, and destruction".

[26] Fritz Kern has shown that primitive society is not exclusively or predominantly built on the idea that right is identical with might or superior muscle power. Many successful attempts are made already during this early stage to set brakes to the struggle for power and humanize relations within a social group. Fritz Kern, *Der Beginn der Weltgeschichte* (Bern, 1953), Ch. XI.

submerged under the surface, and that serious obstacles stand in the way of full human domestication. In Nietzsche's philosophy, however, these obstacles appear as impassable barriers.[27]

Even the ranks of the leaders in human history are not exclusively or predominantly filled with the names of men who have sought power and dominance for its own sake. Nobody will deny that love of power has often been a motivating factor of great strength, and that value symbols — such as freedom, equality, social justice, and universal brotherhood — have been misused by rulers and ruling groups as ideological disguises for ambition and self-aggrandizement. But it is also indisputable that great religious and political figures — such as Buddha, Jesus, Mohammed, Pericles, Trajan, Marcus Aurelius, Cromwell, Jefferson and Lincoln — have utilized their power over the minds, souls or bodies of men for the advancement of religious or ethical ideas, or for the realization of notions of the public good in which they strongly believed.[28] Mankind had judged these men on the basis of their contributions to civilization rather than according to the degree of power which they were able to wield.

The question as to the strength of the power impulse is related to, but not identical with, the problem of aggressiveness in man's basic makeup. Freud was convinced that man is an essentially irrational creature, filled with hostility against his fellowmen, whose transformation into a rational and social being was fraught with great difficulties and hazards. Adler, on the other hand, voiced the belief that altruism and interest in others were built-in elements of the human constitution which could be fostered and strengthened by proper education.

The question is one that does not admit of an easy and clearcut answer. First, the psychic constitution of individuals differs without a shadow of doubt. Egoism and altruism, combativeness and friendliness, acquisitiveness and willingness to share are qualities which are unevenly distributed among human beings, most of whom appear to combine both sets of opposing

---

[27] Heidegger states that, while Hegel had considered rationality as the essence of man, the clue to Nietzsche's thinking is his conception of man as a brute animal. Heidegger, *supra* n. 3, Vol. II, p. 200.

[28] The point that power can be an ennobling force if put in the service of human improvement was made by Arnold A. Rogow and Harold D. Lasswell, *Power, Corruption, and Rectitude* (Englewood Cliffs, N.J., 1963), pp. 130-131, in their criticism of Lord Acton's dictum that "power tends to corrupt and absolute power corrupts absolutely". See also *infra* Secs. 6 and 18.

dispositions in some proportion or other.[29] Secondly, little empirical evidence is available to determine whether aggressiveness and hostility are appetitive traits of human nature or mere reaction-formations to frustrating situations.[30] If the second alternative is true, the chances for controlling destructive behavior are improved; but thus far no panaceas have been devised for eliminating all disappointments in life which may call forth sociopathic responses. Thirdly, it is widely conceded today that political, economic and educational incentives favoring either self-assertive or cooperative attitudes are apt to influence individual and social behavior. This fact again stands in the way of a generally valid determination as to whether man is primarily social or antisocial.

Egocentricity seems to be innately preponderant in early life. The infant is self-seeking, insistent on immediate gratification of his desires and unwilling to share his possessions. In the words of Gordon Allport, "even at the age of two the child is, when measured by standards applied to adults, an unsocialized horror".[31] Between the fifth and seventh year, however, and sometimes earlier,[32] there is already noticeable a marked increase in cooperative behavior and a growing awareness of the rights of others. The child learns that others are not there just to fulfill his demands.[33] He also discovers that joint activities with other children require some *esprit de corps* and mutual adjustments.

---

[29] Views expressing one-sided leanings were propounded by Ardrey and Ashley Montagu. Ardrey speaks of the "probability that man is an innate killer" and also assumes a more or less compulsive drive to gain territory. Robert Ardrey, *African Genesis* (New York, 1961), p. 168; Ardrey, *The Territorial Imperative* (New York, 1966), Ch. 8. Montagu, on the other hand, assumes a strong inborn preponderance of the cooperative impulse. M. F. Ashley Montagu, *On Being Human* (New York, 1951), pp. 43-45, 92-95. Somewhere in the middle between these two positions stands the theory of Karl Lorenz, *On Aggression,* transl. M. K. Wilson (New York, 1963), pp. 48-49, 277. See the suggestive comments by Ludwig von Bertalanffy, "System, Symbol, and the Image of Man," in *The Interface between Psychiatry and Anthropology,* ed. I. Galdston (New York, 1971), pp. 90-96.

[30] It has been suggested but not definitely proved that predispositions to commit violence may be due to chromosomic peculiarities. *Sacramento Bee,* Dec. 27, 1968. The position that aggressiveness and hostility are secondary, purely reactive impulses was taken by Erich Fromm, *Man For Himself* (New York, 1947), pp. 216-218.

[31] Gordon W. Allport, *Becoming* (New Haven, 1955), p. 28.

[32] Bruno Bettelheim, *The Children of the Dream* (New York, 1969), pp. 103-104, describes the playing activities of children over two years of age in an Israeli kibbutz who are left to their own devices in enclosed play pen areas. He found that, although some children are pushed down or crawled over, this Hobbesian state of affairs usually does not last very long, and that successful conditions for cooperative play are soon created by children exhibiting some qualities of leadership.

[33] Allport, *Personality: A Psychological Interpretation* (New York, 1937), p. 425; Wilfried Ver Eecke, "Law, Morality, and Society", 80 *Ethics* 140 (1970).

The inculcation of other-regarding motivations, designed to counterbalance or supplement purely ego-centered inclinations, occurs in a slow process of education and social "conditioning", with varying and sometimes disappointing results. Throughout the range of human history it was found necessary to reinforce the social instinct by the use of legal, ethical and perhaps religious systems requiring human beings to show concern for the interests of others and to desist from acts injurious to them. Such systems have never been fully effective in controlling antisocial conduct. Hostility, greed and a quarrelsome disposition have caused grievous encroachments and untold harm in personal relations. Pugnaciousness, envy and the acquisitive spirit have been responsible for the occurrence of disruptive group conflicts and destructive international wars. Even when a reasonable degree of social harmony and cohesiveness was attained within the boundaries of a particular political society, that same society may have been embroiled in hostile encounters with other organized social units.

These unquestionable facts do not, however, demonstrate that the aggressive and destructive appetites of human beings are so strong that social peace can be achieved only at the cost of the most severe repressions. Hobbes was convinced that only an autocratic government endowed with absolute powers would be able to subdue the innate pugnaciousness of men.[34] But the history of societies which limited governmental power and granted to men a substantial amount of freedom offers proof that he was overly pessimistic. Although the social component of man's nature, according to the available evidence, is in need of external reinforcements, it seems to be sufficiently developed in the majority of men to provide psychological support for the institution of law. Most people do not appear to view the restraints of the law as unnatural shackles upon their nature.

The much-discussed question whether man is basically a competitive or cooperative creature overlaps with the problem of human aggressiveness but is not coterminous with it.[35] The view once widely held in this country that competition in the struggle for existence was an inexorable law of nature has lost a great deal of credibility. It is realized today that human beings are capable of teamwork for a common purpose. A great deal of collaborative effort is, for example, required and often achieved in modern

---

[34] Thomas Hobbes, *Leviathan,* ed. M. Oakeshott (London, 1946), Ch. XVII.

[35] Aggressive self-assertion in competition, unless it becomes tortious in character, is qualitatively different from the aggressiveness exhibited by unlawful forms of antisocial conduct.

large-scale business, governmental and educational organizations.[36] On the other hand, in countries that have based their social order in principle on anticompetitive ideals, such as the Soviet Union, a substantial amount of competition for favored positions, higher pay and admission to higher educational institutions appears to have become an important feature of social reality.

Whether or not the social organization of a country gravitates around competition or cooperation, laws designed to control the antisocial and hyperaggressive impulses of men have always been found a necessity for peaceful social living.[37] It is also worthy of notice that those modern political and social orders which have made a strong effort to replace the competitive pattern by a system of communal cooperation have experienced a need for psychological pressures and legal supports to insure labor discipline and adequate performance.[38] This would tend to indicate that the collective sentiment is not spontaneous and natural in many men but requires for its effectuation a fairly strong set of external inducements. The reply might be made that a long-continued experimentation with cooperative living would gradually fortify the social spirit and trans-substantiate it into a central source of human motivation. The question is, under present circumstances, a speculative one which need not be pursued further for purposes of this book.

These general observations on human nature were designed to set the stage for a more detailed investigation of the anthropological roots of the law.

SECTION 5
The Will to Law as Restraint on Indiscriminate Change

It has been shown that Nietzsche saw the power impulse operative as the prime driving force in the movements of nature as well as in human

---

[36] Cf. Charles K. Ferguson, "Concerning the Nature of Human Systems and the Consultant's Role", 4 *Journal of Applied Behavioral Science* 179, 185 (1968).

[37] *"Ubi societas, ibi ius"* (Where there is society, there is law), said the Romans. On this phenomenon see René Marcic, *Rechtsphilosophie: Eine Einführung* (Freiburg, 1969), pp. 20-21, 138-141.

[38] See, for example, Harold J. Berman, *Justice in the U.S.S.R.*, rev. ed. (New York, 1963), pp. 147-150, 161-162, 291-298, 350-351; Berman, *Soviet Criminal Law and Procedure* (Cambridge, Mass., 1966), pp. 7-9; John N. Hazard, *Communists and Their Law* (Chicago, 1969), pp. 346-347; Jesse Berman, "The Cuban Popular Tribunals", 69 *Columbia Law Review* 1317, 1318-1319, 1350-1354 (1969); Gary J. Edles, "Mobilization of the Masses: A Survey of Communist Chinese Labor Law", 1969 *Washington University Law Quarterly* 394, 400-408.

individual and social life.[1] The whole world, in its inorganic and organic forms, appeared to him as a huge playground for the dynamic and often dramatic encounter of power quanta and power complexes. Since Nietzsche viewed this spectacle as a disorderly welter of clashes and collisions, he was inclined to depreciate the importance of regularity and law in nature as well as human life.

It was pointed out in opposition to Nietzsche's thesis that modern physics, although it has moved away from the classical picture of a strictly law-determined universe, does not support the notion of pervasive lawlessness in the processes of nature. Regardless of whether the laws of nature are of a causal or statistical character, they enable us to predict the movements of large aggregates of physical particles with a high degree of accuracy. It is also well established that nature cannot be solely explained in Nietzschean terms as a jumble of encounters between dynamic power units. Quiescence and inertia are as much a part of the cosmic scene as active force and discharge of explosive energy.

The domain of human individual and social life in certain fundamental respects partakes of the general structure of nature. The uniformities that can be observed in nature find a counterpart in the regularities of human behavior brought about by obligatory rules of law.[2] The inertial principle, which plays such a prominent part in the operations of nature, also projects itself into the conduct of human life. It was shown by the testimony of leading psychologists and psychiatrists that display of energy, fight against obstacles, productive activity and progress are by no means the only, or even the dominant, facets of human existence. The counter-tendency to save energy and preserve an established equilibrium also appears to be an integral part of the human life process.[3]

There can be little doubt that a significant connection exists between the phenomenon of inertia, in its individual and social manifestations, and the institution of law. The connection is particularly strong in the early and primitive stage of the law, its age of childhood. The link becomes weaker as deliberate thinking about the utility and value of legal arrangements in part replaces unreflective habit. And yet, the tie to the past which characterizes individual and social inertia is never wholly severed in the

---

[1] See *supra* Secs. 2 and 4.

[2] There is, however, a difference between the rule of law in nature and in society. If we assume in consonance with the findings of many modern physicists that there are some loopholes in nature's observance of its laws, there are certainly many more breaches of human laws.

[3] See *supra* Sec. 4.

development of the law. This has the consequence that the continuity and relative stability of legal structures always operate as counterweights to rapid progress and sweeping change. It is true that at some point of time in an advancing civilization the desire for comprehensive reform of the legal order will tend to gain the upper hand over the conservative forces in the life of the law. The intrinsic properties of the law are such, however, that the time lag between social and legal growth can rarely be eliminated altogether. Legal institutions usually respond slowly and haltingly to the social needs for change.[4]

The anthropological source of the inertial component in law must be sought in certain predispositions of the human organism which are quite pronounced in early life. It was shown in the preceding section that there is, according to the findings of psychology, a strong human desire to repeat previous experiences, especially those that have been found to be pleasurable. This tendency is very conspicuous in the young child. The following examples are given by Freud to illustrate this phenomenon:

> "The child...never gets tired of demanding from a grown-up the repetition of a game he has played with him before or has shown him, till at last the grown-up refuses, utterly worn out; similarly, if he has been told a pretty story, he wants to hear the same story instead of a new one, insists inexorably on exact repetition and corrects each deviation which the narrator lets slip by mistake, which, perhaps, he even thought to gain new merit by inserting. Here, there is no contradiction of the pleasure-principle: it is evident that the repetition, the rediscovery of the identity, is itself a source of pleasure."[5]

Similarly, in conducting religious rites or celebrating holidays in the home, children are prone to demand strict adherence to previous practices and customs. The lighting of candles or singing of songs is expected to take place at a certain definite time in the festive proceedings. If phrases to be read during a ritual ceremony are altered in their wording or in the sequence of their recital, disappointment or objection are likely to be voiced.

The fact that children are strongly predisposed toward the observance of rules and established procedures offers additional evidence of the same general inclination. It may happen, of course, that the younger members of

---

[4] See Jean Beetz, "Reflections on Continuity and Change in Law Reform", 22 *University of Toronto Law Journal* 129, 130-133 (1972).

[5] Sigmund Freud, "Beyond the Pleasure Principle", in *The Major Works of Sigmund Freud,* ed. R. M. Hutchins (Chicago, 1952), [hereinafter referred to as *Major Works*], p. 651.

a family have never been exposed to regularized modes of family living, and therefore have not experienced the psychological effect of traditional or habitual ways of doing things. Where, however, it is the custom to take the meals at a certain time of the day, or to arrange a trip to the countryside every weekend, or to give a party on each child's birthday, the children themselves will usually be the first ones to insist that such rules or traditions be kept in an undeviating fashion. This same propensity will also make itself felt when household assignments have been distributed among the family members according to a fixed schedule.[6] The setting of a precedent, too, creates an anticipation of a repeat performance on a similar occasion.

Related to these desires for repetitive experience and rule observance in infantile psychology is a strong preference for maintenance of the status quo. Rudolf Bienenfeld in his analysis of "Justice in the Nursery" has furnished us with a good description of this tendency. Every child, he says, tenaciously wants to keep all his possessions and will jealously resist every attempt at an encroachment. The eldest child will vigorously defend any prerogative that has been accorded to him in view of his status. The youngest child will obstinately cling to his privilege of being spoiled as the baby.[7]

These three desires for repetitive experience, rule-adherence, and preservation of the status quo have a firm anchorage in the instinctual constitution of the child and, in some form or another, tend to remain ingrained in the texture of the adult human psyche.[8] All three in their combination constitute important anthropological and psychological foundations for the institution of law. Although they are not, as we shall see, the only building stones furnishing support for the legal structure, the persistency with which mankind has clung to the creation of legal devices

---

[6] See in this connection Gordon W. Allport, *Personality: A Psychological Interpretation* (New York, 1937), p. 170.

[7] Rudolf Bienenfeld, *Rediscovery of Justice* (London, 1947), pp. 20-21.

[8] The persistence of the instinct of repetition in the psychological life of normal adult persons is described by Freud, *supra* n. 5, p. 645. In view of the fact that some biologists and psychologists have denied the existence of human "instincts", it should be made clear that the term is used in this book in the broad and loose sense of an inner inclination or innate readiness to respond to a stimulus coming from within the organism itself. See Freud, "Instincts and Their Vicissitudes", in *Major Works*, p. 412. Cf. also William McDougall, *An Introduction to Social Psychology*, 13th ed. (Boston, 1918), pp. 23-24, 30. Instinctual responses need not be mechanical or automatic; in human beings they are usually affected and to some extent controlled by environmental influences. See Erik H. Erikson, *Childhood and Society*, 2d ed. (New York, 1963), p. 95; Abraham H. Maslow, *Motivation and Personality*, 2d ed. (New York, 1970), pp. 77-95, 103.

and legal arrangements would not be explicable without reference to these instinctual roots of the institution. Especially in early society, as we shall see, the inertial, backward-looking, tradition-oriented tendencies determine the complexion of the law in a decisive fashion.[9]

What are the connecting links between the phenomenon of law and the triad of repetition, rule-adherence and preference for the status quo?

The element of repetition is typical for the law because legal norms are designed to apply to more than one single situation. A statute governing the validity of wills is intended to be followed in innumerable instances involving the making of testamentary dispositions. A code of civil procedure will control the conduct of a large number of trials. A judicial decision dealing with the legality of a restraint on trade will not be limited in scope to the situation actually adjudicated therein; it will serve as a precedent for the appraisal of future cases in which the lawfulness of a similar business arrangement has become the subject of challenge.

The repetitive element in the legal process is closely connected with the practice of rule-adherence in the administration of justice.[10] If legal norms are designed to apply to more than one isolated occurrence, they must possess an attribute of generality which permits an extension of their sphere of operation to a multitude of cases. Some measure of generality is the characteristic attribute of all rules. Every legal system contains a congeries of prescriptions which, because they are couched in general terms, lend themselves to a more or less uniform and standardized application in a number of essentially identical or similar situations. Thus law exhibits the same predisposition towards recurrent regularity which has been found to be a strongly-ingrained propensity in children.

There should be added the caveat, however, that law does not exhaust its significance in the observance and application of rules. It also uses other vehicles of regulation and adjudication, such as general principles, precedents, social policies, and cultural value patterns. All of these additional sources share with legal rules a suitability to serve as evaluative yardsticks in a succession of cases showing identical or similar features.

The very fact that law becomes articulated in the form of rules and other normative propositions produces a pronounced orientation of law-

---

[9] See *infra* Sec. 8.

[10] "Most characteristic of law is the aspect of rule," says Charles Fried in *An Anatomy of Values* (Cambridge, Mass., 1970), p. 124. A legal system without a substantial number of formalized or nonformalized rules is indeed unthinkable. On the rule aspect of law see also Edgar Bodenheimer, *Jurisprudence: The Philosophy and Method of the Law* (Cambridge, Mass., 1962), pp. 168-173.

induced behavior toward the past. The person who wishes to act in compliance with the law, the court which seeks to decide a case in conformity with legal prescriptions, the administrator who is bound to a set of legal rules and procedures in the performance of his duties — they all look out to find for their contemplated action a source or authority which is already in existence; in many cases it is a norm which has been in force for a long period of time.[1] This norm may have sanctioned the exercise of a power or prohibited the doing of an act; it may have provided a framework of administration or put into effect a set of obligatory procedures. Whenever private or official action is taken in reliance on, or under the compulsion of, a norm, the status quo is preserved through compliance with a command originating in the past. Unless and until the applicable norm is changed, the rule of law protects the existing fabric of the political, economic, and social order. As Nietzsche observed in a suggestive formulation: "Where law prevails, a certain state and degree of power is maintained and all attempts at its augmentation and diminution are resisted."[2]

Law, however, has another side which complements its past-bound attributes.[3] While in early and stationary societies customs long adhered to keep the law in a frozen state for centuries, a developing society exhibits features of increasing mobility and differentiation. An adaptation of the law to the changing social and cultural scene will then become a matter of utmost importance. Law in such a society ceases to be experienced as a God-given, immutable reality; it becomes a target of critical appraisal in the light of its problem-solving qualities or potentialities. This process of periodic evaluation is aided by the gradual strengthening of

---

[1] There are retroactive norms which were not in existence at the time when an act or event occurred, but they are not frequent.

[2] Nietzsche, "The Dawn of the Day", in *Complete Works*, ed. O. Levy (London, 1909-1911), Vol. IX, p. 112 (No. 112) [The translation has been slightly changed]. At another place, Nietzsche characterized law as "the will to perpetuate an existing power relation". *Gesammelte Werke*, Musarion ed. (Munich, 1920-1929), Vol. XVI, p. 237.

[3] A German legal sociologist, Franz Jerusalem, was so impressed with the conservative and stabilizing properties of the law that he came quite close to proclaiming an absolute duty on the part of lawmakers and judges to give maximum protection to the status quo. He insisted that the principle of legality permits the reception and incorporation of novel ideas into the law only to the extent that they bear a sufficient similarity to legal principles and institutions already in force. Franz W. Jerusalem, *Die Zersetzung im Rechtsdenken* (Stuttgart, 1968), pp. 20, 30-32, 38-40. Such a one-sided accentuation of the conservative strain in the legal process magnifies a modicum of truth into the dimensions of an extreme and unacceptable dogma.

man's reflective capacity, which is a concomitant of cultural growth and refinement.

It may be helpful at this point to draw a parallel, within the limits set by certain disparities in the two subject matters, between individual and social development. As the child grows older, he acquires a greater awareness of his environment. His curiosity becomes aroused, he seeks to gain some information and knowledge about the world around him, and he sets out to explore some new dimensions of reality. Alongside this increase of conscious perception and purposive volition proceeds, at least in the well-endowed young person, is the development of critical intelligence and judgment. The arrangements of life affecting him will no longer be accepted as given and inevitable data. If they are detrimental to his well-being and happiness, he may make a deliberate attempt to change them. In a later phase of his personality development, the targets of critical evaluation will tend to become broader. Under proper stimulation they will be extended beyond the individual's purely personal concerns to the conditions of the group in which he lives, to the state of his society and nation and — depending on the breadth of his education and interest — to the complex of problems facing mankind as a whole. By using his faculties of observation and discernment, the individual may come to the conclusion that the existing state of affairs is unsatisfactory, that it calls for the initiation of major changes and improvements.

A corresponding evolution from unreflective acceptance of conditions as they are to an increasing reliance on intelligence as a tool for an appraisal of the social structure takes place in society as a whole. In early society, changes in social and legal institutions are approached with reluctance and aversion; strange detours sometimes are taken, as we shall see, to accomplish such readjustments when they become unavoidable. As insight into the workings of the social process increases, resistance to alterations of the status quo is apt to diminish, especially when new arrangements appear to be imperatively necessary. Disparities between the legal system and the existing sociological structure become obvious, and these discrepancies engender pressures for an adaptation of legal institutions to the prevailing state of affairs.[14] An endeavor may also be made to use the law as a deliberate primary tool for transforming an unsatisfactory social and economic structure into a more satisfactory one. This is true although there are groups in every form of society which profit from maintenance of the social or legal status quo and will therefore oppose any attempt to change it.

---

[14] For a detailed discussion see *infra* Secs. 9-11.

The faculty employed by human beings in modifying their environment and improving the conditions of their life is traditionally called *reason*. In the life of the individual, if he is able to overcome the inertia of pure drift or unquestioning submission to external authority, reason is used in coping with the world around him, choosing a life task felt to be commensurate with his capabilities, and determining the ways of self-maximation apt to aid him in reaching his full potential. In the life of a society, if a *bona fide* attempt at ameliorating existing conditions is made, reason is used to determine the directions and ends of an attack on the physical and institutional environment, as well as the suitable means for attaining the goals which have been adopted. With particular reference to the law, reason in a developing civilization functions, in one of its most essential uses, as "the organ of emphasis upon novelty"[15] which seeks to overcome inertial predispositions and to use human powers for creative objectives. From whatever side the pressures for social and legal improvement may come, a rational evaluation of ends and means to be pursued in achieving this task is the hallmark of civilized social behavior.[16]

These considerations are not meant to imply that the growth of intelligence and reflective thinking in individual and social life destroys the instinctual basis to which we have attempted to trace the phenomenon of law. The backward pull of the law, which is anchored in the repetitive appetitions of human beings, remains active as a counteragency against perpetual change and, like the forward push in the opposite direction, receives some reinforcement from rational reflection.

If change is wholly discontinuous and anarchic, it places a strain on the human constitution which cannot be borne for prolonged periods of time. Sudden and far-reaching upsets in accustomed ways of life may call for radical remedies demanding painful adjustments from the population. But there will come a point when the tendency of the organism to relieve pressure and restore a prior equilibrium will assert itself with great force. A clamor will arise for normalization and stabilization of political and social conditions, for the neutralization of tensions which threaten to disrupt the neurological and sociological balance. We find here the biological basis for the historical law that periods of turbulence and revolution are followed by epochs of consolidation and restoration in which a regular rhythm in social life — accompanied usually by a partial regression to earlier forms of

---

[15] Alfred N. Whitehead, *The Function of Reason* (Princeton, 1929), p. 20.

[16] The functions of reason in setting or directing the goals of societal justice and choosing the means for their implementation are discussed by Edgar Bodenheimer, *Treatise on Justice* (New York, 1967), pp. 33-43.

societal organization – is reinstituted. The notion of a "permanent revolution" characterized by incessant social change, as advocated by Leon Trotzky and others, would seem to be thoroughly at odds with the long-range needs of individuals and social groups.

The tendencies in human nature disfavoring indiscriminate change are to some extent coterminous with the psychological forces seeking preservation of life and bodily integrity, protection of family relations and security of possessions. A world in which everybody would exert his power to the limits of his capacity would be one in which life, liberty and property would become targets of frequent encroachments and acts of spoliation. In a whirling collision of power units, the safety of life and the continuity of the private world an individual has built for himself are exposed to constant jeopardy. This becomes manifest in a revolutionary situation when law is temporarily replaced by an unremitting struggle between political groups or social classes. While this state of affairs can be borne by human beings for a considerable period of time, a point will be reached at which the safety needs of men will reassert themselves with great force and press for a restoration of law.

The law, by the very nature of its institutional structure, acts as a brake on perpetual change by its insistence on repetitive observance of rules and other normative restraints. It is, in one of its most essential aspects, an instrumentality of stabilization, designed to protect the general security and to maintain a social equilibrium. Its conservative properties will normally reduce the number of occasions calling for a rapid adaptation of the individual and social organism to new contingencies and unprecedented challenges. If this tendency is carried too far, it produces the danger of "standpatism" and stagnation. If it is kept within intelligent bounds, the restrictive attributes of the law will serve as protective devices for the preservation of mental health in society. Security is a positive value in individual and social life as long as it is not elevated to the rank of an absolute goal which excludes recognition of competing and perhaps counteracting social and cultural values.

The development of the child, again, provides a good starting point for a discussion of the beneficial sides of security. A certain amount of stability, fixity, and continuity is an essential requirement for the child's psychological health and proper growth. Children who are moved about from one home to another or, in case of separation of the parents, are constantly transferred from one parent to the other are apt to suffer grievous damage to their sense of identity. The effects of parental neglect to give children some safe basis of orientation during their formative years are likely to be serious. It has also been found that the emotional haven of a firm cultural setting is necessary to produce a psychosocial state of equilibrium in the child. Children thrive best in an atmosphere in which certain culturally transmitted values, forms and customs impart a fair measure of steadiness and rhythm to life in the family and beyond it.[17]

The child's need for security is related to his urge for repetitive experiences stressed by Freud. His early confrontation with the world has an almost traumatic impact on him and forces him to absorb new impressions in a bewildering succession. He is often baffled by what is going on around him and therefore finds a great deal of comfort and relief in the recurrence of an event with which he is already familiar. Every "reinstatement of something earlier", as Freud put it,[18] may faintly recall in him the carefree protectiveness which he enjoyed in the maternal womb.

The child's desire for security is also related to, and finds its expression in, his aforementioned propensity to favor and follow rules. It is highly significant for purposes of our argument that there exists a great deal of psychiatric evidence pointing to the adverse effect of "anomie", *i.e.* normless modes of upbringing. A child who in his home atmosphere has never been subjected to the restraining influence of rules of conduct is likely to become disoriented and to require psychiatric help later in his life. Children reared under well-defined and reasonable rules which avoid a rigid straightjacketing of his activities have a better chance of becoming productive and creative members of society than children whose training and education has incapacitated them for the acceptance of behavioral limitations and the practice of self-restriction later in life.[19] As Emile Durkheim has shown, the ubiquity of external restraints imposed upon human beings by the environment necessitates the fostering of internal restraints.[20]

---

[17] See Andrew S. Watson, *Psychiatry for Lawyers* (New York, 1968), pp. 196-197; James S. Plant, "The Psychiatrist Views Children of Divorced Parents", 10 *Law and Contemporary Problems* 807, 812-814 (1944); Homer Clark, *The Law of Domestic Relations* (St. Paul, 1968), p. 326; Erikson, *supra* n. 8, p. 412; Cf. also *Final Report of the National Commission on the Causes and Prevention of Violence* (Washington, 1969), p. 40.

[18] Freud, *supra* n. 5, p. 652.

[19] See Stanley Coopersmith, *The Antecedents of Self-Esteem* (San Francisco, 1967), pp. 204-208, 236, 259; Kurt Goldstein, *Human Nature in the Light of Psychopathology* (Cambridge, Mass., 1951), pp. 201-206, 222; Watson, *supra* n. 17, pp. 227-228; Abraham H. Maslow, *Toward a Psychology of Being*, 2d ed. (Princeton, 1968), p. 163.

[20] Emile Durkheim, *Moral Education*, transl. E. K. Wilson and H. Schnurer (Glencoe, Ill., 1961), pp. 43-46, 50-51. See also Stephen Lukes, "Alienation and Anomie", in *Philosophy, Politics, and Society* (3rd Ser.), ed. P. Laslett and W. G. Runciman (New York, 1967), pp. 143-156; Maslow, *supra* n. 8 pp. 39-43.

These findings indicate the existence of another psychological source, closely linked to the other sources already mentioned, which feeds what may be called the "will to law". There is rooted in the inner constitution of human beings a predisposition to submit to limitations on unbounded freedom of action. Man has a desire to live within circumscribed horizons, although the counter-tendency to break out of these limits is also present in his makeup. Even when the drive toward expansion of power drowns out the urge for restriction in the interest of social adjustment, the existence of boundaries to be crossed and barriers to be surmounted is a precondition for the healthy pursuit of self-enhancement. The developing young person ready to test his strength and thrust forward into hitherto unexplored territory will not be satisfied unless some obstacles challenging his alertness and resourcefulness are placed in his way. "Bursting the bounds" presupposes the presence of hurdles to the pursuit of expansive goals. In this sense, Nietzsche's thesis that the essence of life is the overcoming of resistance carries a great deal of persuasiveness.

Confirmation of these propositions can be obtained from persons trained to deal with juvenile delinquents. The young lawbreaker, consciously or subconsciously, expects to be confronted with interdictions against his antisocial behavior. If, due to parental or societal overpermissiveness, he fails to encounter opposition, he will push farther and farther until he meets a barrier. Since there is lodged in him a deep psychological wish for an external halt to his agressiveness, his actions will become more destructive the further he pushes forward into a normative void. His state of mind may be likened to that of a group of explorers in an uncharted sea who are desperately anxious to spot the comforting sight of a shoreline.

The inner need for the security of limits as a necessary counterpoise against the expansive urges of the ego require an acclimatization of the young person to a system of controls which, although originally imposed in part from the outside, will later operate in the form of internalized "superego" restraints tending to become an integral part of the personality. Self-restriction, like self-actualization through active encroachment upon the environment, becomes natural to the individual because, if he were continuously placed in a setting with unlimited choices, he would be overwhelmed and crushed by the vastness of conflicting alternatives and competing possibilities.[21] His will to power, straining to break through the

---

[21] Watson, *supra* n. 17, p. 228; Goldstein, *supra* n. 19, pp. 203-204, 222. Rothacker has pointed out that unbounded freedom is a bottomless pit: a human being must choose among several possibilities and thereby limit himself, introduce form and norm. Erich Rothacker, *Philosophische Anthropologie*, 3rd ed. (Bonn, 1966), p. 197.

hedges of confining forces, is counteracted by his will to law, which as an energy-conserving disposition keeps in check the aggressive and forward-pushing impulses in the interest of acquiring and preserving some measure of inner and outer tranquillity. The workings of these contradictory drives are neither automatic nor uniform. They depend on environmental influences and are affected by educational practices, and their relative strength varies in different individuals.

As the developing individual reaches adulthood, his need for security remains strong. To be sure, as in the case of the child, not *any* kind of security offered to him by his environment will be accepted by him as satisfactory. The protective arrangements desired by him must be related to his fundamental needs, especially his desire to live, to be free from constant fear, to preserve his well-being and that of his family, and to protect his personal possessions. "Human welfare demands, at a minimum, sufficient order to insure that such basic needs as food production, shelter and child rearing be satisfied, not in a state of constant chaos and conflict, but on a peaceful orderly basis with a reasonable level of day-to-day security."[22]

As the invididual enters into more and more contacts with other individuals, he becomes aware that his own security is inextricably bound up with the security of his fellowmen. Already in childhood and adolescence he has come to realize that trespasses committed by him against the bodies and possessions of others are likely to provoke retaliations in kind or other hostile acts which may be harmful to him. His conscious ego, which mediates between his inner drives and the realities of the outer world, suggests to him the practical advantages of observing the Golden Rule.[23] In the words of Flugel, "with increasing experience ... even the most selfish and inconsiderate among us become conditioned to certain elementary forms of respect for the rights, feelings, and conveniences of others".[24] It is discovered by the individual that he must set limits to his own self-assertion in order to gain the respect, affection and cooperation of his fellowmen. The emergence of a conscious realization of this necessity adds

---

[22] *Law and Order Reconsidered: A Staff Report to the National Commission on the Causes and Prevention of Violence* (Washington, 1969), p. 3. On the safety needs of the individual see also Maslow, *supra* n. 8, pp. 39-43.

[23] Allport points out that Freud, who is often considered an extreme irrationalist, preserved for psychology the emphasis upon the ego as the rational agent in personality. Gordon W. Allport, *Becoming* (New Haven, 1955), p. 46.

[24] John C. Flugel, *Man, Morals, and Society* (New York, 1945), p. 242. See also Freud, *The Future of an Illusion*, transl. W. D. Robson-Scott (Garden City, N.Y., 1964), p. 19.

a rational constituent to the instinctual urge for security predominant in childhood. An originally dormant aptitude for social living, in the normal individual, is brought out and developed by experience gained through contact with others and reinforced by a positive mental attitude toward the benefits of sociality.

The progress made in strengthening social interest and mutual helpfulness is always, however, jeopardized by the persistence of egocentric self-assertiveness in its socially injurious manifestations. Even though the maturing individual becomes increasingly aware that reciprocity in evil will be the likely consequence of infringements perpetrated by him upon the person or property of others, human nature is not sufficiently endowed with automatic controls upon its own aggressiveness to prevent the occurrence of anti-social and destructive acts.[25] It may be only a relatively small minority of men in a particular society whose sociopathic tendencies may endanger the safety of life, bodily integrity and property. Nevertheless, their acts of assault, depredation, and spoliation, if left unchecked and unredressed, may wreak havoc with the community's whole fabric of life. The external controls of the law are therefore desired by men in order to reinforce the social and rational components of their nature and thereby strengthen the general security.

The restrictive aspect of behavior control through law was denounced by Nietzsche as a dangerous fetter upon a life-force whose most essential characteristic, in his view, was its explosive dynamism and expansiveness.[26] He did not entirely deny the value of security in the hurly-burly of individual and social activity. But the only security recognized by him as meaningful was, figuratively speaking, that of a mountain climber needing to gain a secure foothold before he can take on the next step in his ascent. Translated into the language of his power philosophy, this suggests that a secure grounding of a power position must be attained in his opinion before the next assault in the great struggle of life can be launched. To accomplish this end, legal arrangements may serve a useful purpose, as long as they are limited to the "exceptional condition" of a temporary pause in the uphill fight for power-expansion.[27]

This position assigns a unduly narrow scope to the human striving for security. To be sure, if an extreme weight is placed on this desire, an

[25] This point was forcefully made by Ranyard West, *Conscience and Society* (New York, 1945), pp. 165-166.

[26] See *supra* Sec. 2 and Nietzsche, *Gesammelte Werke*, Vol. XVI, p. 212.

[27] See *supra* Sec. 2, n. 26.

arrestation of individual and societal development may be the consequence. Daring, taking risks, adventure, and the exploration of new realms of experience have contributed greatly to personality growth and social improvement. Self-realization sometimes demands a departure from accepted social norms, a striking out into untried directions. Only a philistine philosophy would attribute an exaggerated importance to a quiescent attachment to safety and sheltered ways of human existence. The very necessity of changing the law from time to time produces dents in the armor of security by upsetting long-range plans and arrangements that have been made in reliance on the legally protected status quo. Moreover, overlegislation can be as detrimental to the wellbeing of a community as a lack of effective legal controls.[28] A minute regulation of all aspects of life by a tightly-closed legal system, leaving no room for spontaneous, undirected growth, may easily lead to stagnation or regression.

These observations do not, however, detract from the impelling need to impart a measure of continuity and stability to the conditions of life. Habituating people to the more or less mechanical observance of uniform rules of good conduct is a precondition for social peace and the flourishing of all higher forms of culture. As a modern German anthropologist has observed, the stabilization of one basic layer of conduct frees the performance of the higher tasks of civilization from constant attention to problems on a lower level which may interfere with an adequate discharge of these higher functions.[29] By stereotyping one area of behavior to a considerable extent, room is made for variability and flexibility in other spheres of human activity. More concretely expressed, by establishing a rock bottom layer of fundamental rules to be observed without further reflection in the intercourse of men, the law relieves the individual of the need to be constantly on his guard against assaults on his person, invasions of his home and offenses against his property. It thereby enables him to dedicate his best energies to productive work and also to enjoy the amenities of life.

Although the primary effect of legal security is to introduce some degree of orderliness into human affairs and human relations, its effectua-

---

[28] "Where life becomes frozen, legislation towers high." Nietzsche, *Gesammelte Werke*, Vol. XX, p. 237. While Nietzsche by this statement meant to give expression to his general aversion towards law, there appears to be a kernel of truth in this observation which invites reflection. Freund says suggestively that "law is a system for imposing a modicum of order on the disorder of human experience without disrespecting or suppressing a measure of spontaneity, diversity, and disarray." Paul A. Freund, "Rationality in Judicial Decisions," in *Rational Decision* (Nomos Vol. VII), ed. C. J. Friedrich (New York, 1964), p. 114.

[29] Arnold Gehlen, *Der Mensch*, 6th ed. (Bonn, 1958), pp. 69-70.

tion will also have an indirect impact on individual freedom. By guaranteeing to the individual a sphere of activity within which he is safeguarded against encroachments by others, the law at the same time allows him freedom of action and disposition within the protected domain. Within the limits set by the law, he may move about freely, enjoy his property and dispose of it, speak his mind, and enter into transactions with others. The relation between security and freedom becomes particularly clear when we consider the consequences of insufficient governmental protection against violence and crime. The inhabitants of an unsafe city are afraid to leave their homes at night, to visit friends or to attend cultural events. Although they are theoretically free to go where they please, the lack of legal security reduces them to some extent to the status of prisoners.

Although there is thus a definite connection between security and freedom, it is necessary to realize that the striving for freedom, in and by itself, is more closely linked to the power impulse than to the psychological springs feeding the will to law. The most radical form of freedom is the freedom of anarchy which would permit every man "to do his own thing" without any governmental and legal restraints. Such a mode of life would place no obstacles in the path of an individual who sets out to expand his power as far as he can. Freedom may therefore exist in the absence of law, although such a condition of "anomie" would in the long run tend to be self-defeating.[30]

Security, on the other hand, cannot be established without the help of the law. In a state of nature unregulated by law, men would live dangerously and without institutional guarantees designed to protect their lives and individual interests. This insight provides an explanation for the fact that law has never been defined in terms of unrestrained liberty of action. Even those conceptions of law which center around the concept of freedom have emphasized the necessity for limitations. "Every man is free to do that which he wills," said Spencer, "provided he infringes not the equal freedom of any other man."[31] Kant characterized law in a similar way as the creation of conditions under which the free will of one person can coexist with the free will of everybody else.[32] In both of these definitions,

---

[30] This theme is developed at greater length by Edgar Bodenheimer, "Philosophical Anthropology and the Law", 59 *California Law Review* 653, 675 (1971).

[31] Herbert Spencer, *Justice* (New York, 1891), p. 46.

[32] Immanuel Kant, *The Metaphysical Elements of Justice,* transl. J. Ladd (Indianapolis, 1965), p. 35. A view of justice influenced by the Kantian conception of law was developed by John Rawls, "Justice as Fairness", 67 *Philosophical Review* 164 (1958). Reflections on the ideas of Kant and Rawls are found in Fried, *supra* n. 10, pp. 44, 61-66. On freedom and law see also Fried, "Natural Law and the Concept of Justice", 74 *Ethics* 237 (1964).

it is accommodation and harmonization of individuals' rights and powers that is demanded as a prerequisite for justice. Freedom must be bounded so as to prevent abuses which are hurtful to the community. At the same time freedom must be made safe by guarantees against trespassory acts and invasions of private spheres. Thus the security function of law extends to the protection of areas in which the individual is declared to be free from interference by others.

Because of the substantial benefits which legal security confers on human beings living in society, some political and legal philosophers have declared it to be the foremost function of government to provide for its realization.[33] And indeed, the task of safeguarding life, the bodily and mental integrity of the person, and the safety of possessions by an effective system of law is a political task of utmost importance. It is not, however, the *sole* task of government and law to secure orderly conditions of life, as has sometimes been asserted. The law has to fulfill other objectives which also derive from some deep-seated inclinations and needs of human beings. These further anthropological roots of the law will be discussed in the next section.

SECTION 6
The Will to Law as Restraint on Domination

"Commanding and obeying are the fundamental facts," says Nietzsche, and he adds that this facet of reality "presupposes a hierarchy".[1]

In this passage the Nietzschean tendency to attribute to one aspect of the "human condition" the character of an absolute truth again clearly comes to the fore. Nobody will deny that relations of domination and subjection between human beings have existed from the earliest times to the present, on a private as well as on a governmental level. Children in some cultures have been brought up to obey blindly the commands of their parents. In the history of mankind, myriads of slaves and servants have

---

[33] Thomas Hobbes, *Leviathan,* ed. M. Oakeshott (London, 1946), Ch. XVII; Jeremy Bentham, *The Theory of Legislation,* ed. C. K. Ogden (London, 1931), p. 98; Rudolph von Jhering, *Law as a Means to an End,* transl. I. Husik (New York, 1924), p. 380; Luis Recaséns Siches, "Human Life, Society, and Law," in *Latin-American Legal Philosophy,* ed. J. Kunz (Cambridge, Mass., 1948), pp. 118-123.

---

[1] Nietzsche, *Gesammelte Werke,* Musarion ed. (Munich, 1920-1929) [hereinafter referred to as *Gesammelte Werke*], Vol. XVI, p. 146.

carried out the orders of their masters without a murmur or questioning. Many persons, for psychological reasons or because of physiological infirmities, have lived in a state of complete dependency upon another person. Absolute rulers or autocratic governments have often treated their subjects like minors in need of a guardian. Political communities have been brought under the heel of other political communities, continuing their existence as conquered territories, colonies, or satellite nations.

Where hierarchical relations arise among men or between States, either in a factual or legally sanctioned context, their emergence is attributed by Nietzsche to the ubiquitous working of the power impulse. Although, as we have seen earlier,[2] the Nietzschean will to power is not coterminous with the will to dictate to others by peremptory commands — it may find a more spiritualized expression, for example, in the desire of a great painter, composer, or architect to remold the artistic taste of the public in his own image — the determination to dominate men in the commonly accepted sense covers a broad spectrum of life in his scheme of thought. Sometimes the will to power is bluntly defined by Nietzsche as the human desire to overwhelm or pounce upon the weak, to subjugate and exploit others, and to force one's own forms of life upon them.[3] In the relation between States, Nietzsche saw the will to power manifest itself in the determination of every strong nation to "rule as a victorious, tyrannical, and arbitrary nation over other nations".[4] The most outspoken affirmation of Nietzsche's belief in undiluted power is found in his statement that it is the mark of a great man to rule because he wants to rule — and not because he wants to serve his people or realize an impersonal political goal.[5]

Two basic doubts must be raised with respect to the psychological soundness of Nietzsche's position. The first doubt concerns the genetic explanation of situations in which hierarchical structures characterized by relations of dominance and subordination have arisen in the social order. It cannot be conceded that the causes for the creation of such structures must be sought exclusively in the motivations supplied by the power impulse. Under certain historical conditions, especially in times of crisis or

---

[2] See *supra* Secs. 2 and 4.

[3] Nietzsche, *The Will to Power,* ed. W. Kaufmann (New York, 1968), p. 346 (No. 655); Nietzsche, "Beyond Good and Evil", in *Complete Works,* ed. O. Levy (London 1909-1911), Vol. XII, p. 226 (No. 259).

[4] Nietzsche, "The Dawn of the Day", in *Complete Works,* Vol. IX, p. 186.

[5] Nietzsche, *Gesammelte Werke,* Vol. XIV, p. 209.

war, reasonable men not possessed by the power demon may come to the conclusion that a political setup in which the stream of authority runs in a unilateral manner from the top to the bottom will be the only suitable means for coping with the exigencies of the situation. If this contingency occurs, the chosen stewards of a nation need not be motivated exclusively or primarily by lust for domination in exercising the absolute or near-absolute authority conferred upon them. Genuine leaders of world-historical significance will not accept a call to duty simply because they are drunk with a feeling of power. It is more likely that — in contrast to mere politicians — they will be imbued with a sense of vocation or commitment to a worthwhile cause in approaching and discharging their task. It was Nietzsche's denial of the force of ideas and ideals, and his unrealistic belief that these were mere camouflages of power drives, which blinded him to a recognition of this fact.

That a leader committed to an objective which transcends his will to self-aggrandizement may at the same time derive a feeling of great personal satisfaction from a successful handling of the instrumentalities of power employed by him in effectuating his goals is true but a matter of collateral importance. Such a feeling is entirely natural and does not detract from the possible meritoriousness of the undertaking. The salient point is that relations based on subordination or hierarchy may owe their existence, in certain historical contexts, to a considered judgment of objective necessity or political urgency rather than to the subjective seductions of the desire to exercise authority.

The second objection that must be made to Nietzsche's position is more far-reaching and touches the nerve-trunk of his approach to the problems of power and law. Over and over again Nietzsche described the primary life-force in terms of the impulse to conquer, to exploit, to overwhelm, to dominate, to subjugate. But it is also true that most men have a strong desire to be free from domination by others, to avoid being subjugated, to resist being mere objects of exploitation. Although the urge to exercise power over other persons may be quite pronounced in some human beings, their simultaneous desire of not being subjected in their own persons to the arbitrary will of others will probably be just as strongly developed. While both of these tendencies may easily coexist in the same individual, their relative strength will vary with the character traits, upbringing, life histories, and environmental surroundings of different personalities.

Empirical evidence supporting this psychological proposition can be abundantly found in contemporary society as well as in history. Although young children normally accept the authority of their parents without opposition, the growing youngster will often develop a rebellious attitude against certain manifestations of parental power which he views as threats to his independence. Pupils in school may offer resistance in some form or other when the enforced measures of discipline are felt by them to be oppressive. The movements for workers' coalitions in Western civilization were at least in part directed against the unlimited right of employers to set wages, prescribe the conditions of work and dismiss workers at their discretion. ᛁIn social orders sanctioning slavery, the exercise of arbitrary power by the masters was not always accepted by the slaves as a natural and inevitable fact of life. When abuses of this power became widespread, as in certain periods of Roman history, not only local revolts but even large-scale national uprisings by the slave population caused serious disruptions of the political life. Women have frequently fought against disabilities imposed upon them by the rule of the male sex. Nations dominated by other nations have on many occasions put up vigorous struggles to shake off the yoke.

A defender of Nietzsche's philosophy might reply that defiance of the power of another man or group was merely a manifestation of the challenger's will to enhance his own power at the expense of his adversary. On this assumption a group fighting a struggle for freedom and emancipation would be motivated solely or predominantly by the determination to maximize its own strength.

This interpretation overlooks the fact that a person or group seeking a greater share of independence and autonomy may wish to gain a position of increased equality rather than to reverse, if possible, the role of dominant and dominated party in its favor. The relations between human beings cannot be explained primarily in terms of a struggle for supremacy in which the establishment of relations of domination and subjection is the natural outcome.[6] Such a view sees the law of life in incessant strife, followed by conquest and rule. But although contest and strife form a significant part of reality, men also have an inclination to live in peace and tranquillity and meet their fellowmen on the basis of equality and mutual respect. This inclination may exist not only on the part of those who find themselves in an inferior status but may also be present in the minds of those who are in a position to exercise power. The holders of powers may be ready and willing to treat other men as fellow human beings rather than as subordinates or slaves.

---

[6] Nietzsche did not deny that conditions of equality between social groups might be established in a society. Such equality, however, was viewed by him as a mere standoff, a temporary stalemate and armistice preparatory to a new assault in the struggle for power. See *supra* Sec. 2, n. 23.

To Nietzsche, the inequality of men was a phenomenon of such over-powering force that he could think of social organization only in terms of a hierarchy. His emphasis on domineering and obeying as fundamental requirements in human relations therefore conveys a one-sided picture of social reality. The common humanity of men makes it perfectly natural for many of them, in spite of inevitable differences in ability and character, to deemphasize inequality and live together in a fraternal spirit.

It is the upshot of these considerations that a fight of men or groups of men for an equality that has been denied to them is not necessarily or in most instances a fight for the acquisition of superior power. The chief objective of the encounter may be the accomplishment of a more demo-cratic form of society. It may not even be complete equality that is aimed at, but merely a reduction of inequality for the benefit of the previously suppressed group.

A demurrer might be interposed at this juncture of the argument that a social struggle of this character is a struggle for freedom rather than for equality. And indeed, it cannot be denied that freedom is one of the great prizes that is sought after by an individual, group or nation fighting for independence from oppressive power. Any decisive gain made by a dis-favored individual or aggregate of individuals in such a fight is bound to increase the liberty of that individual or aggregate of individuals. For example, when the disabilities imposed by the common law upon married women in the area of contractual capacity were removed by legislation, their freedom to enter into commercial transactions was greatly enlarged. When the barons at Runnymede and their allies extracted from the King the promise that henceforth no freeman's person or property would be seized without due process of law, the impact of this commitment upon the freedom of a substantial number of men was obvious. The struggle of the American colonists against the power of the British Crown ultimately resulted in the promulgation of a constitution which recognized certain basic freedoms of individuals. The equality fought for by men is in many instances an equality of opportunity for self-fulfillment.

It is no accident that Nietzsche, as the champion of a thoroughly hierarchical structure of society, reserved his strongest fire power for a criticism of equality as a social ideal. He denounced equality as a "poison", a most harmful notion. No greater lie could be uttered, he said, than the assertion that human beings are entitled to equality of treatment.[7] He pleaded for restoration of a caste system because such a system would

---

[7] Nietzsche, "The Twilight of the Idols", in *Complete Works*, Vol. XVI, pp. 108-109 (9th essay, No. 48); Nietzsche, *The Will to Power*, pp. 256, 458 (Nos. 464, 860).

furnish the most adequate symbolic representation of the necessity for a gradated order among men.[8] Since power expansion was to him the law of life, and since power was distributed among human beings in highly uneven proportions, any attempt to treat unequal men as equals and thereby to improve the lot of the weaker appeared to him as a supreme form of injustice.

Thus Nietzsche could see that the endeavor to increase equality among men is a potent antidote to an unrestrained roaming of the power impulse. The psychological drive in men which resists submission to power is at the same time a drive for the attainment of greater equality. This drive, like the urge for security described in the preceding section, has an instinctual as well as a rational basis. It asserts itself as an unreflective urge to act as one pleases, free from direction by others, and to be recognized as a person in one's own right, but it is also amenable to rational explanation and justification. One of the strongest arguments in favor of equality is the inability of self-appointed masters to judge the qualifications of large numbers of subordinate people objectively and make valid determinations to the effect that a certain person should be included in, or excluded from, the dominant elite. Wherever hierarchical structures with pronounced rank differentiations have been created, the inevitability of misclassifications (often due to nepotism, poor judgment or faulty testing methods) has cast a cloud over the effectiveness and justice of the system.

The same method of rational evaluation which brings to light the advantages of some measure of equality may also lead to the discernment of necessary limitations on this principle of social organization. Equality of decision-making power, for example, becomes of dubious value where some members of a group called upon to take an important step have a technically superior knowledge of the subject matter which is crucial in the exercise of sound judgment. When a team of men consisting of a few engineers and a large number of laborers is entrusted with the building of a bridge, equality of voting power with respect to matters pertaining to the safety of construction might not produce the most satisfactory results. In an army, soldiers for obvious reasons cannot be given a power of command equal to that of officers, or be given the right to overrule military orders by majority vote. On the other hand, where the matter is one which calls chiefly for the use of common sense in the normal affairs of life or for judgments on general policies for the community, the "one man, one vote"

---

[8] Nietzsche, "The Antichrist", in *Complete Works,* Vol. XVI, pp. 217-219 (No. 57); *Gesammelte Werke,* Vol. XI, p. 218.

principle may provide the most adequate solution for disposition of the problem.

Although recognition of inequality is imperative in some sectors of social life, the striving for equality has played a highly significant role in the history of human civilizations. Most political and social encounters between masters and serfs, governors and governed, employers and employees, academic administrators and students, majority and minority groups have centered around the finding of ways by which the rights of the previously weaker group would be strengthened at the expense of the dominant group, with the result that an increased (though not necessarily complete) equalization would be established between the two groups.

Whenever this sociological situation has arisen, the law has played an important role in the final settlement of a struggle for greater equality. If the gains obtained in the struggle are to be secured on a more than transient basis, some durable legal arrangements must be made in which the newly-recognized rights and duties of the parties are confirmed. Examples that can be gathered from a study of political, social and legal history to illustrate this point are legion. When the strife between the plebeians and patricians in Rome ended in a victory for the former the substantial political and social gains made by the plebeian class were acknowledged and formalized by a series of public laws, some of which remained a permanent part of the Roman republican constitution.[9] The rights wrested from the English Crown by the barons and their allies in the thirteenth century were defined in a famous legal document. Equal voting rights secured by women in the United States found their expression and protection in a constitutional amendment. The fights of workers to bargain collectively with respect to wages and conditions of employment were legalized by statutes. Newly-won rights of students to participate in the governance of their university were often confirmed in the charter or by-laws of academic institutions. In the area of international relations, the liberation of a nation from the sovereignty of another nation has commonly been placed on a legal basis by the recognition and guaranty of the acquired independence by means of a treaty. It can be safely stated that without subsequent legal ratification the winning of greater equality and privileges by any social group or political unit would often have rested on a highly insecure basis.

There exists thus a definite link between the urge for equality, born of a psychological antagonism against subjection to arbitrary power, and the institution of law. The will to law is deeply anchored in the human desire

---

[9] See *infra* Sec. 16, under (a).

to be free from domination by others. It is reinforced by the willingness of ruling groups governed by reason to lay to rest the struggle for power. These manifestations of the will to law may not exist in the same strength and proportion in all human beings. They may be weakly developed in some members of the human race.[10] But there is no doubt that the will to law as clothed in the garb of the antidomination instinct has played a vital part in the great political, social and economic transformations that have accompanied the development of civilization.

The desire of men and groups to face other men and groups on the basis of equality rather than subordination is kept in check and often thwarted, wholly or in part, by the counter-inclination of human beings to gain power over their fellowmen and exercise it with a minimum of restraint. The domineering impulse is always present somewhere as an underground force, ready to explode under propitious circumstances. Regardless of whether or not the will to domination is healthy, as Nietzsche assumed — or pathological, as Adler asserted — it operates as a strong motivating force in a substantial number of human beings. If this were not true, there would have been no tangible target at which the desire of men to be free from domination could have directed its momentum.

The domination instinct cannot be interpreted exclusively in terms of a wholly irrational feeling of gratification at having others placed helplessly at one's own mercy. Its presence, where it occurs, may in part be the byproduct of a clearly discernible ontological phenomenon. Nature has endowed men with physical strength and mental capacities under a highly unequal system of distribution. The desire to exercise superior power may therefore in some, though certainly not all, cases stem from the fact of actual superiority. Those equipped with great physical vigor, determination of will, and mental resourcefulness may deem it their birthright to govern those who are less vigorous and clever. Where, due to the peculiar ethos of a particular group or society, this feeling is not mitigated by moral and rational considerations regarding the worth of man and the desirability of mutual benevolence, the will to power may easily display itself in a highly virulent form.

Where this situation obtains, the will to law is drowned out by a determination on the part of the ruling group to deny the benefit of rights

---

[10] There are probably many persons who have a conscious or unconscious desire to be led. This does not mean that they wish to be coerced into actions or be hindered in the execution of their personal aims by men who have power over them. It means only that they are easy targets of persuasion for charismatic leaders, without necessarily becoming their inert tools. Victor Kraft, *Die Grundlagen der Erkenntnis und der Moral* (Berlin, 1968), pp. 115-116; Alfred Verdross, *Statisches und Dynamisches Naturrecht* (Freiburg, 1971), p. 97.

to those ruled by it, or certain groups among them. A governing elite which is in a position to impose its will upon the weaker members of society without bridles and to enforce it without fear of effective opposition is not in need of resort to the law. Law is in its very essence a restraint on power because the generality of a normative pronouncement, if it is more than pure rhetoric, binds the addressees to a certain kind of conduct in the future.[11] The exercise of arbitrary power, on the other hand, is necessarily *ad hoc*. The capricious sultan in *The Arabian Nights* wanted to be free to pronounce a death sentence whenever it suited his whim of the moment, and not according to the terms of a statute defining the elements of a capital crime. The corsairs of the Barbary Coast were determined to seize ships whenever they coveted the goods carried by them, and not pursuant to a maritime code laying down the conditions under which prizes might be taken. Those intent upon exercising power without restraint are contemptuous of rules, precedents, and regularized procedures.

The will to power, in its undiluted form, therefore stands in antithesis to the will to law. This becomes manifest particularly when the effects of pure power rule are compared with the consequences of rule by law. Although pure power rule may occasionally be helpful in achieving needed transformations in society, its exercise over long periods of time will usually result in conditions of oppression. The rule of law, on the other hand, unless it has become deformed by tactics of Machiavellian manipulation, is for the most part beneficial to the interests of the weaker groups in society.[12]

In reality, if past experience is a safe guide to judgment, neither power nor law will ever reign supremely and unqualifiedly in a society. Since men have both the desire to exercise power and to curb power, a battle on the political and social plane between these two conflicting impulses will tend to keep intact enclaves of ill-controlled power even in societies intent upon being governed by the rule of law.

The will to law has presented itself in the preceding investigations in a two-fold shape. One of its manifestations is a human inclination to guard against indiscriminate and chaotic change by the creation of a normative structure which permits men to live under conditions of relative stability and security. The will to law also makes its appearance in the form of a

---

[11] See in this connection Lon L. Fuller, *The Morality of Law*, rev. ed. (New Haven, 1969), Ch. II.

[12] This will be shown in some detail in Secs. 16 and 17.

social defense mechanism against the exercise of arbitrary, unfettered power by men over other men. How do these two anthropological and psychological roots of the law relate to each other? Are there any connections between the desire for stability and the wish for equality which lend a modicum of unity to the goals of the law?

At first sight it might seem that the sense of security and the antidomination instinct would tend to push the development of the law into different and perhaps even opposite directions. The striving for constancy aims at preserving things as they are; it is averse to change unless the need for making adjustments obtrudes itself with great cogency. The desire to eliminate repression and power rule would appear, in contrast thereto, to involve a determination to revamp the law in the direction of greater equality. Thus one of the two drives would tend to hold back, and apply a brake to, the dynamic forces in social and legal life, while the other one would operate so as to push the law forward along the road toward active reform.

This first impression is misleading, however. It is true that a struggle for emancipation from stifling forms of power rule is aimed at the accomplishment of political and social change. But in order to safeguard any success won by the formerly weaker side in this struggle, demands will be made for a legal ratification of the new state of affairs. Examples of consolidations of newly-won power positions by means of legal enactments have already been given.

It is at this critical point that some sort of a confluence takes place between the two streams from which the will to law is being fed. Although the antidomination instinct may press for social change in order to redress forms of inequality felt to be oppressive, the conservative, inertial predispositions of the human psyche come to the fore again when the time arrives for a legal termination of the power struggle. The main effort will then be directed at a perpetuation and regularization of the status quo which has emerged as the result of a new balance of forces. The repetition-seeking, past-oriented attitude takes over when the law appears on the plane to replace power in a major readjustment of human political, social and economic relations. The values of security and equality converge in the insistence that the rights and freedoms created by the new order of things be enforced firmly, regularly and equally in favor of all persons entitled to them.

It must also be kept in mind that the stabilization and regularization of human relations by means of legal rules prevents one man from exercising his free, untrammeled volition in dealing with his fellowmen. For example, the fixation of the feudal serf's duties by the customary law of the manor, reserving to him some time for attending to his own affairs, prevented the lord from exploiting the serf solely for his own purposes and pushing him around according to his changing moods. In the area of contemporary employment relations, a determination of wage rates and working hours by statute or enforceable contract denies to the employer the power to make allowance and extent of compensation dependent from day to day on unchallenged compliance by the employee with whatever orders the employer happens to issue to him. Adherence to the rules of a criminal code restrains the government from seizing and punishing a person solely for the reason that by some action of his he has incurred the displeasure of the authorities. Whenever norms are observed and enforced with a certain degree of continuity and consistency, an element of predictability is imparted to human affairs which puts men in a position to know what is expected of them and what kind of action they must avoid in order to protect themselves against adverse consequences. In this sense, a structuring of social relations by norms exhibiting some measure of stability (subject, of course, to overriding needs for change) is an indispensable condition for securing and implementing the function of the law to act as a brake on arbitrary power. It is not, however, a *sufficient* condition for the achievement of this goal: to the extent that the rules governing human relations are unreasonable, unjust or oppressive, the rule of law in society is jeopardized or defeated.

It appears from the preceding considerations that the two chief anthropological roots of the law have a tendency to grow together and become intertwined, although they will continue to remain distinguishable. This insight permits us to make some generalizations about the law which a comparative study of its operation and effects in the history of social groupings would seem to confirm. The law attempts to stabilize and secure human relations against the onrush of chaotic, uncontrolled and potentially destructive forces of change. It also seeks to curb the will to power by reducing natural inequalities which, in their political and social consequences, may give rise to the tyrannical rule of men over other men. By performing these functions, the law will reduce friction and keep down disruptive strife between individuals, groups and nations. As a refrigeration machine preserves food by keeping it cool, the law decreases the heat engendered by struggles for personal advantage, power or supremacy and thereby prevents premature social decay and decomposition. Since the law is never wholly effective in discharging its task, the cooling-off process it seeks to initiate and maintain by consolidation of political and social relations will always be subject to interruptions and disturbances.

In contrast to the tension-relieving tendencies of a workable order of law, an unrestrained rule of power is likely to augment rather than reduce friction in social life. Where an individual, group or nation seeks to exercise an unfettered and essentially arbitrary dominion over other individuals, groups or nations, resistance and strife may be expected to result from this state of affairs. In the long run, the stresses, tensions and dislocations brought about by conditions of personal or collective oppression are apt to break out into explosive conflagrations, on a small or large scale. As in nature, the constant generation and application of heat in political, social and international life will produce weariness and exhaustion. If consuming fires burn in society over prolonged periods of time, the attempts to control and extinguish them will strain the nervous energies of men to the utmost.[13] Finally, men will turn again to the processes of the law to restore physical, mental and social homeostasis.

It is one of the chief objections to Nietzsche's philosophy that he overemphasized and at the same time glorified the "hot", stress-producing, explosive forces in nature and human life, paying only scant and usually derisive attention to the countervailing factors. Life was for him struggle, war, power rule and chaotic change. He had no commendatory words for social harmony, peace, fraternity and stable conditions of law. Apart from possible moral criticisms of this position, its biological dubiousness is evident. A Nietzschean society would consume itself rapidly in a heat death caused by unceasing friction. A social order which avails itself of the social pacifier called law only in "exceptional" situations, as he demanded,[14] has little chance to survive for long. It lacks the moderation and limit-setting ingredients which are essential requirements of a viable and durable social structure.[15]

In the context of this analysis of the nature of law, the inertial properties of the law discussed in Section 5 appear in a new and some-what unexpected light. The modern social scientist is inclined to regard any symptoms of inertia in social life as signs of standstill and lack of progress. The natural scientist, on the other hand, in appraising the role of inertia in the structure of the cosmos, does not share his colleague's derogatory attitude towards the phenomenon. He is aware that the inertial forces keeping stellar bodies in a fixed orbit tend to prevent them from

---

[13] "Absolute quietude is death, absolute tension is unbearable." Erich Rothacker, *Philosophische Anthropology*, 3rd ed. (Bonn, 1966), p. 197.

[14] See *supra* Sec. 2, n. 26.

[15] See in this connection Albert Camus, *The Rebel*, transl. A. Bower (New York, 1956), pp. 294-297, 301-302.

taking off on a course of collision with other celestial bodies. A legal system, by inducing regularized and norm-oriented behavior and thereby decreasing the frequency of unpredictable random motions in the social body, accomplishes a function very similar to that performed by cosmic inertia. The law has registered considerable successes in curbing individuals and groups within an organized society from embarking on a course of conduct leading to potentially destructive clashes and hostile encounters. It has also attempted, with much less success, to restrain sovereign national units from coming to blows with each other. It would seem clear, in view of these observations, that the inertial attributes connected with the operation of the law, if kept within reasonable and proper bounds, carry with them decided benefits for the social process, at least in a healthy and well-balanced societal order.

The next chapter of the book will address itself in greater detail to the conservative tendencies in the law and at the same time discuss the devices used to counteract their socially disadvantageous effects. The third chapter will pursue further the problem of equality and domination taken up in the present section. In addition to some more general comments on this problem, an outline will be presented of some major scenes in the historical drama in which men have struggled for power, freedom and equality, accentuating in particular the role which the law has played in these struggles.

CHAPTER II

STABILITY AND GROWTH IN THE LAW

SECTION 7
Preliminary Observations

It was pointed out in the first chapter that a reasonable amount of security in the conditions of life is an indispensable requirement of a healthy social life. Although there are times when highly unsettled conditions and crisis situations prevent the maintenance of such basic security, the nervous strain placed on human beings by prolonged periods of chronic unrest and strife will ultimately produce a strong desire for return to a stabilized way of life.

It was also shown that the wish of most human beings to be free from oppressive forms of domination and to enjoy the right to shape their lives without constant interference from others is related to the striving for basic security. Men have always attempted to solidify the gains made in the struggle for a greater share of freedom and equality by a consolidation of newly-won rights in order to secure their continued recognition.

The yearning for security in social life engenders the need for stability in law. If law were nothing but an ephemeral, *ad hoc* arrangement good only for a day or a week, it would not be possible to guarantee to human beings that minimum amount of sheltered existence which is prerequisite to their physical and mental health. It would also be impossible to spell out their rights and obligations with that degree of certainty which will permit them to plan their lives in anticipation of the consequences likely to result from their conduct.

It is implicit in the nature of things, however, that the stability afforded by law can only be partial and relative. The interactions of men and groups in social reality produce changes, realignments, shifts of direction and unforeseeable problems that impart a measure of uncertainty and fluidity to the course of human events. The law cannot insulate itself from this dynamic element in the history of the human race.

It is to be taken into account, on the other hand, that the changes and variations that take place in social reality rarely effectuate a complete transformation of the objects exposed to their impact: they usually affect some parts of a social structure and leave other parts unimpaired.[1] This gives the law a chance to preserve those components of social organization that exhibit features of relative constancy. Furthermore, the legal system, by formulating rules and precedents to be followed in the future on a regular basis, offers some inertial resistance to the sweep of change. But, as Lins correctly points out, "although law has static structural elements, it also partakes of the variation".[2] If its inhibiting effect on change were absolute or rigid, the law would come to represent a social reality which is irretrievably gone. It would be a monument of the past without sufficient relevance to the life of the present.

Roscoe Pound has said that "all thinking about law has struggled to reconcile the conflicting demands of the need of stability and of the need of change".[3] It is not the purpose of this book to restate these well-known ideas.[4] What will be attempted in this chapter is to reassess the problem in terms of the dichotomy between power and law and the polarities incident to this distinction. The basic theme to be developed with some specificity is the interaction of power forces and legal structures within a social "field". It will be suggested that power factors operating from outside the law are more likely to push the legal system in the direction of needed basic change than can be expected from the repair work performed by the internal management of the law.

When law develops as a result of "internal, silently-operating forces"[5] under a system based on custom and tradition, change is bound to be imperceptibly slow. When an attempt is made to entrust the adjustment of law to the shifting social scene to the organs charged with the administration of justice (such as the judiciary and the law enforcement officers), change is likely to be gradual, small-scale in scope and uneven.

When, on the other hand, transformations of the legal system are accomplished from the outside by the activity of organs endowed with political power to effectuate change, the dynamism of the process is increased. A legislature not tied down by very detailed and rigid constitu-

---

[1] See Mario Lins, *The Philosophy of Law: Its Epistemological Problems* (Rio de Janeiro, 1971), p. 43.

[2] *Id.*, p. 43. Suggested as an historical study of the interplay between inertial drift and creative use of the law is J. Willard Hurst's *Law and Social Process in United States History* (Ann Arbor, 1960).

[3] Roscoe Pound, *Interpretations of Legal History* (Cambridge, Eng., 1930), p. 1.

[4] For a survey see Edgar Bodenheimer, *Jurisprudence: The Philosophy and Method of the Law* (Cambridge, Mass., 1962), pp. 218-220.

[5] Friedrich C. von Savigny, *Of the Vocation of Our Age for Legislation and Jurisprudence,* transl. A. Hayward (London, 1831), p. 30.

tional restraints can reform the law to a far-reaching extent. A constitutional body freed from the dead weight of the past can achieve a basic regeneration of the legal order. A Government invested with extensive power can, under favorable circumstances, effectuate necessary alterations on a large scale, but power that has become absolute may lead to a dangerous infusion of arbitrariness into the law.

These considerations have prompted the introduction of a distinction between the external and internal dynamics of the law, which is designed to pinpoint the varying strength of the interpenetrations between change and stability in the life of the law.[6] There are elements of puzzlement and mystery in the exact working of this process. The result of the interaction of the two opposing forces seems to be, however, that law is neither primarily an instrument of social change nor in its essence an organ for the perpetuation of the status quo. Its function has always been to curb deleterious manifestations of discontinuity and to direct the dynamic, power-charged forces of social life into controllable channels. But in discharging this function the law has had to absorb the impact of these external forces pressing upon its stable nuclei, and under favorable circumstances this impact has been sufficiently strong to prevent stagnation and a disadvantageous prevalence of regressive tendencies in societal development. Thus we must make a distinction between the expansive, kinetic forces in social and legal development and the restrictive, limit-setting devices which resist or slow down the momentum of these forces and mitigate their explosive effect.

It will be explained in the following sections what roles are played by the various instrumentalities operative in the legal process — such as custom, legislation, equity, judicial action, law enforcement practices — in maintaining and readjusting the equilibrium between continuity and change in the life of the law.

SECTION 8
Custom and Early "Immutable" Law

The thesis was advanced in the first chapter that there exists in human beings, on an individual level, an inclination to repeat earlier experiences, especially those that were found to be satisfactory, and that this urge for

---

[6] The distinction is introduced at the beginning of Sec. 9, *infra.*

reinstatement of a past event was particularly strong in the child.[1] It was also shown that there is a countertendency toward growth and self-enlargement which slowly but surely, along with the development of awareness, motivates the normal person to seek new experiences or renew earlier ones in an improved form. Significant parallels to these psychological phenomena may be found in the social and legal history of mankind.

Repetition of past practices, often attaining an almost compulsive force, dominates the collective life of early man. It is a commonplace statement, denied by hardly anyone, that custom was a social force of great significance in primitive society. Firmly established tradition was generally viewed with awe, its faithful observance was often reinforced by religious beliefs and sanctions, and alterations occurred slowly and reluctantly.[2] According to the Bible, the Medes and Persians went so far as to reject the idea of change in their law altogether.[3]

Among the reasons casting the halo of sanctity upon custom and law was their connection with the cult of ancestor-worship. Not only did primitive people pay reverent homage to their forbears but they tended to believe that these remained alive in their graves, needing to be supplied with food, clothing and utensils.[4] Deviation from usages and forms of life approved and practiced by the departed was viewed as sacrilegious. Since it was thought that the dead, and especially the former chiefs among them, were still watching over the tribe, it becomes understandable why in the mind of primitive man, on frequent occasions, "the wisdom of his ancestors can control against the most obvious evidence of his own opinions and actions".[5]

----

[1] See in particular *supra* Sec. 5.

[2] See, among many others, Paul Vinogradoff, "Custom and Law", in *Anthropology and Early Law,* ed. L. Krader (New York, 1966), pp. 19, 28; Sidney Hartland, *Primitive Law* (London, 1924), pp. 78, 137, 203-214; Max Kaser, *Das Altrömische Ius* (Göttingen, 1949), pp. 22-34; Max Gluckman, *Custom and Conflict in Africa* (New York, 1966), pp. 17-18; Jacob C. Vergouwen, *The Social Organization and Customary Law of the Toba-Batak of Northern Sumatra* (The Hague, 1964), pp. 140-141.

[3] Daniel 6:8.

[4] N. D. Fustel de Coulanges, *The Ancient City,* 10th ed., transl. W. Small (Boston, 1901), p. 15; Edward B. Tylor, *Primitive Culture* (London, 1920), Vol. II, pp. 113-120; Lucien Lévy-Bruhl, *The 'Soul' of the Primitive,* transl. L. A. Clare (New York, 1966), pp. 232, 241-242, 271; Vergouwen, *supra* n. 2, pp. 140-141.

[5] Tylor, *supra* n. 4, Vol. I, p. 156.

The objections voiced by Bronislaw Malinowski against the "Custom is King" theory of early society were directed against certain exaggerations and overgeneralizations indulged in by some of its proponents rather than against its central core. First, Malinowski protested against the view, put forth with particular emphasis by Sidney Hartland, that the savage accepts the fetters of custom as a matter of course and never seeks to break them. As Malinowski points out, rules of law are defied or evaded in every type of human society, including its primitive forms. Secondly, Malinowski doubted that the rules and customs of early law were as closely tied to religion as had sometimes been assumed. He pointed out that the enforcement of early law depended to a far-reaching extent on the secular principle of reciprocity which made legal compliance highly desirable as a matter of self-interest. He did not deny that the force of habit, "the awe of traditional command and a sentimental attachment to it" had a strong sway in all primitive societies, although this did not mean that the crust of custom was rigid, solid and impenetrable.[6]

It is not only the practice of ancestor-worship that accounts for the persistence of custom in ancient law. The deep uncertainty and insecurity pervading life at a time when there was dearth of knowledge about the most elementary facts of nature made it particularly desirable for men to live within a framework of usages and institutions which were firmly established and therefore reduced the perplexity and fear which was otherwise their normal state of mind in a poorly comprehended world. Custom performed a "burden-relieving" function,[7] because by stabilizing certain conditions in the outer world, it set free human energies for coping with new and unprecedented tasks confronting the community. Constant improvisation and the making of individual decisions in many diversified situations places a great deal of discriminative strain on human beings, which will be partly alleviated by repetitive and routinized adherence to firmly-laid grooves of behavior patterns.

As was pointed out earlier, such stabilizations of the normal course of life also release human powers for the higher cultural activities, such as art and reflective thinking. To be sure, they carry with them the drawback that the community selects certain more or less fixed modes of conduct

---

[6] Bronislaw Malinowski, *Crime and Custom in Savage Society*, ed. C.K. Ogden (Paterson, N. J., 1964), pp. 10-15, 22-32, 51-52, 122-123.

[7] See *supra* Sec. 5, n. 29 and Arnold Gehlen, *Urmensch und Spätkultur*, 2d ed. (Frankfurt, 1964), pp. 19-25, 42-44. On the cultural necessity of selection from the total of human potentialities see also E. Adamson Hoebel, *The Law of Primitive Man* (New York, 1954), pp. 10-13, 17.

and action out of the totality of possibilities and variables and decrees them to be the people's "way of life". But we might well agree with the anthropologist Arnold Gehlen that some degree of selective goal fixation in the creation of communal life-forms becomes inevitable if chaos in society due to wholly inconsistent and conflicting normative patterns is to be avoided. Gehlen also points out that consolidation of customary practices that have been found workable compensates in part for the plasticity and indeterminate vagueness of human instinctual reactions, which contrast rather sharply with the sureness and automation of instinct-directed animal behavior.[8]

Custom thus has a solid anchorage in the human impulse of security which was found to be one of the chief psychological roots of the law.[9] But the security afforded by customary ways of conduct is always a tenuous and precarious guaranty. Social systems can never be static, although the rate of change at which they develop will by no means be uniform. Warfare with neighboring tribes may force a primitive community to change its former peacetime habits. A prolonged drought may bring about modifications in the techniques of tilling the soil. A resourceful member of the tribe may suggest new ways for the herding of cattle. Adverse experiences with certain types of sexual practices may dictate their abandonment. Contacts with more advanced cultures may result in a substantial overhauling and improvement of the social system. Novel problems of a legal character may come up which call for the charting out of untried modes of disposition.

It is particularly in the last-mentioned instance that the reluctance of early societies to opt for open and aboveboard change becomes manifest. To overthrow or revise an accustomed legal procedure or rule of customary law is painful for primitive man. He prefers to maintain his belief in the immutability of a God-given law and to accomplish desired changes *sub rosa* and through the use of *fictions*.[10]

The histories of Roman as well as Anglo-American law are replete with examples of fictitious devices designed to cast a concealing veil over departures from legal tradition. Sometimes such devices were employed for

---

[8] See Gehlen, *supra* n. 7, p. 21.

[9] See *supra* Sec. 5.

[10] On the role of fictions in law see Henry J. S. Maine, *Ancient Law,* Everyman's Lib. ed. (London, 1917), Ch. II; Lon L. Fuller, *Legal Fictions* (Stanford, 1967). On fictions in ancient Roman law see Rudolph von Jhering, *Geist des Römischen Rechts,* 5th ed. (Basel, 1894), Vol. IV, pp. 301-310.

the purpose of covertly expanding the jurisdiction of a court with strictly defined competences of adjudication. The litigational powers of the urban praetor in Rome, for example, were restricted to disputes between citizens. In order to make it possible for noncitizens to avail themselves of the important and popular action of conversion, they were granted permission to file complaints with the urban praetor in which possession of Roman citizenship was intimated (although not explicitly asserted). Similarly, the jurisdiction of the Court of Exchequer in medieval Britain was limited to controversies between taxpayers and the Crown, and matters affecting the King's property. In order to extend the court's jurisdiction to ordinary personal actions, such as an action to collect a debt, the writ of *Quominus* was invented. The plaintiff would make a fictitious allegation that he was indebted to the King for unpaid taxes. It was then stated that the defendant had refused to discharge a liability owing to the plaintiff, and that in consequence thereof the plaintiff was less able to pay his taxes to the King. Thus, the appearance of a question involving the royal revenue was created, and the court assumed jurisdiction.

In other instances, fictions were used as a method for covering up changes in substantive or remedial law. For example, the *Twelve Tables* in Rome provided no method by which a father could emancipate a son from the parental power but decreed that if the father sold the son three times as a slave, the son was to be free from his power. In order to enlarge the scope of emancipation, the courts allowed the father to make three fictitious sales of the son to a friend, in one and the same ceremony; the first two sales being followed by immediate release of the son by the friend, while the third one, according to the letter of the law, resulted in emancipation. Also, under the Roman civil law, an heir had an effective action for recovery of goods forming part of the deceased person's estate. Other persons did not have this convenient action, but it was granted to them by the praetor in certain circumstances under the fictitious assumption of legal heirship. In English common law, the action of trover, enabling a plaintiff to recover the full value of a chattel appropriated by the defendant, originally lay only in cases where the plaintiff had lost a chattel and the defendant had found it and converted it to his own use. Subsequently the scope of the action was enlarged so as to include acts of conversion other than unlawful detention of a lost chattel. But for many centuries after this extension of the action, the fictitious (and incontrovertible) allegations of loss and finding remained an indispensable part of the writ and declaration in trover.

The persistency and longevity which may accompany the incrustation of a fiction in the body of the law is well illustrated by the history of the

action of ejectment in Anglo-American law. In the early common law, the
action of ejectment could be maintained to recover a leasehold interest but
was not available to a freeholder of land. Inasmuch as ejectment soon
proved to be an expeditious and popular remedy, a strong demand arose to
allow the action to the holder of a freehold interest who had been ousted
from possession of his land. The common law courts were perfectly willing
to accede to this demand but unwilling to enlarge the action openly
beyond its traditional scope. For many centuries they insisted that a
freeholder wishing to use ejectment must make a fictitious lease to a friend
willing to cooperate. The friend would go on the land, waiting to be
evicted either by the occupant or (in a later stage of the development) by a
put-on ouster ceremony staged by a second friend called the "casual
ejector". The fictitious lessee would then sue the occupant for recovery of
the land and, if he was successful, hand over its possession to the real party
in interest. After 1660, the courts dispensed with the necessity of an actual
lease and ouster *mise-en-scène*. The fictions became a matter of pleading
rather than of realistic enactment, and the courts did not permit the
defendant to controvert the fictitious allegations of lease, entry and ouster
in the complaint. This sham procedure was used in England and in the
United States until the second half of the nineteenth century.[11]

As Lon Fuller has pointed out, the introduction of such strange
contrivances into court procedure was not done with an intent of
deliberate deception.[12] The lawyers, the parties, the legal scholars and
many members of the public knew that, notwithstanding the form of
words appearing in the respective complaints, trover was used against
converters other than finders of chattels and ejectment was used by
plaintiffs other than lessees of the land. Why, then, were the fictions
preserved for so many centuries?

The answer may simply be that judges have traditionally considered
themselves mere mouthpieces of the law, unable to change it by direct and
unconcealed fiat.[13] But this answer does not quite exhaust the depth of
the problem. In Rome as well as in England, legislatures had ample
opportunity to step into the breach caused by judicial unwillingness to

[11] For a more detailed account of the history of ejectment see William Blackstone,
Commentaries on the Laws of England, ed. T. M. Cooley (Chicago, 1899), Bk. III, pp.
200-207; William S. Holdsworth, *A History of English Law*, 3rd ed. (Boston, 1925), Vol.
VII, pp. 10-13.

[12] Fuller, *supra* n. 10, pp. 6-9.

[13] This is in essence the point made by Alf Ross, "Legal Fictions", in *Law, Reason, and
Justice*, ed. G. B. J. Hughes (New York, 1969), pp. 232-233.

engage in lawmaking. After all, it was a rather unedifying spectacle to have men who were not even parties to the action of ejectment surreptitiously go on other people's land and feign the occurrence of an eviction, or to fill innumerable court complaints with statements everybody knew to be false. But apart from a few utilitarian rationalists like Jeremy Bentham,[14] nobody including the legislative organs of the State seemed to take offense at the perpetuation of rather questionable procedures. The ultimate reason for the acquiescence, especially on the part of the legal profession, must be sought in that human penchant for continuity which we found to be a powerful source from which the will to law is fed. The mental attitude underlying consent to the use of fictions is the conscious or unconscious feeling that the new should be engrafted upon the old by a process which reduces the gap between the two to the lowest degree of visibility.

The use of fictions is most widespread in early periods of legal history when unreflective attachment to the habits of the past is strongest. It tends to decrease with the growth of rationality in legal thinking. And yet, even in our own time the role of fictions is not played out entirely. In many States of the Union, for example, the pleadings in divorce proceedings still have little relation to the actualities of the pertinent matrimonial troubles.[15] Recovery by parents against tortfeasors for loss of the services of children in most cases does not depend upon whether or not such services were actually rendered.[16] But deliberate efforts are being made throughout the legal system to eliminate the fictional element as far as possible.

The force of inertia in the law also finds confirmation in the tests which were developed by the common law courts with respect to the proof of legally relevant customs. The establishment of a custom as a valid rule of law required evidence, in the words of Blackstone, "that it have been used so long, that the memory of man runneth not to the contrary. So that, if any one can shew the beginning of it, it is no good custom".[17] Moreover, the custom must have been practiced perpetually and without interruption to qualify for recognition by the legal system. The Roman jurists took a

---

[14] See Jeremy Bentham, *Works*, ed. J. Bowring (New York, 1843), Vol. I, p. 235, where a vigorous attack on the use of fictions is made.

[15] See Brigitte M. Bodenheimer, "Reflections on the Future of Grounds for Divorce", 8 *Journal of Family Law* 179, 182-183 (1968).

[16] William L. Prosser, *Handbook of the Law of Torts*, 4th ed. (St. Paul, 1971), p. 883.

[17] Blackstone, *supra* n. 11, Introd. p. 77.

similar position by holding that only customs of long duration were capable of being elevated to the rank of law.[18]

Under this conception of customary law, the age and continuity of a certain practice invests it with a halo which makes it worthy of acceptance by a judicial tribunal. Just as old wine is expected to be good wine, an ancient custom is presupposed to be a desirable one. Although the English courts have never strictly adhered to the rule that custom, in order to be provable in a court of law, must have existed from time immemorial, they have generally insisted on the presentation of evidence showing long and general usage.

It is true that antiquity is not the only standard used in determining the legal validity of a custom. Among other criteria, reasonableness was viewed as an appropriate test at the time of Blackstone in the sense that the court had power to reject a custom if this test was not met. And yet, a custom with a sound rational basis would not have been admitted unless the requirement of antiquity was also fulfilled.

The significance of custom for the legal system has diminished considerably in our own time. Statutes, judicial decisions and administrative regulations have supplanted customary law, which in early periods functioned as a major source of adjudication. But vocational and business usages, as well as customs of a local character, do sometimes find their way into courts of law today. It is symbolic of present-day resistance to the inertial conception of law that the test of antiquity in the proof of custom has, for the most part, received an inhospitable treatment at the hands of American courts.[19]

SECTION 9
The External Dynamics of the Law I: Legislation

At this juncture of the discussion, a distinction will be introduced which thus far has found no firm anchorage in the vocabulary of jurisprudence. It is the distinction between the external and internal dynamics of the law, which appears to have a particular usefulness in analyzing the relation between stability and change in the legal order.

----

[18] Friedrich C. von Savigny, *System des Heutigen Römischen Rechts* (Berlin, 1840), Vol. I, p. 146.

[19] See Edwin W. Patterson, *Jurisprudence: Men and Ideas of the Law* (Brooklyn, 1953), p. 227.

There is an essential difference, obscured sometimes in modern juris-prudential writings, between the making of law by a political body, such as a constitutional convention or legislative assembly, and an innovation in the law effected from within the legal system by the decision of a judicial tribunal or administrative agency in a legal controversy. Both are examples of legal dynamics, because the continuity of the law is being interfered with by a deliberate act of change. The difference stems from the fact that a tribunal deciding a legal controversy is less free to make a drastic break with legal tradition than a political organ charged with the task of creating new law. Although both have at their disposal something in the nature of a dynamo capable of generating movement and modification in the law, the horsepower embodied in the lawmaking machinery of the litigation-deciding tribunal is considerably weaker than the kinetic energy level at which a genuinely legislative entity may operate. The distinction between the internal and external dynamics of the law is coterminous with this difference.

Legislative power, on a governmental plane, may be vested in one man, or an oligarchic council of men, or an elected representative body. It may also, on a private or semi-public level, reside in organizations of employers and employees acting conjointly, in corporations adopting by-laws, in private universities enacting regulations on faculty and student conduct and other matters. In a third layer, legislative power is exercised in the international domain by the making of treaties between two or more nations which lay down binding norms for the reciprocal conduct of these nations toward each other. When such treaties are entered into between all or most nations of the world, they amount for all practical purposes to an international code, although the subject matters dealt with by a multilateral treaty will not nearly be as embracive as the areas of regulation dealt with by a national code of laws.

The volume of policy-making discretion allocated to lawmaking entities may show extremely wide variations and disparities. At one end of the spectrum stands the power of a constitutional convention in a country which has just succeeded in gaining its political independence, such as the United States after the Revolutionary War or an African State which in the twentieth century severed its colonial ties with England or France. There would seem to exist in this situation a maximum of freedom on the part of the constitution-making authorities to break away from tradition and to set up an entirely new framework of societal organization. The men entrusted with this awesome responsibility might almost be tempted to claim for themselves the attributes of Nietzsche's "highest man", whose exultation has its source in the fact that he "determines values and directs the will of millenia".[1] Legally at least, since they are fashioning the supreme law of the land and not bound to respect any preceding charter of government, the liberty of the constitution-makers to shape the new society in their own image would appear to be at a maximum.

On closer scrutiny, however, this seemingly boundless discretion of the founding fathers of a country melts down to somewhat more modest dimensions. Many different and often weighty factors and conditions will reduce the alternatives open to the framers of a basic law in selecting a suitable political, economic and social structure for their country. It can be said with assurance, for example, that the men who drafted the Constitution of the United States were not "free" to adopt a hierarchical feudal setup following the English medieval model for the white settlers in the colonies. The expectations of the colonists to be treated as free and equal citizens, which formed a major motive for their immigration, imposed some definite limitations on choices for fashioning the political and economic matrix. Moreover, the ideological predilections of the founding fathers were strongly influenced — although probably not conclusively determined — by the English heritage in their education and upbringing, the books that had made an impact on their thinking, the prevailing spirit of the times, and the natural and social conditions of their country. Last but not least, the necessity of securing ratification of the constitutional document from the legislatures of at least nine of the thirteen States impelled anticipation of possible objections and consideration of the views of those whose votes were needed to transform the document into operative law.

Sociological factors of a different kind will affect the setting up of a social structure in a newborn African country. The lack of a proper educational system under previous colonial conditions, resulting in widespread illiteracy among the population, may make it impossible to establish a Western-style democratic system in which intelligent participation in the political decision-making processes depends upon prior schooling imparting some skill in understanding and discussing fairly sophisticated issues. Tribal enclaves may exist in some parts of the country, which may require special political treatment. The compelling need to enter into close economic relations with another nation may make it inadvisable to adopt a political or economic structure which would alienate the sympathies of that nation's dominant circles.

The upshot of these considerations is that a legally unfettered power to pursue political objectives or accomplish social transformations may find its

---

[1] Nietzsche, *The Will to Power,* ed. W. Kaufmann (New York, 1968), p. 519 (No. 999).

extralegal limits in public opinion, the mores of the time, the actual state of economic and intellectual development, and the necessity to appease the feelings of certain influential groups whose cooperation or consent is needed.

In spite of these natural limitations, the scope of innovative power possessed by the architects of a constitution is very extensive. The debates in the American Constitutional Convention of 1787 demonstrate clearly the manifold choices which the delegates had before them when they set out to fashion a system of government. In a similar vein, the comparative method used in several of the new African countries by the framers of the basic norms for social organization enabled them to select, without in any manner neglecting the indigenous heritage, some solutions adopted in other and perhaps heterogeneous social orders which they thought would have a good chance of working successfully in their own country.[2] There is no better example of potentially trailblazing and creative lawmaking through the use of external, *i.e.* political, dynamics than the case of framing a fundamental charter for the governance of a country.

The constitution of a State, in addition to setting up a scheme of government and defining the functions of its organs, will often place some substantive restrictions on the authority of the legislative bodies. It may provide, for example, that they shall make no laws abridging freedom of speech or assembly, or impairing the obligation of contracts. It may guarantee to individuals certain rights capable of being enforced against the judicial or executive agencies of the Government, and prohibit any legislative tampering with these rights. It may restrain the lawmakers from levying certain kinds of taxes or from condemning property without due compensation.

When a legislature is compelled to operate within a network of constitutional restrictions, its power to effectuate change in the law is not as extensive as that of the constitution-making bodies. An additional curtailment is suffered by virtue of the aforementioned sociological factors which constitute a brake on all forms of lawmaking. Especially in a democratic polity, the force of public opinion, the desire to please the voters, the determination not to antagonize powerfully entrenched interest groups will often operate as strong impediments to legal innovation and reform. When

---

[2] See Antony Allott, "The Unification of Laws in Africa", 16 *American Journal of Comparative Law* 51, 62, 78, 86-87 (1968); Cliff F. Thompson, "The Sources of Law in the New Nations of Africa", in *Africa and Law*, ed. T. W. Hutchison (Madison, 1968), pp. 163-164; John N. Hazard, "Negritude, Socialism and the Law", 65 Columbia Law Review 778 (1965); Norman J. Singer, "Modernization of Law in Ethiopia", 11 *Harvard International Law Journal* 73, 80, 88-90 (1970).

the inertial forces placing barriers in the path of needed changes become excessively strong, the successful accomplishment of such changes will sometimes have to wait for the advent of cataclysmic occurrences.

In spite of these sociological impediments, the changes in the law that have been accomplished, for example, through Congressional legislation in almost two hundred years of United States history are truly impressive. It is of special interest to consider in this connection that the whole body of modern social legislation was created under the aegis of a constitutional charter which, unlike the basic charters adopted by other countries in more recent times, did not contemplate or require the recognition of social rights to be secured by welfare legislation. State legislatures, too, accomplished many basic reforms in the face of State constitutions containing checks on legislative authority which often surpassed in specificity those embodied in the Federal Constitution. However detailed its provisions may be, the basic charter of government in a political society will probably never form a straitjacket on the exercise of legislative power to the same extent that a detailed code of statutory law will constitute a bridle on the exercise of judicial power.

When we move to the more subordinate forms of lawmaking, the framework of restrictions on policy-making discretion is apt to become tighter. An administrative agency of the Government may have the right to promulgate regulations defining the procedures it will use in discharging its functions. The President of the United States may be empowered to issue an executive order on trading with enemy and neutral countries in wartime. But in both instances there may exist a statutory scheme which keeps administrative or executive latitude within narrow confines, reducing it more or less to the filling in of details. Surprisingly enough, the power to accomplish desired results in this area of delegated public legislation may sometimes be smaller than in some domains of private or semi-public lawmaking, such as the conclusion of collective bargaining agreements regulating wage rates, hours of work and general conditions of employment in a certain industry. In spite of this fact, we are still moving here within the orbit of the external dynamics of the law, because political power (though of a limited scope) is used to set up a system of norms providing procedural or substantive standards for the decision of individual cases.

While the process of enacting legislation well exemplifies the dynamic, forward-moving forces which press upon the legal system from the outside, the enacted norms themselves serve in the main the opposite purpose of stabilizing social motion. When, for example, procedures for the disposition of legal controversies are fashioned by a legislature, these will constitute a firm, binding, and lasting framework for judicial action in circumscribed classes of cases. When individual rights, such as freedom of speech or religion, and social rights, such as old-age benefits or workmen's compensation, are granted by a constitutional or legislative body, this is done with the understanding that these rights will be protected on a lasting and continuing rather than a merely ephemeral basis. Generally speaking, whenever political power is transformed into law, the underlying purpose is to steer the chaotic flux of free-wheeling societal forces into controllable and durable channels.

If many types of legal arrangements, as has been suggested earlier, aim at promoting the security of the conditions of life, legislation would appear to be a particularly suitable instrumentality for the achievement of this objective. By spelling out in an articulated and formalized statement the essential content of the rights and duties to be enforced by the law, a legislative enactment gives notice — albeit an incomplete one because of the imprecision of human language — to the addressees of the laws as to what they may expect from their Government in the event they are harmed or imposed upon, or charged with injuring others. Furthermore, while a judicial decision in an individual case in many instances defines the existence or nonexistence of a right, duty, or legal relation in an *ex post facto* manner, a duly-promulgated piece of legislation announces its position beforehand and with intent to serve as a reasonably secure guide to future action by the subjects of the law. It phrases its dispositions in general terms, thereby designating the classes of people to which they are made applicable. It can carve out from the rule a set of exceptions, while the judge can write qualifications into a rule chosen by him only to the extent made necessary by the narrowly circumscribed facts of the case.[3]

Because of these beneficial features, legislation is, on an overall view, a fairly reliable guarantor of what Lon Fuller has called "the internal morality of the law".[4] This attribute of the law requires articulated and intelligible statements of generalized norms of conduct, publicized in advance of their operativeness and prospective in their effect, and providing a reasonable amount of security to the citizens by aiming at least at a "temporary permanence".[5] Of course, as Fuller has pointed out, these safeguards of

---

[3] For further comments on the differences between legislative and judicial lawmaking see *infra* Sec. 11.

[4] Lon L. Fuller, *The Morality of Law*, rev. ed. (New Haven, 1969), pp. 33-94. My own semantic preference is to reserve the term "morality of law" entirely to the substantive content of legal norms, instead of extending it to extrinsic guarantees of the rule of law.

[5] This phrase was used by an able judge of the Supreme Court of Utah, James H. Wolfe, in a personal conversation with the author in 1953.

rule by law are meaningful only if there is congruence between the precepts as announced and their actual application and enforcement in legal practice.[6]

Legislation is also well adapted to the furtherance of the second cardinal lodestar of legal ordering: the goal of equality. Clear delineations of permissible and prohibited forms of conduct contribute significantly to the realization of equal treatment under the law, which is one of the basic requirements of justice (though by no means the only one). By designating the classes of people and the categories of acts to which a normative regulation is applicable, a legislative enactment draws lines of demarcation for its enforcement which are helpful in dealing with similar situations in a similar way. This is most obvious in the field of criminal law, in which the superiority of codified law over judicial determinations as to what constitutes criminal conduct is no longer a controversial question. But the merits of legislation are also conspicuous in the civil rights area, when a previously disfavored group succeeds in fighting its way up from the depths of discrimination to a place in the sun and insists on definitions of its newly-won equality.

If the instrumentality of legislation is of such beneficial use in helping to achieve the principal goals of legal ordering, a question arises which thus far has received little consideration in jurisprudential literature. The two most influential systems of the world, Roman law and Anglo-American common law, during many centuries of vigorous growth, did not employ legislation as the chief tool of legal improvement. The celebrated classical law of the Romans, which served as a model for the modern civil law of continental European and Latin-American counties, was not primarily a statutory or codified law. Its unfolding was due in the main to a process of collaboration between the praetors, who were the principal magistrates of the judicial system, and a professional group of private Roman jurists. These jurists supplied the praetors (who were not trained lawyers) with legal advice and also wrote carefully worked-out opinions for the benefit of the parties and lay judges (who rendered the final decision in a lawsuit on the basis of legal instructions by the praetor). These opinions, called *responsa*, were collected and came to assume an authority which went far beyond the actual case in which they were rendered.

There was, to be sure, another very important source of law in Rome which had some of the earmarks of legislation. At the beginning of his one-year term of office, the praetor issued an edict in which he announced the types of civil actions which he would permit to be brought in his court

---

[6] Fuller, *supra* n. 4, pp. 39, 81-91.

and the pleas which he would recognize as defenses to these actions. Such an edict was legislative in the sense of a preannounced general statement, different from an individual judgment in a litigated case, which defined the scope of legally enforceable rights. But until the relatively late date of approximately 130 A.D., when the praetorian edict was cast into a more or less permanent form, it varied from typical codified law by being restricted in its operative validity to the praetor's one-year term of office.[7] Moreover, the praetorian edict was for the most part no more than a list of remedies and counterremedies (defenses) and thus dealt only with a limited segment of the legal order as a whole. It was, however, supplemented by many enactments of the regular legislative bodies (popular assembly, senate, later the emperor) which settled numerous specific questions, especially in the fields of criminal, procedural, and public law, without any attempt at comprehensive code-making.[8]

In the earlier development of Anglo-American law, too, legislation played a relatively subordinate role. The chief vehicle of growth in the formative period of the English common law was the issuance of writs by the Chancery. These writs were applied for by individual litigants and, if granted, signified authorizations to the courts to try the cause of action outlined in the writ. The Register of Original Writs contained a collection of the causes of action available to plaintiffs and, therefore, like the edict of the Roman praetor, had a quasi-legislative effect.[9] It left unanswered innumerable legal questions that might come up in the course of a trial, again resembling in this respect the praetorian edict. These problems had to be solved by the courts in a slow and gradual process of small-scale lawmaking. As in Rome, the courts were sometimes aided in this task by special enactments passed by the national legislature.

Considering the previously-discussed advantages of legislation in implementing the "will to law", where do we find the explanation for the

---

[7] However, the freezing of the edict by the *edictum perpetuum* during Hadrian's reign was foreshadowed by the earlier practice of the praetors to repeat most of the declarations contained in their predecessor's edict, so that in this way a fixed stock of norms was carried over from one edict into the next — another example of the inertial properties inherent in the law.

[8] Good accounts of the Roman sources of law are found in Herbert F. Jolowicz, *Historical Introduction to the Study of Roman Law,* 2d ed. (Cambridge, Eng., 1952), pp. 91-99, 365-383; Wolfgang Kunkel, *An Introduction to Roman Legal and Constitutional History,* transl. J. M. Kelly (Oxford, 1966), pp. 81-103; Max Kaser, *Römische Rechtsgeschichte,* 2d ed. (Göttingen, 1967), pp. 128-155.

[9] See Frederick W. Maitland, "The History of the Register of Original Writs", in *Collected Papers,* ed. H. A. L. Fisher (Cambridge, Eng., 1911), Vol. II, pp. 110-173.

sparing use of legislation, for long periods of time, in the history of the two major legal systems of the world? Several reasons suggest themselves to account for this phenomenon. First of all, a legislative organ is a person or body "external" to the law.[10] By the exercise of political power, it may inject itself decisively and drastically into the autonomous development of the law. For reasons discussed in the preceding section, men in earlier times might have deemed it undesirable to disturb legal continuity and stability, beyond an absolutely necessary minimum, by open, deliberate interference with the "internal, silently-operating forces" of the law.[11] The danger of breaching the organic unity of the law and destroying its roots in popular custom and consciousness by politically-motivated commands of the sovereign was presumably apprehended as a real and substantial one.

Secondly, the very thought of a stream of official commands regulating the most varied aspects of life was foreign to the mentality of men in a social structure in which State power was not as yet fully and strongly developed. Especially in the feudal phases of Roman and English economic history, the holders of landed estates enjoyed a considerable amount of private power and legal autonomy. The time was certainly not then ripe for a typical effort at comprehensive legislation which, on the basis of equality of all men before the law, authoritatively determines their rights, powers and obligations in the fields of contracts, torts, property, family relations and inheritance.

Last but not least, a codification of the law presupposes, as an initial venture, the accumulation of a large stock of judicial decisions capable of serving as a basis for the fashioning of statutory generalizations. Unless the draftsman of legislation has at his disposal such a body of empirical materials, he will be at a loss to determine the categories of factual situations that should be included in, or excluded from, the scope of an abstractly formulated rule. In addition to this storehouse of illustrative examples, effective codification requires a degree of sophistication and synthetic mental skills that are acquired by civilized men only slowly and gradually after their culture has entered into the more mature stages of its development. The early codes of mankind do not as yet demonstrate the possession of these qualities by their makers. They are, for the most part, rather crudely and inartistically drawn, reveal the prevalence of rudi-

---

[10] Henry J. S. Maine, *Ancient Law,* Everyman's Lib. ed. (London, 1917), p. 17.

[11] Friedrich C. von Savigny, *Of the Vocation of Our Age for Legislation and Jurisprudence,* transl. A. Hayward (London, 1831), p. 30.

mentary ideas of justice, and display the human power of abstraction in an inchoate and somewhat clumsy form.[12]

The reasons responsible for the lack of adequate and comprehensive legislation in older times are no longer valid today. We are quite disinclined to view the large-scale imposition of prescriptions by an external political body as an undue interference with the constancy and continuity of the law, two qualities which earlier generations valued as sacred attributes of the legal order. Furthermore, the weakness of State power, which at one time left much quasi-legislative power vested in private hands or non-governmental institutions, has been replaced by a definite trend in the opposite direction, removing a further obstacle to a wider exercise of legislative authority. Thirdly and lastly, there is now at our disposal a wealth of casuistic determinations of specific legal problems, enabling legislative draftsmen to draw upon a rich diet of empirical source materials.

It is most likely that, in the centuries to come, legislation will become the chief vehicle of legal development and legal reform in the Anglo-American orbit. If this prediction turns out to be correct, the English-speaking countries will thereby fall into step with the lawmaking policy current in other developed countries in the contemporary world. The chief consequence of this trend — which has already become quite visible in an incipient form in a number of American States, especially California — will be an increased reliance on wholesale codification as a method of structuring and rationalizing the legal system. Whether this result, in federations like the United States, Canada and Australia, will be achieved through a full-scale use of federal power or rather by means of more or less uniform compilations of State laws is a matter of secondary importance.

As far as the United States is concerned, the main reason why comprehensive codification is likely to occur within the next one hundred years is a proliferation of judicial decisions which is rapidly assuming unmanageable proportions. Already in 1836, it seemed ominous to Judge Joseph Story, penman of a historic report published by the Legislature of the State of Massachusetts, that

> "...at present the known rules and doctrines of the common law are spread over many ponderous volumes. They are nowhere collected together in a concise and systematic form, having a positive legislative

---

[12] These characterizations would appear to be applicable to the *Twelve Tables,* an early Roman code, whose text is found in *Sources of Ancient and Primitive Law,* ed. A. Kocourek and J. H. Wigmore (Boston, 1915), pp. 465-468. Our evaluation of the *Twelve Tables,* however, is hampered by missing sections and doubts as to the authenticity of some of its parts.

sanction. They are to be gathered from treatises upon distinct and independent subjects, of very different merit and accuracy; from digests and abridgments; from books of practice and from professional practice; and above all, from books of reports of adjudged cases, many hundreds of which now exist, and which require to be painfully and laboriously consulted in order to ascertain them."[13]

He added the observation that "a vast deal of time is now necessarily consumed, if not wasted, in ascertaining the precise bearing and result of various cases which have been decided touching a particular topic".[14] If this last remark, which was designed to provide support for his Commission's plea to codify the common law of the State, was perhaps something of an overstatement at the time when it was made, it certainly amounted to an accurate prediction of things to come in the twentieth century.

Today, the "wilderness of single instances" has reached such dimensions that conflicting and contradictory authorities can be found on countless points of law. The "vast deal of time...now necessarily consumed, if not wasted, in ascertaining the precise bearing and result of various cases" increases the cost of lawsuits and contributes to the fact that many members of the public shun litigation like a loathsome disease. For this and other reasons, many attorneys in private or public utterances have expressed their sympathy and support for the idea of codification. Some distinguished judges have added their voices to the growing chorus of spokesmen favoring an increased use of legislative power in the future.[15]

Section 10
The External Dynamics of the Law II: Equity

It was the opinion of Sir Henry Maine that, in the history of the progressive societies, legislation was the last in time of three principal

---

[13] State of Massachusetts, House of Representatives Report No. 17, reprinted in *Codification of the Common Law: Letter of Jeremy Bentham and Report of Judges Story, Metcalf and others* (New York, 1882), p. 50.

[14] *Id.*, p. 51.

[15] Henry J. Friendly, "The Gap in Lawmaking", 63 *Columbia Law Review* 787, 791 (1963); Roger J. Traynor, Comment, in *Legal Institutions Today and Tomorrow*, ed. G. M. Paulsen (New York, 1959), pp. 48-50; Traynor, "Reasoning in a Legal Circle", 56 *Virginia Law Review* 739, 741 (197). A British voice is Patrick Devlin, *Samples of Law Making* (London, 1962), p. 23.

reformatory agencies used to bring the law into harmony with the needs and exigencies of the social whole. The two earlier ones were fictions and equity, serving as instrumentalities of legal change in this temporal order.[1] The sequence of discussion adopted in this book with respect to these three tools of law-improvement does not follow Maine's chronological arrangement. Fictions and legislation have already been discussed.[2] Equity will be the subject of investigation in the present section.

It must be emphasized, first, that Maine's theory, although it contains a substantial ingredient of truth, cannot be accepted as a generally valid scheme of historical analysis. Fictions, equity, and legislation did not succeed each other as vehicles of law reform in the sense that each of them occupied a certain stage in legal history to the more or less complete exclusion of the two others. A few intimations by Maine show that the great jurist was aware of this fact; but some of his more sweeping generalizations, such as the statement, "My own belief is that remedial Equity is everywhere older than remedial Legislation"[3] make it desirable to restate his theory in a loosened and substantially revised version.

Sir Henry Maine's sociology of legal evolution takes its concrete illustrations principally from the histories of Roman and Anglo-American law, although he also drew upon Hindu law — with which he was well acquainted — in his inquiries. Maine was fully familiar with the fact that a famous piece of legislation, called the *Twelve Tables*, formed an early mainstay in the edifice of Roman law. In fact, he believed — not quite in consonance with the present state of our historical knowledge — that this code marked the beginning of the Roman law system as properly defined.[4]

In spite of his otherwise ample use of the comparative method, Maine did not in his discussion of ancient codes refer to the enactments of the Anglo-Saxon Kings, which were important early milestones of English legal history.[5] Since the Norman Conquest of England resulted in an almost complete break with the preceding legal development, he was perhaps justified in ignoring these codes for purposes of his argument. He might, however, have compared the *Twelve Tables* with another piece of English

---

[1] Henry J. S. Maine, *Ancient Law,* Everyman's Lib. ed. (London, 1917), p. 15.

[2] *Supra* Secs. 8 and 9, respectively.

[3] Maine, *supra* n. 1, p. 15.

[4] *Id.*, p. 4. The most elaborate modern study of the early Roman law preceding the *Twelve Tables,* with particular emphasis on basic underlying conceptions, is Max Kaser, *Das Altrömische Ius* (Göttingen, 1949).

[5] The earliest code was the Code of Ethelbert, promulgated in 600 A. D., followed by the laws of Ine, Cnut, and several other compilations. See William S. Holdsworth, *A History of English Law,* 3rd ed. (Boston, 1927), Vol. II, pp. 19-21.

legislation, the *Magna Carta* of 1215, which owed its origin to a somewhat similar sociological constellation.[6]

If the history of Roman as well as English law was characterized by the appearance of codes at an early time (although these codes were incomplete and fragmentary), how can this fact be fitted into Maine's general theory, according to which legislation was a latecomer in the succession of law-improving devices? A thorough study of his argumentation will disclose that he assumed the existence of a foundation of compiled legal precepts which the further development of the law would use as a launching pad. In orther words, the alternation of fictions, equity, and legislation as agencies of law reform would not commence until there was some basic stock of rules which, as time went on, would be in need of modification; and this substratum of recognized norms would ordinarily, though not necessarily, consist of an ancient code of law.[7]

Unfortunately, this reading of Maine's theory by no means solves all the difficulties which his scheme of legal evolution presents to us. It appears, for example, that when equity appeared on the scene in Rome and England, fictions did not abdicate their functions in the work of the courts; in some instances, their use became broadened instead of declining in importance.[8] At the same time, the growth of equitable jurisdiction in

---

[6] The *Twelve Tables* constituted a legal compromise between the patrician and plebeian orders in Rome after a struggle of large dimensions had taken place between the two classes. See *infra*, Sec. 16, under I. The issuance of *Magna Carta* was preceded by a civil war between the forces of the King and the feudal magnates, ending in a charter of concessions made by the King.

[7] A comparison of Chapters 1 and 2 of Maine's work, *supra* n. 1, would appear to support this interpretation.

[8] The Roman law fictions discussed in Sec. 8 remained in full force while the Roman praetor was changing the ancient civil law by granting new equitable remedies. Even in the relatively late epoch of classical law, fictions were still being used. See, for example, Kaser, *Das Römische Privatrecht* (Munich, 1955), Vol. I, p. 369. The English writ of *Quominus*, also discussed in Sec. 8, made its first appearance in the Court of Exchequer in the fourteenth century, the same period in which the equitable jurisdiction of the King's Council began to develop, but the use of fictions connected with the writ did not get into full swing until the seventeenth century. See Harold Wurzel, "The Origin and Development of Quo Minus," 49 *Yale Law Journal* 39, 53, 63 (1939); Holdsworth, *supra* n. 5, Vol. I, p. 240. The use of the highly fictitious Bill of Middlesex in the Court of King's Bench likewise did not predate the exercise of equitable jurisdiction by the Council. See Holdsworth, *id.,* p. 219. The fictitious allegations of loss and finding in the declaration of trover were introduced in the sixteenth century, postdating the beginnings of equity. See Thomas A. Street, *The Foundations of Legal Libility* (Northport, N.Y., 1906), Vol. III, pp. 164-166; Cecil H. S. Fifoot, *History and Sources of the Common Law* (London, 1949), pp. 104-105. The fictions surrounding the action of ejectment originated in the sixteenth century. Holdsworth, *supra* n. 5, Vol. VII, pp. 10-11. They were persistently used in England and the United States until the nineteenth century.

the two legal systems did not exclude the use of legislation in the Roman popular assembly or the English Parliament. Although the number of statutes passed in the Roman Republic after the *Twelve Tables* which directly affected private law was not large, there was a fairly substantial amount of legislation dealing with problems of public law, criminal law, and procedure.[9] In England, the legislative activity of the King's Council and that larger body known as *Magna Curia* (which finally developed into Parliament) was considerable throughout the formative and post-formative period of equity.[10]

While Maine conceded that two of his three law-improving instrumentalities might sometimes be found operating together in a legal system, he seemed not to have visualized the possibility of concurrent use of all of them at the same time.[11] It can no longer be doubted, however, that in Rome as well as in England there was legal growth through simultaneous reliance on fictions, equity, and legislation.

It must be concluded, in view of these facts, that the truth embodied in Sir Henry Maine's theory is limited to the very broad outlines of the development portrayed by him. Fictions are for the most part invented in early periods of legal history. While some of them may exhibit considerable persistence and longevity, they tend to decrease in importance in the era when law reaches its maturity. This epoch shows acceleration and multiplication in the use of legislation as a tool of legal improvement. There is also a middle period which, without displacing the two rival devices, unfolds a vigorous activity of innovation through the use of equity.

Maine's chart of natural legal evolution was influenced by certain assumptions of a social-psychological nature. Maine was convinced that the employment of fictions was congenial to the infancy of societies, an age at which law is considered immutable and deliberate change frowned upon. When the epoch of equity arrives, an open and avowed interference with the law takes place by the superimposition on its basic structure of flexible equitable principles designed to soften its rigor. On the other hand, equity

---

[9] Rudolph von Jhering, *Geist des Römischen Rechts,* 5th ed. (Basel, 1894), Vol. II, pp. 40-43; Wolfgang Kunkel, *An Introduction to Roman Legal and Constitutional History,* transl. J. M. Kelly (Oxford, 1966), pp. 30-31; Herbert F. Jolowicz, *Historical Introduction to the Study of Roman Law,* 2d ed. (Cambridge, Eng., 1952), pp. 83-84.

[10] For details see Howard L. Gray, *The Influence of the Commons on Early Legislation* (Cambridge, Mass., 1932), Chs. IV, VI, VIII; James F. Baldwin, *The King's Council in England during the Middle Ages* (Gloucester, Mass., 1965), Ch. XII, Holdsworth, *supra* n. 5, Vol. II, pp. 435-484; See also Theodore F. G. Plucknett, *A Concise History of the Common Law,* 5th ed. (Boston, 1956), pp. 320-324.

[11] Maine, *supra* n. 1, p. 15.

differs from legislation, the agent of legal improvement which comes after it, "in that its claim to authority is grounded, not on the prerogative of any external person or body, not even on that of the magistrate who enunciates it, but on the special nature of its principles, to which it is alleged that all law ought to conform".[12]

If it is true that there was considerable overlapping of equity jurisprudence with the use of fictions by the courts, in Rome as well as in England, that some novel fictions were created by the judges at a time when new blood was being injected into the law by the introduction of equitable principles, and that the use of fictions did not terminate after the law had long outgrown its stage of infancy, then Maine's interpretation cannot face up to the test of historical reality. Why would fictions not disappear from the legal scene, or at least cease to be newly invented, after the myth of an immutable law had given way to the new philosophy which guided the administration of equity?

It is the distinction between the external and internal dynamics of the law that can furnish us with a clue to the solution of this puzzle. The use of fictions was a feature of the internal development of the law, which commonly takes place by way of gradual, cautious adaptation and modification of pre-existing rules and remedies through court action in litigated cases. Not only during the infancy of legal systems but far beyond the life span of this period can we observe a disinclination on the part of the courts to arrogate to themselves an openly proclaimed power of lawmaking. This phenomenon will be discussed and explained in the next section. Suffice it to state at this point that in 1600 the Court of King's Bench declared that it could "qualify a tort, but not increase a tort".[13] This case involved an extension of the action of trover to a case of trespassory taking of a chattel by a converter. Previously, the scope of the action had been restricted to cases of loss and finding,[14] and the declaration in the suit was framed in the required traditional form. Although the summary of the reasoning of the court in the report of the case is terse and not entirely clear, it appears that the court was unwilling to enlarge the ambit of the tort but ready to "qualify" its elements by not allowing the defendant to contradict the fictional allegations of loss and finding. This decision is not an isolated occurrence, but typical of the approach of courts in cases where

---

[12] *Id.*, pp. 16, 17.

[13] *Bishop v. Montague*, Cro. Eliz. 824, 78 Eng. Rep. 1051 (1600). On this case see Street, *supra* n. 8, Vol. III, p. 165.

[14] See *supra* Sec. 8.

feigned assertions were used to conceal an unquestionable alteration in the law. One must concur with the comment by Alf Ross that fictions of this type may reflect a reluctance to make open use of judicial lawmaking power.[15]

While the courts in Rome and England carried on such exercises in legal inertia, there occurred at the same time an infiltration of new, untraditional, and equitable principles into the law which modified and rejuvenated it to a far-reaching extent. In Rome, the same authority (namely, the praetor) who administered the *ius civile*, i.e. the regular legal system composed of statute and customary law, also forged the equitable remedies through the instrumentality of the *ius honorarium*, by which he superimposed a new and flexible system of law upon an old and stabilized one. In England, a bifurcation of legal development took place in the fourteenth century. While the common law administered in the regular courts became stale and rigid, the King and his council used their reserve power of jurisdiction by granting remedies outside the scope of the traditional law of the realm. Why was such innovative power, both in Rome and England, freely used in one area of the legal system, while in another the judicial agencies persisted in displaying a conservative attitude towards legal improvement?

In trying to answer this question with respect to the Roman law, it is of great significance that the main body of this law, known as *ius civile*, was applicable only to citizens of Rome. Prior to 212 A.D. (a late stage in the history of Roman law) it was not available to the inhabitants of the territories conquered by the Romans and added as provinces to their Empire. The residents of these territories were called provincials and did not enjoy citizenship rights. There were also natives of foreign countries who came to Rome and entered into business transactions with Roman subjects.

When litigation arose in Rome between a Roman and a non-citizen, or between two non-citizens, the Roman praetor in charge of such lawsuits, known as the *praetor peregrinus*, could not apply the rules of the *ius civile*. Since the two or more litigants involved in the lawsuit usually possessed different nationalities, he also did not apply the law of any particular province or foreign country. What he did was to fashion a legal system which was neither traditional Roman law nor foreign law, and which was designated by the name *ius gentium*. In some of its parts, this *ius gentium* incorporated institutions which were common to the Roman law and the

---

[15] Alf Rose, "Legal Fictions", in *Law, Reason, and Justice*, ed. G. B. J. Hughes (New York, 1969), pp. 223-224, 232-233.

legal systems of the provinces or surrounding foreign countries. For the most part, however, it was an independent legal structure which included actions and defenses unknown to the traditional Roman law.[16] This body of law was, on the whole, less formalistic and more elastic than the ancient *ius civile.*

It seems that, in the course of time, the freer and often more equitable rules of the *ius gentium* found their way into the administration of justice by the domestic counterpart of the *praetor peregrinus,* who was known as the *praetor urbanus.*[17] It is not difficult to guess at the reasons why this apparent reception of the *ius gentium,* which in its beginnings was more or less independent from Roman law proper, into the *corpus* of the latter system of law took place. The *ius gentium* was more modern, more progressive, more flexible than the law of Rome itself. A Roman citizen suing a foreigner might avail himself of one of its equitable remedies or defenses. But the same citizen might be denied the benefit of that equitable action or defense if he were to sue another Roman citizen on a similar state of facts. The differences in the nationality of the adversaries can hardly be said to provide a rational basis for discriminatory treatment with respect to the remedies available in lawsuits against them, especially since both the *ius civile* and the *ius gentium* were branches of Roman law in the wider sense of the term. To deny the remedy in the domestic suit while allowing it in the foreign suit was probably felt to be a violation of a cardinal principle of justice, a principle which demands that equal or essentially similar things be dealt with in an equal or essentially similar manner.

Even though the *ius gentium* was a part of Roman law in an extended sense of the phrase (because it was shaped by an organ of the Roman State, the *praetor peregrinus*) it was nevertheless a body of equitable law outside the bounds of the genuine national law of the Romans. Because of its external character, the Roman legislature did not touch the *ius gentium* and limited itself to legislative measures affecting the *ius civile.* The urban praetor, on the other hand, although he possessed no outright legislative powers, appears to have adapted the national Roman law to the equitable

---

[16] Max Kaser, *Römische Rechtsgeschichte,* 2d ed. (Göttingen, 1967), pp. 134-138; Franz Wieacker, *Vom Römischen Recht* (Stuttgart, 1961), p. 115; Jolowicz, *supra* n. 9, pp. 100-105.

[17] The version of the origin of Roman equity presented in the text reflects the majority view held by Roman law scholars, but (because the beginnings of praetorian jurisdiction are shrouded in some uncertainty) has been questioned by some writers. Discussions of the problem are found, among many others, in Kaser, *supra* n. 8, Vol. I, pp. 179-182; Kaser, *Das Römische Zivilprozessrecht* (Munich, 1966), pp. 109-110; Wieacker, *supra* n. 16, pp. 115-116; Kunkel, *supra* n. 9, p. 78.

law fashioned by his colleague in charge of foreign lawsuits. If this under-standing of a somewhat obscure historical development is correct, it was not an internal, organic evolution of the indigenous law of Rome but in a certain sense an importation, for reasons of fairness and justice, of prin-ciples of a rival system administered by a special organ in the same city. Once the *ius gentium* had been absorbed into the *ius honorarium*, it received the same cautious and conservative treatment at the hands of the praetors that was customarily accorded to the *ius civile*.[18]

The story of English law shows even more clearly than Roman law history that the growth of equity jurisprudence was, in its decisive initial phases, a phenomenon of the external rather than the internal dynamic of the law. This statement may raise the eyebrows of some legal scholars, but there is a great deal of evidence to support it. Many of the early petitions asking the Government to secure justice where it would not be secured by the ordinary processes of the common law were addressed to the *Magna Curia* (the predecessor of Parliament), especially during the fourteenth century.[19] The *Magna Curia* sometimes disposed of them by an act of general legislation providing the new remedy sought for; in other instances it enacted a private bill which confined the redress of injury to the individual case before it.[20] When this legislative body became swamped with petitions of this kind, it referred a substantial number of them to the King's Council, a smaller group of trusted advisers chosen by the King from the membership of the larger assembly. There were also petitions addressed to the King's Council, or to the person of the King, in the first place, whose number increased in the course of time. The petitions received by the King or his Council were usually transmitted to the Chancellor, who until the end of the fifteenth century (when a separate Court of Chancery arose) disposed of them, not as a judicial officer, but as executive secretary of the Council and with the cooperation of other members of the Coun-cil.[21] Sometimes the King himself would preside at meetings convoked for this purpose.[22]

---

[18] It has been mentioned already that the actions and defenses permitted by the annual edict of the praetor were usually retained in the next edict with only minor modifica-tions. See Kunkel, *supra* n. 9, p. 89. Furthermore, the praetor was not authorized to alter the *ius civile* directly.

[19] Plucknett, *supra* n. 10, p. 179; Baldwin, *supra* n. 10, pp. 242-243.

[20] See Gray, *supra* n. 10, pp. 47-48.

[21] Frederick Pollock, *The Expansion of the Common Law* (London, 1904), p. 68; Geoffrey R. Y. Radcliffe and Geoffrey Cross, *The English Legal System*, 4th ed. (London, 1964), pp. 114-118; Baldwin, *supra* n. 10, pp. 244-245.

[22] George Spence, "The History of the Court of Chancery", in *Select Essays in Anglo-American Legal History* (Boston, 1908), Vol. II, pp. 227-228.

It is of greatest importance for an understanding of the nature of early equity to realize that the King and his Council, during the fourteenth and fifteenth centuries, shared the legislative power with the larger body which after 1400 became known as the English Parliament. Although a rivalry for the exercise of this power developed between the two organs of government which was ultimately resolved in favor of the legislative supremacy of Parliament, the petitions for special relief addressed to the Council were often disposed of in the form of a statute.[23] Such a statute may have been in the nature of a private act granting relief in the special case only for which it was passed. But the choice of this way of disposition shows that the Council, in acting on the petitions, considered itself as an instrument of the royal (legislative or executive) prerogative, rather than as a judicial organ making new law in derogation of the law administered by the common law courts. The very mode in which the petitions were phrased furnishes additional support for this interpretation. They generally asked for relief "for the love of God and in the way of charity",[24] thus invoking the extraordinary powers of the King rather than some rule of law providing the basis for action on a judicial level.

The conclusion must therefore be drawn that the incisive changes wrought in the body of English law by equity jurisprudence during the first two hundred years of its existence, through the allowance of remedies wholly unknown to the common law of the time, were an emanation of the political prerogative of the King, whose undefined scope fused legislative, executive, and judicial powers in a somewhat indiscriminate fashion. This development cannot be explained in terms of a large-scale overhauling of the legal system through an innovative exercise of what today would be regarded as a typical exercise of judicial power.[25] It was not until 1474

---

[23] *Id.*, pp. 230-231. See also Baldwin, *supra* n. 10, pp. 318-320.

[24] Frederick W. Maitland, *The Constitutional History of England* (Cambridge, Eng., 1931), p. 222; Spence, *supra* n. 22, p. 229.

[25] Legal historians have shown that the common law, prior to the stagnation it experienced by the end of the thirteenth century, had exhibited a great deal of equitable ferment. Harold D. Hazeltine, "The Early History of English Equity", in *Essays in Legal History*, ed. P. Vinogradoff (London, 1913), pp. 261-285; Holdsworth, *supra* n. 5, Vol. II, pp. 245-249, 334-347. It is not clear from these accounts why certain remedies of an equitable nature were used by the common law courts in an early time and then simply abandoned, leaving these remedies to be monopolized by the Chancellor. It is not disputed, on the other hand, that much of the flexibility of the early common law was due to the willingness of an executive agency outside the common law courts, *i.e.* the Chancery, to grant writs for the filing of common law actions on a much more liberal basis than was possible after the imposition of Parliamentary restrictions on the writ-making power, beginning in 1258.

that decrees in equity were made by the Chancellor on his own authority, and at approximately that time a separate court headed by him had come into being.[26] But at this juncture of the development, the great novel remedies and other legal institutions introduced by equity — such as specific performance, injunctions, uses and trusts of land, relief against fraud and mistake — had already achieved a firm place in the texture of the system.[27]

The transformation of equity from an extraordinary into an ordinary jurisdiction was accompanied by a gradual regularization and crystallization of its adjudicatory processes. To be sure, after the Chancellor had set up a court independent of the King's Council by the end of the fifteenth century, there was vigorous development and elaboration of the equitable remedies introduced into the system at an earlier time. But the Court of Chancery was no longer a "fountain of unlimited dispensations",[28] exercising the political prerogatives of the King and his council; it had attained the status of a regular court of judicature which followed precedents and imparted some degree of predictability to its decisions. Furthermore, after the intense struggles waged in the seventeenth century between the Court of Chancery and the common law courts had subsided,[29] equity ceased to be a source of frequent interferences with, and disturbances of, the common law. It evolved into a system which, for the most part, simply supplemented the remedies afforded by common law courts. This is, in essence, the meaning of Blackstone's statement that "equity follows the law":[30] equity was not supposed to set aside any rule or disposition of the common law, but to recognize their validity and grant redress only in cases where the remedy at law was inadequate.

The new attitude assumed by the Court of Chancery after the storms of the seventeenth century is well reflected in the following passage from a judicial opinion by Lord-Chancellor Eldon:

"The doctrines of this Court ought to be as well settled and made as
    uniform almost as those of the common law, laying down fixed

---

[26] See Holdsworth, *supra* n. 5, Vol. I, pp. 404, 409.

[27] *Id.*, Vol. IV, pp. 419-420, Vol. V, pp. 287-288, 292.

[28] Frederick Pollock, "The Transformation of Equity", in *Essays in Legal History*, ed. P. Vinogradoff (London, 1913), p. 293.

[29] For a description of these battles see Radcliffe and Cross, *supra* n. 21, pp. 123-126.

[30] William Blackstone, *Commentaries on the Laws of England*, ed. T. M. Cooley (Chicago, 1899), Bk. III, p. 430.

principles, but taking care that they are to be applied according to the circumstances of each case. I cannot agree that the doctrines of this Court are to be changed with every succeeding judge. Nothing would inflict on me greater pain, in quitting this place, than the recollection that I had done anything to justify the reproach that the equity of this Court varies like the Chancellor's foot."[31]

Although Lord Eldon's judicial philosophy was probably more conservative than that of some of his predecessors and successors in the office of Lord-Chancellor, it was nonetheless not out of line with the prevailing spirit in equity courts in England and the United States discharged their functions in the eighteenth and nineteenth centuries.[32] It is to be noted in this connection that Lord Eldon in his statement did not advocate a complete homogenization of the judicial methods used at the common law and in equity. Although the principles of equity were to be stable and uniform, they should in his opinion "be applied according to the circumstances of each case". This adaptation of fairly well-defined but essentially flexible principles to concrete and unique fact situations has to this day remained a quality of the administration of equity distinguishing it from the more rigid texture of the common law.

In 1905, Roscoe Pound published an illuminating article entitled *The Decadence of Equity*.[33] In this article he pointed out that there was going on in the Anglo-American system of justice a progressive erosion of the function of equity as a rejuvenating force in the law. He attributed this decline of the institution to the conception of equitable adjudication held by Lord Eldon. He demonstrated that in its early formative period equity had been a "justice without law",[34] a discretionary modification of the strict law by the infusion of individualized fair play according to the needs of the particular litigated situation. The crystallization of equity into a system of general rules — even though these rules were somewhat more elastic than those of the common law — had interfered with the performance of equity's original mission. Equity, according to Pound, gradually took on an increasingly technical character, signaling the danger of its

---

[31] *Gee v. Pritchard,* 36 Eng. Rep. 670, 674 (1818).

[32] See William S. Holdsworth, *Some Makers of English Law* (Cambridge, Eng., 1938), pp. 176-210; Duncan M. Kerly, *An Historical Sketch of the Equitable Jurisdiction of the Court of Chancery* (Cambridge, Eng., 1890), p. 1.

[33] Roscoe Pound, "The Decadence of Equity", 5 *Columbia Law Review* 20 (1905).

[34] *Id.,* p. 20.

ultimate fossilization. In terms of the terminology and sociological analysis used in the present book, Pound's thesis confirms the fact that the transmutation of equity from an externally-imposed, roving dispensation of the royal prerogative into an instrumentality of the internal dynamics of the law has infused into equity certain inertial ingredients typical for judicially-administered law in general.

Can it be said that the equity administered by American courts in the twentieth century has overcome these regressive tendencies? There has, no doubt, been some reactivation of equitable initiative in fields like protection of political freedoms, privacy and other personal rights of a non-property character.[35] The injunction in equity has been used as a formidable weapon by the courts in desegregation and reapportionment cases. Since we are concerned, however, with the power of equity to devise new rules and remedies, we must distinguish between the exercise of injunctive power by courts in aid of the enforcement of constitutional commands or statutes on the one hand and cases where rights or remedies were fashioned by way of original judicial creation. Injunctions in desegregation and reapportionment cases belong to the first category. They are issued to implement the equal protection clause of the Federal Constitution, as reinterpreted by the United States Supreme Court in recent times, and not in support of the enforcement of non-constitutional, non-legislative, court-invented categories of rights. In a similar vein, injunctions issued for the purpose of safeguarding the voting rights of minority groups were for the most part based on the Congressional civil rights legislation of 1966. Are there instances, in the twentieth century, of creative lawmaking by courts exercising equitable powers which are comparable to the fashioning of uses, trusts and specific relief in contract cases by the King's Council in the fourteenth and fifteenth centuries?

The most conspicuous example of judicial innovation that comes to the mind of the student of modern American legal history is the right to privacy. Recognition of the right to be free from unwarranted and distasteful publicity was for the first time demanded in a law review article by Warren and Brandeis in 1890.[36] A number of States, through decisions of

---

[35] There was a time when equity limited itself to a far-reaching extent to the protection of property rights. See William F. Walsh, *A Treatise on Equity* (Chicago, 1930), pp. 213-214, 259-262.

[36] Samuel D. Warren and Louis D. Brandeis, "The Right to Privacy", 4 *Harvard Law Review* 193 (1890). Among the more recent legal and general discussions of the right of privacy are William L. Prosser, *Handbook of the Law of Torts*, 4th ed. (St. Paul, 1971), Ch. 20; Charles Fried, "Privacy", 77 *Yale Law Journal* 475 (1968); *Privacy*, ed. J. R. Pennock and J. W. Chapman, Nomos Vol. XIII (New York, 1971).

their highest courts, adopted the position that there was a legally enforceable right of this character, while others, including the pivotal State of New York, relegated the protection of this right to action by the legislature. Since the right to privacy, in those States in which it has been judicially recognized, can be enforced by an action at law for damages as well as by an injunction in equity, it cannot be termed a typical creature of equity; its development is due to an exercise of general judicial power to adjust the law to changes and refinements in community sentiment, a matter to be discussed in the next section.

In the vitally important field of environmental control, much good has been done by courts exercising equitable powers in reducing the adverse effects of water and air pollution in individual litigated cases. Obviously, however, the problem cannot be solved by isolated court actions, which will be limited in their effect to particular industrial plants and will consume much time and financial resources. Pervasive legislative regulation is indispensable for coping with a matter which involves the well-being and even the survival of exceedingly large numbers of people.

On an overall basis, the judgment of Sir Henry Maine, confirmed by Roscoe Pound, stands up well to historical scrutiny. Equity proved its valor as an instrument of incisive legal change at a time when its innovative devices and procedures were engrafted upon the law from the outside by the exercise of political prerogatives. To the extent that equity became gradually incorporated into the regular processes of the judicial system, it lost a great deal of its original creative momentum and encountered some of the inertial resistance which, as the next section is designed to show, is a conspicuous attribute of the internal administration of the law.

SECTION 11
The Internal Dynamics of the Law I: Judicial Innovation

The statement was made in the preceding section that "not only during the infancy of legal systems but far beyond the life span of this period can we observe a disinclination on the part of the courts to arrogate to themselves an openly-proclaimed power of lawmaking". The validity of this assertion is borne out by many pronouncements of judges and leading textwriters during the formative and classical periods of the common law. Coke, Hale, Mansfield, and Blackstone, for example, were convinced that courts never make law, but merely declare, and furnish evidence of, what the law is on any particular point in controversy. The law itself, they believed, to the extent that it had not been positivized in a legislative enactment, must be found in popular usage, reason, and the community's sense of justice.[1] The same view was held in early United States history by Alexander Hamilton, Chancellor James Kent and Chief Justice John Marshall. Marshall's formulation of this conception of the judicial function is particularly trenchant and suggestive:

> "Judicial power, as contradistinguished from the power of the laws, has no existence. Courts are mere instruments of the law, and can will nothing. When they are said to exercise a discretion, it is a mere legal discretion, a discretion to be exercised in discerning the course prescribed by law; and when that is discerned, it is the duty of the Court to follow it. Judicial power is never exercised for the purpose of giving effect to the will of the Judge: always for the purpose of giving effect.....to the will of the law."[2]

In the case in which this statement appears, the "will of the law" had found expression in an act of Congress. But Marshall apparently meant to say more than merely restate the commonplace truth that courts are bound by the legislative will embodied in a valid law. The passage quoted above is preceded by the assertion that the judicial department "has no will, in any case". If these words are interpreted literally, they amount in effect to a denial that law possesses any internal dynamics of its own. Once law has sprung into being, by constitutional mandate, legislative decree, or popular practice hardened into custom, the judiciary has to accept it as it is and cannot reshape or improve it by deliberate action designed to serve the common good. The function of law to provide stability becomes in this view the lodestar of judicial activity.

An extreme antithesis to this position is presented by a movement in political and legal thought which reached a climax in the 1960's, and which one of its most outspoken representatives has labeled "political jurisprudence".[3] Several variations of this theory can be found in the pertinent literature, and in some of its most influential expressions it has formed an

---

[1] Pertinent quotations are found in Edgar Bodenheimer, *Jurisprudence: The Philosophy and Method of the Law* (Cambridge, Mass., 1962), pp. 286-288. See also William S. Holdsworth, "Case Law", 50 *Law Quarterly Review* 180, 182-189 (1934).

[2] *Osborn v. Bank of the United States*, 9 *Wheaton* 738, 866 (1824). See also *The Federalist*, ed. J. E. Cooke (Middletown, Conn., 1961), pp. 523-526, where Alexander Hamilton expressed a similar view.

[3] See Martin Shapiro, "Political Jurisprudence", 52 *Kentucky Law Journal* 294 (1964).

alliance with what is often referred to as the "neo-behavioral" approach.[4] The theory has found more adherents in the ranks of political scientists and law teachers than among judges and attorneys, but its educational impact upon the legal profession, especially its younger members, has been sufficiently strong to warrant close attention. An attempt will be made to depict the most essential tenets of faith of this movement, without encumbering the presentation too much with an analysis of the numerous shadings and nuances which a careful study of the literature will reveal.

The "political process" approach to the judicial function assumes, in the words of a leading spokesman, that "judges share with legislatures, chief executives, and heads of major administrative departments the political power and responsibility to make policy decisions that reflect certain priorities of values".[5] The first important ingredient of this statement is the propagation of the idea that the power conferred upon the judiciary is a *political* power, comparable to the power possessed by Presidents, congressmen and many administrators, though perhaps distinguishable from the latter varieties by the specific modes and techniques in which it is exercised. The second significant element of the proposition is the expression of a conviction that judges are *makers of policy,* and not merely executors of policy-determinations that have become articulated in constitutional provisions, statutes, and other relevant sources of law. The implication of this position is that judges, in the numerous cases where choices are left to them by the indeterminacy, vagueness, ambiguity, or incompleteness of the positive law, will choose among alternative solutions by giving preference to certain values to which they assign a high priority, and from the implementation of which they expect the realization of pragmatically desirable consequences.

Both the political and behavioral versions of this approach seem to converge in the assumption that judicial choices among conflicting values are made on the basis of individual predilections of judges rather than some

---

[4] Schubert, a widely read political scientist, has described his judicial philosophy as a mixture of the "political process" approach — which he calls the "conventional" attitude in contemporary political science — and the behavioral research method. See Glendon A. Schubert, *Judicial Policy-Making: The Political Role of the Courts* (Chicago, 1965), pp. 158-159, 161-165.

[5] Schubert, *supra* n. 4, p. 1. A similar view is expressed in a more radical formulation by Shapiro, *supra* n. 3, p. 296: "The core of political jurisprudence is a vision of the courts as political agencies and judges as political actors". The logical consequence of this position is that the critic of court decisions, too, merely gives expression to his political preferences. "It may well be that the real test of Supreme Court performance in every area of its jurisdiction is whether or not one likes the results it achieves." Shapiro, *Law and Politics in the Supreme Court* (Glencoe, Ill., 1964), p. 327.

objectively discernible scheme of axiological priorities immanent in the social structure. This leads to the further supposition that, whenever judges are placed in a position where they have to uphold, invalidate or otherwise pass upon certain measures originating with other decision-makers, they will be prone to accept these measures if they are personally in agreement with the policies embodied in them. If they reject these policies, their conflict with other branches of the government will be likely to find its expression through an activist exercise of judicial review (or perhaps other means available to the judges, such as whittling down the scope of an enactment by means of restrictive interpretation). The basic premise underlying such views of judicial behavior is that judges are primarily oriented by goal values which are the same as those which motivate other political actors.[6]

A court which is frequently called upon to make decisions affecting the political and social value structure of the country is the United States Supreme Court. It is therefore understandable that a great deal of the writing on political jurisprudence has centered around this Court. Miller and Howell have proposed, for example, that this Court, acting as a sort of national conscience, should "help articulate in broad principle the goals of American society".[7] Schubert has claimed that the justices of the Supreme Court, with very few exceptions, can be assimilated to Harold Lasswell's category of the "political type", *i.e.* a specimen of man who is intent upon playing a political role that will permit him to enjoy the power and deference for which he is craving.[8] Furthermore, in the light of the assumption that the justices are motivated chiefly by their personal value preferences, their voting records have been dissected by neo-behaviorists with a view to ascertaining their social and economic philosophy. The possibility of making scientifically valid predictions of future decisions based on the liberal or conservative leanings of the members of the Court has sometimes been proclaimed with great self-assurance.[9] It has been

---

[6] See Schubert, *supra* n. 4, pp. 153-157. See also Shapiro, *supra* n. 3, pp. 310-311: "If judges are viewed as policy-makers, then it is natural to ask of them as one asks of other policy-makers, how do their individual value preferences affect their policy decisions".

[7] Arthur S. Miller and Ronald F. Howell, "The Myth of Neutrality in Constitutional Adjudication", 27 *University of Chicago Law Review* 661, 689 (1960).

[8] Schubert, *The Judicial Mind* (Evanston, Ill., 1965), p. 12; Harold D. Lasswell, *Power and Personality* (New York, 1948), p. 38.

[9] See, for example, the detailed charts designed to serve as patterns for such forecasts in Schubert, *supra* n. 8. Schubert notes, however, certain "paradoxes" in the conservative philosophy which complicate the task of prognostication. *Id.*, pp. 273-274.

asserted, for example, that in cases arising under the Federal Employers'
Liability Act economic liberal members of the Court have consistently
voted to uphold the claims of workers, while the economic conservatives
have seen fit to deny them.[10]

Although the United States Supreme Court has served as the focal point
for testing such notions, the political-process approach has not remained
restricted to an appraisal of the work of this Court. The logic of the theory
itself requires its extension to other categories of tribunals. State supreme
courts, like the highest court of the land, often have to pass with final
authority upon constitutional questions that have a bearing upon the
political liberties and economic well-being of the people. The lower federal
and State courts have to adjust their methods of adjudication to the
judicial mores of the higher courts and therefore cannot escape the impact
of the judicial philosophy which governs the decision-making processes of
the courts of last resort. It seems therefore safe to state that the tenets of
political jurisprudence and the neo-behaviorist theories associated with
them are meant to be applicable to all layers of the judicial system.[11]

One of the foundation stones of the political-process approach is a
strongly-held belief that law is in no sense an independent organism that
can be insulated from the battle of contending political forces. This view
places the law — with the exception perhaps of its purely technical parts —
in the midst of the struggle for power.[12] In the federal sphere, this notion
tends to assign to the United States Supreme Court the role of a
competitor with Congress and the Executive for the maximation of
political decision-making authority. It is interesting to note that Adolf
Berle, who can be identified with this viewpoint, declared in 1967 that in
this contest the Supreme Court had emerged as the unmistakable victor.
"Ultimate legislative power in the United States has come to rest in the
Supreme Court of the United States."[13] Although Berle realizes that the
Federal Constitution has not assigned the legislative power to this Court or
any other judicial organ, he contends that the Supreme Court by the force
of circumstances could not have escaped the position in which, according

---

[10] Schubert, *supra* n. 4, p. 122.

[11] See Shapiro, *supra* n. 3, p. 318: "It is easier to get Americans to grasp a political or
governmental context for the Supreme Court than for other courts. But that does not
mean that in reality other courts are less political". See also Schubert, *supra* n. 4, pp.
1-3.

[12] See Miller and Howell, *supra* n. 7, p. 691; Shapiro, *supra* n. 3, pp. 294-295.

[13] Adolf A. Berle, *The Three Faces of Power* (New York, 1967), p. 3.

to his interpretation, it finds itself today. In arrogating to itself the paramount political power in the country, Berle states, the Supreme Court has taken on the functions of a "revolutionary committee", an event with consequences which, by and large, he regards as desirable.[14]

The first question to be discussed in the light of such theories is whether the basic assumptions of the political-process approach constitute a correct reflection of actual contemporary judicial policy as practiced particularly by the highest court of the land. The three main areas in which an exercise of a politically-inspired legislative power by the Supreme Court of the United States (and some other courts following its lead) allegedly has taken place are school desegregation, reapportionment and the administration of criminal justice.

Berle declares that "the school segregation cases were and perhaps still are the most spectacular exercise of legislative power".[15] Schubert believes that the Supreme Court in *Brown v. Board of Education* became the active agent of "policy-making" while other political organs were standing pat.[16] Rosenblum expresses the view that the Supreme Court's ruling outlawing segregation in public education can hardly be clothed with a purpose that is vitally different from that pursued by a legislative body.[17]

An appraisal of these statements should proceed from the premise that there is little point in imputing to the Supreme Court a policy of incisive encroachment upon the functions of other government departments if its decisions can be explained on grounds which do not suggest an abandonment of the traditional judicial function by the Court. The *School Segregation Cases*[18] involved an interpretation and application of the Equal Protection Clause of the Federal Constitution, which prohibits unreasonable discriminations based on race, sex, religion or other factors. Regardless of whether one agrees or disagrees with the particular interpretation of the Fourteenth Amendment adopted by the Court in this instance, it would seem clear that the Court did not move beyond the confines of the task imposed on it by the framers of the Constitution. As Alexander Hamilton

---

[14] *Id.*, p. 10. See also Berle, *Power* (New York, 1969), Ch. 4, entitled "Judicial Political Power." Berle holds that the fusion of judicial and legislative power which, in his opinion, has occurred in the Supreme Court carries with it certain dangers for the future which he seeks to meet by proposals for a redistribution of judicial power.

[15] Berle, *supra* n. 13, p. 15.

[16] Schubert, *supra* n. 4, pp. 133-136.

[17] Victor G. Rosenblum, *Law as Political Instrument* (Garden City, N.Y., 1955), p. 10.

[18] *Brown v. Board of Education*, 347 U. S. 483 (1954).

said in *The Federalist:* "The interpretation of the laws is the proper and peculiar province of the courts. A constitution is in fact, and must be, regarded by the judges as a fundamental law."[19]

The impression created in some circles that the Supreme Court in the *Brown* case "legislated" the desegregation of the public schools stems from the fact that the Court, in an earlier decision,[20] had found the establishment of separate facilities for black school children consistent with the requirements of equal protection. It was argued that the reversal of this decision, resulting in a clear-cut break with judicial precedent, was indicative of an intent on the part of the justices to make new law in an essentially legislative manner and thereby to usurp the functions entrusted under the Constitution to Congress or the state legislatures.

There are two reasons why this argument lacks persuasive force. First of all, during the greater part of common law history in England, and throughout the history of law in the United States, courts have been held to possess a legitimate power to overrule precedents deemed to have been based on error.[21] If the Supreme Court in the *Brown* case came to the conclusion that its earlier inconsistent decision rested on a faulty or unreasonable construction of the Constitution, its abandonment of that construction cannot be said to amount to a usurpation of legislative powers.

There is a second way of justifying the *Brown* decision from the point of view of proper use of the judicial method. The position might be taken that at the time of *Plessy v. Ferguson* participation of black children in public education was still too recent an event to allow the formation of a fully-informed judgment on the effects of segregation. The Court at that time assumed that no problem of equal protection was presented as long as the school facilities afforded to whites and blacks were commensurate in quality. The experiences and studies made in the following fifty years demonstrated that a segregated school system, regardless of the comparative quality of white and black schools, creates conditions of inherent inequality between the races and also produces the typical psychological consequences of discriminatory treatment. Furthermore, the fifty years intervening between the first and second decision had furnished a great deal of proof that, in spite of an initial cultural handicap, blacks are capable of

---

[19] Hamilton, *supra* n. 2, p. 525 (Essay No. 78).

[20] *Plessy v. Ferguson,* 163 U.S. 537 (1896).

[21] Even Blackstone, a conservative writer and judge, admitted an exception from the binding force of precedent "where the former determination is most evidently contrary to reason ... But even in such cases the judges do not pretend to make a new law, but to vindicate the old one from misrepresentation", William Blackstone, *Commentaries on the Laws of England,* ed. T. M. Cooley (Chicago, 1899), Bk. I, p. 70.

intellectual attainments equal to those of white people. In the words of the Court, "many Negroes have achieved outstanding success in the arts and sciences as well as in the business and professional world".[22] This statement is relevant to the conclusion reached by the Court in the sense that the Equal Protection Clause does not require an equal treatment of persons and situations which in the very nature of things are unequal. Viewed in the light of such considerations, the overruling of *Plessy* in the *Brown* case did not constitute judicial legislation in the area of race relations, but rested on a finding of unreasonable discrimination in contravention of the Fourteenth Amendment. This finding was substantiated by evidence and social experiences which were not to the same extent available at the time of the earlier decision.

Reapportionment is a second critical area for testing the alleged usurpation of non-judicial functions by the Supreme Court. When the Court enunciated in a series of holdings the principle that failure to apportion legislative districts on the basis of population violates the Federal Constitution and, in the absence of effective legislative action, warrants imposition of an equitable scheme of representation by the courts, some writers suggested — either by way of approval or disapproval — that the Court had entered into the political thicket and rendered a policy decision of an incisively lawmaking character.[23] Here again, it was claimed by the critics that the Court, even more abruptly than in the *School Desegregation Cases*, had reversed its earlier position on the question.[24] Adverse comment also was generated by the Court's action in excluding certain factors, such as balancing of urban and rural power in the legislatures, insuring effective representation of sparsely settled areas, or giving weight to economic or other group interests, from consideration in drafting and adopting a plan of reapportionment.[25] The question was raised as to whether the Court, in its

---

[22] *Brown v. Board of Education,* 347 U. S. 483, 490 (1954).

[23] See *Baker v. Carr,* 369 U. S. 186 (1962); *Wesberry v. Sanders,* 376 U. S. 1 (1964); *Reynolds v. Sims,* 377 U. S. 533 (1964). Berle, *supra* n. 13, pp. 10, 15, 25, describes the cases as spectacular exercises of legislative power but expresses his agreement "in general". Strong reservations are voiced by Phil C. Neal, "Baker v. Carr: Politics in Search of Law", 1962 *Supreme Court Review* 252, 253, 327. See also Robert G. McCloskey, "The Supreme Court, 1961 Term: Foreword", 76 *Harvard Law Review* 54, 64-74 (1962).

[24] In *Colegrove v. Green,* 328 U. S. 549 (1946), the Court refused to review a challenge to Congressional apportionment. The case did not, however, reach the argument under the Equal Protection Clause, which figured prominently in the reapportionment cases of the 1960s. The *Colegrove* decision might be explained on the ground that there was want of equitable reasons for judicial intervention under the particular circumstances of the case.

[25] See *Reynolds v. Sims,* 377 U. S. 533, 579-580 (1964); *Davis v. Mann,* 377 U. S. 678, 692 (1964).

insistence on an almost undiluted size-of-population principle, had imposed upon the country a political scheme of representation preferred by the majority of the justices, instead of simply giving effect to the "will of the law".

The question raises highly complex issues which take the interpreter into the borderland between political and legal action. The basic notion underlying the rulings in the reapportionment cases is that, apart from the special situation created by the Federal Constitution for elections to the United States Senate, the votes of all citizens in State and Congressional elections should carry an approximately equal weight. For State elections this conclusion was derived by the Court from the command of the Equal Protection Clause. With respect to elections for the House of Representatives, it was based on Art. I, § 2 of the Constitution, providing that representatives shall be chosen "by the People of the several states" and shall be "apportioned among the several states....according to their respective Numbers".[26] Although Mr. Justice Harlan questioned the applicability of these provisions and the soundness of the Court's analysis of the will of their framers, it cannot be said that the Court's conclusion as to the basic principle controlling the apportionment of legislative seats was reached in a constitutional void. Notwithstanding the fact that the particular provisions relied on by the Court do not directly prescribe the general solution which it chose to adopt, these provisions need be construed in the context of a document designed to create a fundamentally democratic commonwealth, in which there should be no unreasonable disparities in individual voting strength.

Doubts may be voiced, however, with respect to the Court's position that, although mathematical precision was not required in implementing this equality, the Constitution prohibits dilutions of the equal-population principle designed to insure some degree of representation to area or other group interests, even though these departures do not submerge population as the controlling principle of an apportionment plan.[27] Whether the Federal Constitution really sought to enjoin the states from organizing the second chamber of their legislature along lines of representation somewhat different from that of the first chamber is at least debatable. The doubts are increased by the fact that the Federal Constitution is not a charter averse to the idea of minority protection. The Fourteenth Amendment, on which the court so strongly relied, is one of the chief instrumentalities for

[26] *Reynolds v. Sims,* 377 U. S. 533, 568 (1964); *Wesberry v. Sanders,* 376 U. S. 1, 7-18 (1964).

[27] The only departure permitted by the Court is to enable the State to use political subdivisions as bases for electoral districts. *Reynolds v. Sims,* 377 U. S. 533, 578-579 (1964).

affording this kind of protection. By engrafting an almost undiluted majority rule upon the total system of state elections, the Court did perhaps not remain true to its own premise that equal protection demands complete equivalence of voting strength. It is generally assumed that under its rulings urban and suburban power will be overrepresented in relation to rural and agricultural interests. Even though the Court would have been fully justified in applying the axe of judicial review to wholly unreasonable reapportionment plans, there is a doctrinaire element in the criteria it laid down in its decision which does not seem to be firmly anchored in the constitutional provisions on which the Court relied.[27a]

The administration of criminal justice is another field in which a use of judicial power by the Supreme Court for unadulterated purposes of law-making is claimed by some observers of the Court's work to have occurred. Decisions dealing with the scope of the privilege against self-incrimination have often been referred to in support of this contention. The Fifth Amendment to the Federal Constitution provides that no person "shall be compelled in any criminal case to be a witness against himself". In *Miranda v. Arizona*,[28] the Supreme Court set out to prove that this provision made it mandatory upon police officers to inform persons who had been taken into custody, as a prerequisite to lawful interrogation, of their right to remain silent and avail themselves of the assistance of counsel. Since these requirements were held to be applicable to situations in which no actual compulsion to speak was involved, the conclusions reached by the Court could not be derived from the text of the Constitution by an act of direct deduction. The Court attempted to show, however, that the atmosphere prevailing in police stations during interrogations of suspects was inherently coercive, so that indirect pressures were apt to be exerted upon the arrested person which could easily undermine his will to resist and induce him to reveal the secrets of his case. In *Griffin v. California*,[29] the Court struck down as a violation of the privilege against self-incrimination a rule of the California Constitution which permitted the prosecutor and court in a criminal case to comment upon the defendant's failure to take the stand to explain or deny evidence against him. While it is possible to support the court's holding in *Miranda* by a broad construction of the privilege as defined in the Fifth Amendment, it is difficult in the second case to relate the decision to the language and meaning of that amendment.

[27a] While this book was on the press, the Supreme Court, in *Mahan v. Howell*, 93 Sup. Ct. 979 (1973), has initiated a trend towards greater flexibility in adjudging the constitutionality of reapportionment schemes.

[28] 384 U. S. 436 (1966).

[29] 380 U. S. 609 (1965).

Other instances in the field of criminal justice in which assumption by the Supreme Court of somewhat freewheeling lawmaking powers has been asserted are the imposition upon the States of standards of procedure previously developed in the federal domain and the invalidation of numerous State and federal convictions upon technical grounds in cases where the guil of the defendant was beyond a reasonable doubt, and where the infringement of procedural rules was neither blatant nor obvious and deliberate. In the face of this line of decisions, a federal judge has cautiously intimated that the Supreme Court, without a clear warrant contained in the Federal Constitution, has promulgated a rather detailed code of criminal procedure and rendered it binding upon the fifty States.[30]

In passing upon such criticisms, it must be realized that the problems faced by the United States Supreme Court in constitutional cases present special features and difficulties, because in this area the relation between law and the country's political and social value patterns is particularly close. Important legal pronouncements in the constitutional field therefore tend to produce momentous consequences for the political life of the country and its social institutions. Moreover, constitutional clauses are often flexibly and even vaguely formulated in order to secure their maximum adaptability to the varying conditions of life. Their wording therefore often leaves room for alternative interpretations which attempt to discern their meaning and spirit in the light of the values to be served by them.

The United States Supreme Court, during the period when the stewardship of the Court was entrusted to Chief Justice Earl Warren, was strongly inclined to construe the provisions of the Federal Constitution relating to criminal procedure in favor of the persons accused of crime. The charge was leveled against the Warren Court by many laymen and members of the legal profession that the Court failed to strike a fair balance between society's need for protection against crime and the interests of defendants in criminal proceedings.[31] The reply might be made to this accusation that it was the purpose of the Constitution to give maximum protection to individual liberties; that the Bill of Rights contains no reference to the concept of the public interest; and that for these reasons a broad and liberal interpretation of the procedural guarantees has less of a "political"

---

[30] Henry J. Friendly, "The Bill of Rights as a Code of Criminal Procedure", 53 *California Law Review* 929 (1965). Cf. also Walter V. Schaefer, "Police Interrogation and the Privilege against Self-Incrimination", 61 *Northwestern University Law Review* 506 (1966).

[31] A discussion of the criticisms to which the Warren Court was subjected is found in Clifford M. Lytle, *The Warren Court and Its Critics* (Tucson, 1968).

flavor than reading into these amendments a command to balance individual against collective interests.

If this line of argumentation is persuasive — and it would seem to possess at least some *prima facie* plausibility — it would lead to an appraisal of the Warren Court's work in the criminal field quite different from the criticism to which the Court was frequently subjected. It would tend towards the conclusion that the Court cannot be accused of usurping political power for the purpose of shaping the criminal procedure of the federal and State courts in its own image of desirable law for the future. The implication would rather be that the Court followed tradition in interpreting the procedural guarantees of the Constitution in the light of a Jeffersonian individualism which could not have foreseen the vexing problems of maintaining public order in a complex, urban society.

When we leave the field of constitutional adjudication and turn to the work of the courts in ordinary litigation, the element of volitional, purely result-oriented policy-making moves further into the background. Courts are in a very significant sense the guardians of legal security. The effectuation of this key value of the legal order requires a reasonably strong possibility of reliance on preannounced standards of decision-making which cut down the range of contingency and surprise. The chances for predicting the outcome of actual or potential lawsuits correctly should be substantially larger than the odds in forecasting passage or defeat of a legislative bill. This is one of the main reasons why judges for the most part measure the events in litigation before them by yardsticks — such as statutes or judicial rules of decision — which were already in existence at the time when these events happened.

Subject to important exceptions and qualifications to be discussed later, reason requires a predominantly past-oriented attitude on the part of judges. In its absence, the legal relations and transactions of men would always be in a state of uncertainty and suspense. Nobody entering into a legal arrangement with another person could be assured that a court in the future would judge the validity or legal consequences of the transaction on the basis of criteria which were known, ascertainable, or foreseeable at the time of its making. Long-range planning would frequently be frustrated by shifts and reversals in judicial policy, and expert advice on whether or not to engage in litigation would be practically useless. That modicum of security in the conditions of life which is indispensable to human well-being and mental health would be non-existent or in serious jeopardy.[32]

---

[32] On the advantages of a reasonable amount of legal security see *supra* Sec. 5.

The value of equality is also not furthered by a philosophy which tends to be overly hospitable to individual policy-making ventures by judges. Equal treatment of equal situations, which is a postulate of justice deeply ingrained in the human mind, is not possible in the absence of objective, impersonal standards limiting decisional freedom. If allocation of powers, duties, and rights among men were primarily a function of free-wheeling individualized adjudication, the perpetration of gross inequalities would result from a medley of uncoordinated judicial philosophies. Even though some degree of unification would be achieved through the guidance provided by a supreme appellate court, the consistency and continuity of policy-oriented lawmaking by this court would always be jeopardized by changes in composition and shifting judicial majorities. It is likely that an excessively individualized dispensation of justice, grounded on the judges' personal viewpoints concerning various aspects of the world, would in the long run result in the disintegration and breakdown of the legal system.

Limitation of judicial discretion is thus a cardinal prerequisite of order as well as justice.[33] More than that, it is an integral component of the very notion of law as a device for restraining power. Although the effectuation of a rule of law which guarantees security and equality to free men through the promulgation and enforcement of a normative structure designed to curb arbitrariness is an ideal which can never be fully attained, it makes a great deal of difference whether or not the judicial function is conceived and exercised in a manner conducive to the vigorous pursuit of this ideal. A judicial philosophy which preaches or exalts policy-making by individual judges or judicial majorities cannot be considered a suitable vehicle for the achievement of the basic goals of the law.

A rejection of the main tenets of political jurisprudence nevertheless leaves room for creative innovation by the judiciary. It does not imply a return to a mechanistic jurisprudence which, by insisting on strict, syllogistic enforcement of existing rules, is oriented exclusively toward the past and oblivious of the judge's task to do justice between the parties. While the legal order, and particularly the judicial process, in the words of Paul Freund, "puts a premium on continuity in the midst of change",[34] there remains the need for steering a safe course through a strait of

---

[33] Limitation of judicial discretion is not the equivalent of straitjacketing. There are areas in the law where a great deal of leeway, within the confining bounds of general guidelines, must be left to the judge. On this problem see Edgar Bodenheimer, "Classicism and Romanticism in the Law," 15 *U.C.L.A. Law Review* 915, 928-930 (1968).

[34] Paul A. Freund, "Rationality of Judicial Decision", in *Rational Decision* (Nomos Vol. VII), ed. C. J. Friedrich (New York, 1964), p. 117.

navigation flanked by two menacing rocks: sterile, progress-negating immobility on the one side and precipitous, indiscriminate dynamism on the other.

The occasions for judicial innovation, within the limits dictated by the general functions of law, arise from the fact that some norms embodied in constitutional provisions, statutes and precedents will become frozen in the absence of reinterpretation and readaptation to a social scene which moves on (like the shifting scenery in some Wagnerian operas) and produces new relationships and alignments between individuals and groups. The result of this often-occurring discrepancy between law and social reality, if it remains uncorrected, will be an application of legal provisions to situations which were not within the original contemplation of their framers and, if they had been, would in all likelihood have caused a revision or qualification of the norm. This general proposition will be illustrated by several examples.

In a simple, preindustrial economy, it was not necessarily unreasonable to place the assumption of risk in a sales transaction on the buyer. In most cases he was probably able to discover defects in the object sold to him by a careful inspection. In an age of highly developed technology, in which complex machinery and gadgets, canned foods and packaged goods are produced, such an inspection can no longer be expected and demanded of the purchaser. A retention of the *caveat emptor* rule would under these changed circumstances bring about highly iniquitous results never envisaged by the makers of the rule.

The law of leases furnishes another example of a gap between legal and social reality. It originated in England in the context of a feudal order in which relations between men were appraised chiefly in terms of their position within a hierarchical system of landholding. A lease was construed as investing its holder with a limited (but usually long-continuing) ownership right in the leased premises, with the consequence that he was largely responsible for keeping his property in a state of appropriate maintenance and repair. In our own day, a lease is in its essential social significance a contract by which the owner of property grants the use of it to another person for a limited and often short period of time. Unlike the feudal tenant, the modern lessee does not acquire anything like a landed estate and is therefore less free than his remote predecessor to deal with the property at his pleasure. It would seem fair under these circumstances to impose, as a general rule, the burden of maintenance and care on the owner-lessor. In many States of the Union, however, the law of leases has not been purged of the remnants of medieval feudal law, and this failure to adapt the law to a modern institution essentially different from the old one

but carrying the same name has produced some unfortunate consequences
and hardships.[35]

The third example relates to the inferior status of women which, prior
to the twentieth century, was a conspicuous feature of the common law in
England and the United States. A rule requiring ratification by the husband
of all transactions entered into by his wife might have been plausible and
acceptable in a period of civilization in which the notion of inequality of
the sexes was for the most part concurred in by both men and women, and
was perhaps consonant with the division of functions in an agricultural age.
When such beliefs gave way to an assumption of essential equality, application of the restrictive rules, before they were abandoned by legislative or
court action, resulted in many unreasonable discriminations violative of
fundamental justice.[36]

The lesson to be derived from these examples may now be summarized. When a judge applies a rule of the past to a situation which is within
the original purview of this rule, he thereby promotes certainty and
calculability of the law, values which the judge is bound to respect even
though he may question the soundness of the precedent. But when he
practices blind adherence to a norm reflecting social relationships or arrangements which have become extinct or decisively modified by super-
vening developments, such action may produce a degree of unfairness
which is no longer outweighed by the security interest intrinsic to the law.

When an earlier rule of law which has become obsolete is incorporated
in a statute, Anglo-American legal doctrine does not authorize the judge to
ignore the enactment unless good grounds exist for a constitutional
challenge. He will have to wait for amendatory action by the legislature.
The British, from 1898 to 1966, took the position that even judicial rules
laid down by their highest court could be overturned by parliamentary
statute only.[37] The adoption of this position was prompted by the consideration that a judicial reversal of a precedent, since it affects a past
transaction by a retroactive ruling, always takes by surprise one of the
parties who had relied on the status quo secured by the earlier rule. But
the counterarguments against an absolute prohibition of judicial overruling
were found so persuasive that the British House of Lords decided to change

---

[35] See "Legal Problems of Landlord and Tenant", 3 *University of California, Davis Law
Review* 31-87 (1971).

[36] An area of domestic relations still filled today with many antiquated rules is the law
of minors' disabilities. See, for example, Robert G. Edge, "Voidability of Minors' Contracts: A Feudal Doctrine in a Modern Economy", 1 *Georgia Law Review* 205 (1966).

[37] *London Street Tramways Co. v. London County Council,* [1898] A. C. 375.

its rigid position in 1966.[38] First of all, it was probably taken into account that legislatures are so often preoccupied with matters yielding an immediate political advantage that they might easily neglect problems in the politically neutral areas of the law. Secondly, there are usually on the scene some economic or professional interest groups which profit from maintenance of the status quo and will bring pressure to bear upon legislative bodies to preserve it.

When a reasonable inference can be drawn that the community standard of justice has substantially changed, the courts may under certain circumstances be justified in adjusting the non-statutory case law to the revised mores of society. It would seem proper to hold that they may do so when legislative reform, due to preoccupation of the lawmakers with vital political problems, pressures exerted by special interests, or simple inattention, is not forthcoming and cannot be expected to take place within a foreseeable time. Even in this situation, judicial innovation is not ordinarily undertaken in the absence of a determination that, considering all aspects of the case in which a plea for an overruling of precedent has been made, the need for achieving fundamental justice significantly outweighs the interest in legal security and continuity.

It might be helpful to analyze certain reformatory actions of American courts in the torts field in the light of these standards of judicial action. In a gradual, decidedly non-abrupt development, the courts, in tort actions by consumers of goods against their makers or suppliers for defects causing injury, have dispensed with the necessity of proving negligence and have imposed a strict liability upon the manufacturers and other sellers.[39] One reason for this step was the extreme difficulty facing the plaintiffs in actions against producers in discharging their burden of proof with respect to the occurrence of negligence in the manufacturing process. Many serious obstacles stand in the way of securing persons who are familiar with the defendant's production methods and at the same time willing to bring to light defects in these processes. The plaintiff seldom, if ever, has any direct evidence of what went on in the defendant's plant. He therefore finds himself, with respect to this type of suit, in a position of serious inequality as compared with plaintiffs in other kinds of negligence actions.

During the reign of the negligence doctrine, the courts came to the

---

[38] Announcement of Lord Chancellor Gardiner on July 29, 1966, 110 *Solicitor's Journal* 584 (1966).

[39] See, among many other cases, *Spence v. Three River Builders,* 90 N. W. 2d 873 (Mich. 1958); *Goldberg v. Kollsman Instrument Co.,* 191 N. E. 2d 81 (N. Y., 1963); *Greenman v. Yuba Power Products,* 59 Cal. 2d 57 (1963). Cf. William L. Prosser, *Handbook of the Law of Torts,* 4th ed. (St. Paul, 1971), Ch. 13.

plaintiff's aid by applying the doctrine of *res ipsa loquitur,* which permitted the judge or jury to infer negligence without substantiated proof. But this doctrine was of little use when someone other than the maker of the defective part (who might be unknown) was sued, and the courts therefore searched for a broader basis of liability.[40] They held that in an age of highly developed technology consumers are helpless to protect themselves against dangerous defects in products, and that makers and suppliers should be held to warrant to the general public that such products are safe and suitable for use. The public sentiment strongly supported such holdings. Since the legislatures in most States failed to come to grips with the problem, the courts were thoroughly justified in adopting an innovation which, though it resulted in the overthrow of many earlier decisions of long standing, greatly promoted the achievement of justice.

The abandonment of the doctrine of sovereign immunity by court action in a number of States furnishes another example of a revision of law which is within the proper bounds of the judicial function.[41] The notion that the State and its political subdivisions are exempted from liability for torts committed by their agents originated in England at a time when official political doctrine proclaimed that the King was God's chosen vice-regent on earth who, because of divine investiture, was incapable of doing wrong. This theory was without much critical reflection received into the law of the American colonies and States. It probably did not cause an excessive amount of harm during the time when governmental activity that might give rise to claims for negligence was fairly well limited. In this century, however, when federal, State and municipal enterprise in the fields of gas and electricity, atomic power, transportation, and hazardous military production is extensive, freedom from governmental liability is apt to cause inequities of the most grievous kind to the victims of accidents resulting from the operations of governmental facilities. Here again, legislative inertia prompted the courts to take the lead in the repeal of obsolete doctrine.

Another immunity which was stricken from the law by a number of courts through the abrogation of precedents was the rule which barred family members from suing each other in tort.[42] The abolition of this

---

[40] See William L. Prosser, "The Assault upon the Citadel", 69 *Yale Law Journal* 1099, 1114-1117 (1960).

[41] See *Muskopf v. Corning Hospital District,* 55 Cal. 2d 211 (1961); *Molitor v. Kaneland Community Unit District,* 163 N. E. 2d 89 (Ill. 1959); *Myers v. Genesee County Auditor,* 133 N. W. 2d 190 (Mich. 1965). In some States, the legislature partially restored the immunity lifted by the courts, by way of limits on the amount of recovery or selective allowance of actions.

[42] *Klein v. Klein,* 58 Cal. 2d 692 (1962); *Goller v. White,* 122 N. W. 2d 193 (Wis. 1963); *Gelbman v. Gelbman,* 245 N. E. 2d 192 (N.Y. 1969); *Immer v. Risko,* 267 A 2d 481 (N. J. 1970).

immunity makes it possible for a wife or child injured in an automobile accident caused by the family father's negligence to recover damages from him. In an age in which the taking out of liability insurance has become a common feature of societal life, this revision of the law by the courts will save many families from being plunged into serious financial distress; this consideration would seem to outbalance any benefits that might result from preservation of the old rule.

Robert Keeton has aptly said with reference to judicial innovation that "superficially it may seem that the functions of changing the law and guarding its stability are mutually repugnant. But closer examination discloses that occasional legitimated changes in the law are essential to continuity itself".[43] If a rule which was suited to the social conditions of a bygone age is applied in a contemporary setting in which it will produce results incompatible with its original purpose, a discontinuous break with the justice of the past will have been accomplished.

An adjustment of the law to basic principles of contemporary justice, public policy, or communal mores is presumably not the type of volitional freedom which Chief Justice Marshall had wished to see excised from the judicial domain. His pithy statement that "courts can will nothing"[44] may be interpreted to mean that judges should refrain from acting as legal politicians who, in disposing of a controversy, consider it their chief aim to give effect to their personal convictions or idiosyncratic preferences. Marshall thought that judges should endeavor to find the *ratio* of their decisions in an impersonal configuration called the legal system. Since the norms of this system are frequently surrounded by an aura of ambiguity, vagueness, and opacity, and since competing social values have sometimes to be weighed against each other for the purposes of determining priorities, a truly creative element may inhere in the discernment of that rationale of decision which, in view of the totality of factors to be appraised, is deemed to lead to a just and proper result. It should also be noted that the extension of a well-established general principle to an entirely new situation represents, in its practical effects, a form of judicial innovation.[45]

Notwithstanding this creative component in the judicial process, the range of lawmaking tasks which courts are unable to perform is immense. The very fact that a court has before it one concrete case with its particular facts and circumstances, and is supposed to decide this single

[43] Robert E. Keeton, *Venturing To Do Justice* (Cambridge, Mass., 1969), p. 24.

[44] *Osborn v. Bank of the United States*, 9 Wheaton 738, 866 (1824). See *supra* n. 2.

[45] An example is the extension of the well-known principle that persons whose rights are to be affected by an administrative proceeding are entitled to notice and a hearing to civil proceedings for attachment and garnishment. See *Fuentes v. Shevin*, 407 U. S. 67 (1972); *Randone v. Appellate Department*, 3 Cal. 3rd 536 (1971).

case and no other, forms in and by itself a barrier to a broad use of quasi-legislative rulemaking power.[46] Courts are reluctant and not well equipped to lay down in their decisions general principles which go far beyond the need of finding a justification for the result reached in the individual case. A court may wish to proscribe an entire category of acts of unfair competition, but feels constrained by the scope of its authority to do no more than to enjoin the particular practice challenged in the case (and others which cannot on any reasonable ground be distinguished from it). A court also is prevented from promulgating detailed instructions to executive or administrative agencies as to how they should go about performing their functions. This is the reason why the creation of the law of social insurance and workmen's compensation, which necessitates the setting in motion of a complicated administrative apparatus, was accomplished by statute. The fashioning of entirely new legal institutions has generally remained the prerogative of the legislature, especially when such action requires an accommodation of many competing interests.[47] In the words of a distinguished judge: "Legislatures can break sharply with the past, as need be, as judges ordinarily cannot. They avoid the wasteful cost in time and money of piecemeal litigation that all too frequently culminates in a crazy quilt of rules defying intelligent restatement or coherent application."[48]

It is difficult to draw a sharp line between situations suited for change at the hands of the judiciary and those in which legislative action is called for. Speaking in general terms, it might be stated that courts are apt to refrain from decreeing alterations in the law which bear the taint of arbitrariness. For this reason, the courts have usually refused to set up or modify specific time limitations for the bringing of actions and other purposes.[49] They also have — at least in cases of ordinary litigation not

---

[46] Congress and the legislatures of several States have sometimes empowered the courts to promulgate rules of procedure. This constitutes, of course, a delegation of outright legislative authority to the courts, and the drafting of such rules is an activity outside the scope of the judicial function.

[47] See in this connection Wolfgang Friedmann, "Legal Philosophy and Judicial Lawmaking," 61 *Columbia Law Review* 821, 839-842 (1961).

[48] See Roger J. Traynor, "The Courts," 42 *Journal of the State Bar of California.* 817, 819 (1967). Judge Traynor points out that, because of the need for a coherent and coordinated statement of the law in some of its most important areas, "it fell to the legislators to spell out whole statutes such as insurance codes and the uniform laws dealing with negotiable instruments, sales, bills of lading, warehouse receipts. stock transfers, conditional sales, trust receipts, written obligations, fiduciaries, partnerships, and limited partnerships". *Id.,* p. 818.

[49] See the comments of Chief Justice Charles E. Hughes in *Coleman v. Miller,* 307 U. S. 433, 451-456 (1939).

involving the interpretation of the Constitution — tended to shy away from
making innovations when the need for reform with respect to the subject
matter in question was debatable or controversial.

A court will, on the other hand, be inclined to overrule earlier case law
or adopt a new legal norm when it has reason to assume that the
community's sense of justice would be shocked or grievously disappointed
by a perpetuation of the status quo. Thus the New York Court of Appeals,
in *Woods v. Lancet*,[50] allowed a suit on behalf of an infant for tortious
infliction of prenatal injuries in reversal of an earlier negative position and
justified its action by declaring that, since the legislature had failed to act,
it was "the duty of the court to bring the law into accordance with present
day standards of wisdom and justice". But even in situations where imperative considerations of justice would seem to demand a change in the law,
the courts may leave the task of accomplishing it to the legislature. They
may feel that several reasonable alternatives for the solution of the problem
are open, and that the choice among them depends largely on considerations of political or social expediency. The conclusion may also be reached
that the problem cannot be satisfactorily disposed of within the
acknowledged limitations of the judicial function, which necessitate a
tailoring of the remedy to a narrowly circumscribed fact situation. Courts
will normally be unable to set up a comprehensive system of regulation, to
decree exemptions of qualifications not directly related to the facts of the
case, or to take into account interests which are not represented in the
litigation at hand.[51]

The foregoing considerations are designed to show that it is possible as
well as necessary to make a fundamental distinction between judicial justice
employed in the settlement of past controversies and legislative justice
geared to the improvement of society's future state of well-being. This
distinction is related to the dichotomy between the external and internal
dynamics of the law. A legislature reforming the law from outside by the
exercise of political power has a latitude of teleological, goal-oriented
discretion not to the same extent open to the judicial custodians of the
legal system. While the volitional freedom of legislators may be hemmed in
by constitutional restraints and deference to the opinion of constituencies,
the range of choice possessed by judicial officers is much more narrowly

---

[50] 102 N. E. 2d 691, 694 (1951), citing *Funk v. United States*, 290 U. S. 371, 382
(1933).

[51] Cf. the observations of Justice Louis D. Brandeis in his dissenting opinion in
International News Service v. Associated Press, 248 U. S. 215, 262-278 (1918). See also
Ogle v. Heim, 69 Cal. Rptr. 579, 583 (1968).

confined by the existence of numerous standards of adjudication.[52] Although part of the judge's activity moves in a twilight zone in which the lines between lawfinding and lawmaking are blurred, and although there are important occasions for innovative achievements on the part of judges, it is in the nature of the adjudicatory function that truly activist "leaps forward" amounting to genuine law reform remain a relatively rare phenomenon. In the maintenance of a balance between legal stability and growth, the scales in the internal administration of the law are, as a general rule subject to exceptions, tipped in favor of stability.

SECTION 12
The Internal Dynamics of the Law II: Law Enforcement

Legislative reform, equitable emendation, and judicial innovation are not the only means by which a legal system can be improved and (within the limits set by the inertial tendencies in the law) kept abreast with the changing times. The policies and practices followed in the field of law enforcement may also have a marked impact on the legal development of a society. It may happen that the norms laid down in statute books and judicial decisions are ignored, bypassed, or selectively executed by public prosecutors, grand juries, tax collection bureaus, police officers, or other enforcement agencies. Since these governmental organs and officials are functionaries who have been set up within the legal system for the purpose of carrying out statutory or judicial mandates, the effect of their actions on the course of the law is a phenomenon of the internal dynamics of the law.

Examples of manipulatory tactics that may be employed by law enforcement agencies with the aim and consequence of modifying or immobilizing parts of the ordained normative structure are not hard to find. Public prosecutors in a certain State or country, consistently and for many decades, may refrain from taking violations of the usury statutes by financial and lending institutions to the courts. District attorneys' officers may adopt a policy of not prosecuting certain sexual offenses, such as fornication, seduction, and adultery, or they may take action against certain types of offenders, such as homosexuals, only rarely and sporadically. Tax

---

[52] These standards of adjudication include formalized pronouncements, such as constitutional provisions, statutes, regulations, and precedents, as well as nonformal sources, such as basic principles of public policy and justice, fundamental value patterns of the social order, prevalent modes of societal behavior. Reliance on such nonpositive sources does not stamp the attribute of "political" upon the judge's decision. On the non-formal sources of law see Bodenheimer, *supra* n. 1, Ch. XVI.

collecting agencies may exhibit leniency in scrutinizing the income tax returns of economically powerful individuals or corporations. Regulatory agencies established for the purpose of watching over the pricing or manufacturing practices in certain industries affected with a public interest may assume a protective rather than supervisory attitude toward the regulated enterprises. Grand juries, in communities where racial prejudice runs high, may refuse to file indictments against members of the dominant majority who have committed serious acts of violence against persons belonging to the disfavored minority. Police officers in a certain city may follow a policy of proceeding against users of certain narcotics while sparing the sellers of these drugs. Some such practices of non-enforcement or discriminatory execution of laws have occurred in the United States as well as in other countries.

The motivation underlying such policies may variously be deference to changes in community sentiment with respect to the desirability of some laws, a feeling that the statutory minimum penalty is too severe, response to community prejudices, desire to give special protection to certain privileged groups, or simply inability, due to overloading or undermanning of the legal apparatus, to enforce all laws with equal vigilance.

Decisions by law enforcement agencies not to invoke the legal — especially the criminal — process may be lawful or unlawful, depending upon the constitutional, statutory, and judicial norms controlling the activities of the agency concerned. There are statutes and police department regulations in a considerable number of States and cities in the United States which declare that the police shall at all times detect and arrest violators of the law and enforce all criminal laws of the State and ordinances of the city.[1] There are also statutes which impose a duty of full enforcement in specifically designated areas of the law.[2] The purpose of such enactments is to deny the police discretion to refrain from invoking the criminal process with respect to certain offenders or classes of offenders. In practice, however, it has been found impossible to comply with such mandates, especially those which extend the duty of unrestricted enforcement to the entire field of the criminal law. While the rate of crime has constantly risen in the United States, the resources allocated to the battle against it have not been commensurate with the gravity of the problem.[3] The means are lacking in many places for employing an

[1] Citations to such statutes and ordinances are found in Joseph Goldstein, "Police Discretion Not To Invoke the Criminal Process", 69 *Yale Law Journal* 543, 557-559 (notes 26-27).

[2] See Wayne R. LaFave, *Arrest* (Boston, 1965), p. 77.

[3] On the relation between under-enforcement and over-criminalization see Harry W. Jones, *The Efficacy of Law* (Evanston, Ill., 1969) pp. 33-34.

adequate number of policemen, and the actual members of the work force often do not have the training and qualifications needed to perform their task effectively. This is perhaps the most important, but not the only reason why selective enforcement of the law has become a more or less accepted fact. Among the other reasons, a feeling that there are some obsolete laws in the penal codes which the community no longer wishes to see enforced plays a rather conspicuous role.

While the law in the United States, at least in theory, regards policemen as ministerial officers charged with a strictly-defined duty, it takes a different attitude towards the prosecuting authorities. The discretion of the American district or county attorney to decide when to prosecute and when not to prosecute an offender is given recognition in the case law.[4] Although in this area, too, some legislatures have enacted statutes which seem to impose an absolute duty upon State attorneys to initiate proceedings under certain circumstances or with respect to specific offenses, these statutes have rarely received a literal construction at the hands of the courts.[5] It may be assumed that clear abuses of the prosecutor's discretion not to prosecute are remediable in one way or another, especially by *mandamus*. The remedy is infrequently used, however, and the low visibility of many decisions not to proceed decreases its utility.

There is no doubt that an administrative determination not to proceed against certain offenders may decisively affect the vitality of some parts of the legal organism. This is not the case, of course, where such determination is based on the conclusion that sufficient proof of the offense in an individual case was unlikely to be secured. Where, on the other hand, a broad-gauged policy decision is made to the effect that it would be undesirable to enforce certain segments of the legal order, this amounts virtually to an exercise of the power to reform the law. The social and economic impact of such policy may be far-reaching and momentous. A lagging effort to enforce the antitrust laws may, over prolonged periods of time, bring about a shift of economic development in the very direction which the law sought to block off. Acquiescence by a regulatory administrative agency in certain unlawful practices engaged in by the regulated industry may have the effect of legalizing these business patterns for all practical purposes in contravention of the written law. A consistent refusal

---

[4] See LaFave, "The Prosecutor's Discretion in the United States", 18 *American Journal of Comparative Law* 532, 536 (1970).

[5] See Frank W. Miller, *Prosecution* (Boston, 1970), pp. 166-167; Newman F. Baker and Earl H. De Long, "The Prosecuting Attorney", 24 *Journal of Criminal Law, Criminology, and Police Science* 1025, 1056-1060 (1934); Note, 30 *Indiana Law Journal* 74, 80-82 (1954).

to invoke the legal process against offenders in certain areas of the sex laws might in some instances produce a change in the sexual mores of the society similar to that which a repeal of these laws would have achieved.

The non-enforcement of laws by agencies set up for the very purpose of carrying them into effect raises, of course, a problem of major importance. More than forty years ago, Thurman Arnold noted that "the idea that a prosecuting attorney should be permitted to use his discretion concerning the laws which he will enforce and those which he will disregard appears to the ordinary citizen to border on anarchy".[6] When it is considered that such discretion is exercised not only by public prosecutors, but also by police chiefs, patrolmen, grand juries, and administrative agencies, the probability is increased that some basic objectives of the law may become frustrated by non-execution of legal mandates. Is it desirable, is it consistent with the idea of a rule by law to vest far-reaching powers of non-action or selective policy-making in the organs charged with its enforcement?

In trying to find an answer to this question, it is necessary to distinguish between three major and essentially different sets of problems which have not been sufficiently kept apart in the literature on the subject. The first of these three rubrics is concerned with the enforcement of old or obsolete laws which people in all classes or sections of the population who possess any information and judgment on the matter would in all likelihood wish to see disregarded by the legal authorities. The second group of questions relates to situations in which this condition is not fulfilled, and where selective or discriminatory practices are engaged in by the authorities for the purpose of favoring a special interest group or disfavoring a certain minority group. A third class of cases is presented when there exists perfect readiness on the part of law-enforcing agencies to perform all of the duties entrusted to them, but where insufficient resources have been allocated by the legislature to enable them to carry out their appointed tasks.

The endeavor to find an adequate solution for the first group of problems would benefit greatly from a careful reconsideration by the United States Supreme Court of certain overbroad dicta found in its opinion in *District of Columbia v. John R. Thompson Co.*[7] In this case, the defendant had been prosecuted, under statutes passed by the Assembly of the District of Columbia in 1872 and 1873, for its refusal to make its

---

[6] Thurman W. Arnold, "Law Enforcement — An Attempt at Social Dissection", 42 *Yale Law Journal* 1, 7 (1932). See also Sanford H. Kadish, "Legal Norms and Discretion in the Police and Sentencing Processes", 75 *Harvard Law Review* 904, 906-915 (1962); Edward L. Barrett, Jr., "Police Practices and the Law", 50 *California Law Review* 11 (1962).

[7] 346 U. S. 100 (1953).

eating facilities available to Negroes. The statutes in question made it a misdemeanor for any restaurant keeper to refuse to serve any person on account of race. The Court of Appeals took the position that the statutes were beyond the authority of the District's Assembly to enact. The court also commented that the statutes "having lain unenforced for 78 years, in the face of a custom of race disassociation in the District, the decision of the municipal authorities to enforce them now, by the prosecution of the instant case, was, in effect, a decision legislative in character".[8] The United States Supreme Court disagreed with the lower court. It held that the District's Assembly had been delegated power by Congress to enact the statutes. It also concluded that the statutes had not been abrogated by non-use. In connection with the second holding, the Court laid down a broad rule to the effect that "the failure of the executive branch to enforce a law does not result in its modification or repeal".[9]

It is submitted that the result reached by the Supreme Court in the *Thompson* case was correct, but that the sweeping declaration just quoted was not necessary to the decision. When a statute has been enacted for the purpose of protecting a racial or other minority group against certain manifestations of community prejudice, the statute clearly does not lose its force by persistent non-invocation in deference to such prejudice. In making this determination in the context of the *Thompson* case, it is not irrelevant to note that the reasons which prompted the enactment of the District of Columbia laws affording the members of the black race equal access to eating facilities were still fully valid and subsisting eighty years later when the Supreme Court rendered its decision.

An entirely different situation is presented when a law which at the time of its passage responded to certain strongly-held convictions or sentiments of the population becomes outdated and obsolete because of a general and pervasive change in community attitude. Suppose, for example, a law prohibiting the playing of any outdoor game on Sundays was passed in 1850 in a State in which rigid views concerning the sanctity of the Sabbath were held in all classes and sections of the population at that time. Let us assume, further, that after a period of rigid enforcement the law gradually falls into disuse because the beliefs of the community with respect to permissible Sunday activities have become increasingly secularized. If some persons were prosecuted and convicted under this law in 1970 for playing a game of tennis in a public park on Sunday, would a court be justified in overturning the conviction on the ground that the

---

[8] *John R. Thompson Co. v. District of Columbia,* 203 Fed. 2d 579, 592 (1953).

[9] *Supra* n. 7, at 113-114.

statute has lost its force by non-use in the face of a manifest change in community sentiment?

The post-classical Roman law subscribed to a doctrine known by the technical name of *desuetudo*. It was formulated in Justinian's *Corpus Iuris Civilis* as follows: "Statutes are abrogated not only by the voice of the legislator, but also by the tacit consent of all through desuetude."[10] Some but not all of the modern civil law countries incorporated this doctrine into their legal system, and it probably received its most careful elaboration in Germany.[11] It became a well-established principle in German law that consistent non-use of a statute may result in its abrogation if a general customary law contrary to the statute has succeeded in securing a firm hold in the community's sense of justice.

The policy rationale behind the doctrine of desuetude, according to Justinian's Code, is the idea that "statutes...bind us for no other reason than because they have been accepted by the judgment of the people".[12] When the considerations which originally prompted the enactment of the statute have lost their force because the fundamental conceptions of the people have undergone a fundamental change, a good case can be made out in favor of an eventual cessation of the statutory rule after a prolonged period of consistent and uncontradicted non-enforcement. With respect to non-statutory law developed by the courts, the notion that "when the reason for the law ceases, the law itself also ceases" is by no means a stranger to Anglo-American ideas of fairness and justice, and occasional decisions have extended this principle to the statutory field.[13] In general, however, the anti-desuetude position of the *Thompson* case has firmly held its ground in American case law.

If properly limited, a reception of the late Roman doctrine would probably cause considerably more good than harm in the administration of justice. The separation of powers doctrine would not offer a significant

---

[10] Dig. 1. 3. 32. 1. There is some evidence that the doctrine was not as yet recognized during the classical period of Roman law. See A. Arthur Schiller, "Custom in Classical Roman Law", 24 *Virginia Law Review* 268, 279-282 (1938); Fritz Schulz, *Principles of Roman Law,* transl. M. Wolff (Oxford, 1936), p. 14. Recognition in classical times is affirmed by Herbert F. Jolowicz, *Historical Introduction to the Study of Roman Law,* 2d ed. (Cambridge, Eng., 1952), p. 364.

[11] See Arthur E. Bonfield, "The Abrogation of Penal Statutes by Nonenforcement", 49 *Iowa Law Review* 389 (1964).

[12] Dig. 1. 3. 32. 1.

[13] See *Funk v. United States,* 290 U. S. 371 (1933); *Phipps v. Boise Street Car Co.,* 107 Pac. 2d 148, 151 (1940); Bonfield, *supra* n. 11, p. 393.

obstacle to its acceptance, since a legislative intent to prolong the statute beyond the period of its usefulness need not be presumed. One major advantage in recognizing desuetude would be to provide doctrinal legitimation for a salutary non-invocation practice by law enforcement agencies which otherwise would clearly bear the stamp of illegality.

It must be insisted, however, that any application of the *desuetudo* principle should be restricted to the fairly infrequent situation where rejection of the policy rationale behind an old statute is well-nigh universal. Where such disapproval is confined to certain classes or groups of the population – even though they may be large in number – the conclusion that the statute has been abrogated by non-use would not be acceptable. Thus, a prolonged dormancy of a statute prohibiting the playing of outdoor games on Sundays may justify reliance on the desuetude doctrine. This doctrine may also, in the light of the prevalent sexual mores, apply to statutes penalizing all forms of fornication.[14] The failure to enforce a prohibition of usury, on the other hand, would not fall within its purview. Where an organ of law enforcement refrains from carrying out a statutory mandate for the benefit of a powerful interest group, such action lacks legitimacy if the general community sentiment with respect to the desirability of the prohibition has not changed.

Desuetude of the law also cannot be recognized where the object of an enactment is protection of a racial or other minority, and its non-enforcement by government agencies is motivated by deference to majority feelings. This was the situation in the *Thompson* case,[15] where the statute which for many years remained ineffective was designed to afford racial minorities equal access to eating facilities. In this type of a situation, the size of the section of the population opposed to enforcement would appear to be immaterial, since the principle of majority rule is in such instances shoved aside by a legislative determination to safeguard the rights of a minority group, whether or not that group is large or small in numbers. It might be observed in passing that this legislative objective was not present in regard to the law prohibiting recreational outdoor activities on Sundays. Even though there may still, at this time, exist some very small groups opposed to such activities, it was not the purpose of this legislation to protect the religious feelings of such groups.

---

[14]In many cities of the United States, there were no arrests for fornication in 1948. Morris Ploscowe, *Sex and the Law* (New York, 1951), pp. 155-157. It is certain that the evidence in favor of desuetude has increased rather than decreased since that time. With respect to more controversial kinds of sexual conduct, such as homosexuality between consenting adults, legislative action is probably needed to settle the problem.

[15]*Supra* n. 7.

The foregoing considerations may be summarized in the conclusion that the non-invocation practices of law-enforcing organs should be regarded as legal where a total change of general community sentiment has occurred regarding the justice of the non-enforced measure. There may also be other situations where instances of discretionary non-enforcement may be justified by equitable considerations or other persuasive reasons. Such practices must be deemed illegal, on the other hand, when they are actuated by the desire to protect special interest groups; they also violate the law when designed to frustrate the purpose of an enactment granting equal protection to minority interests.

This leaves for discussion the situation where selective policies of non-enforcement are due to a lack of adequate financial resources. If in this situation the officers of the law choose to concentrate on the prosecution of relatively minor infractions and neglect enforcement with respect to the most grievous offenses against the public order (such as homicide, arson, robbery, aggravated forms of burglary), this course of action should be said to bear the stamp of illegality. Apart from this requirement, it would seem futile to charge such officials with unlawful conduct if their policies were impelled by reasons beyond their control. It is reasonable under these circumstances to advert to the old realistic maxim "Necessity knows no law", and to take the position that a meaningful evaluation according to the "lawful-unlawful" test is impossible.

The objection may be raised to the account here presented that a division of law enforcement practices into "lawful" and "unlawful" ones is useless not only in this last instance but in all cases where the practice in question remains unreversed and may thus be said to constitute "the law" for the persons directly affected by them. It has become quite fashionable in some quarters — which are by no means restricted to the unsophisticated sections of the population — to equate the law with the actual doings of the officers of the law. When the provisions of the penal code dealing with assault and homicide are not invoked against members of a racial majority committing acts of violence against a racial minority,[16] this is by some declared to be a feature of the "living law". When tax laws remain unenforced against certain powerful economic interests, the law as such is often denounced as unjust. This identification of law with the facts of legal life is by some critics carried beyond the scope of non-enforcement practices to all situations where illegal acts that remain unredressed are

---

[16] See in this connection the report of the U. S. Commission on Civil Rights entitled *Law Enforcement: A Report on Equal Protection in the South* (Washington, 1965), pp. 8-13, 43-45.

committed by an organ of the legal system. Since the maintenance and propagation of this view has broad and far-reaching implications for the attitude of people toward the institution of law in general, it requires discussion in a book concerned with the basic constituent elements of law.

It should be viewed as axiomatic that an exercise of arbitrary or unauthorized power by the officials of the law, contrary to a valid normative standard, can under no circumstances be denominated an act of "law". It makes no difference whether the illegal act remains unredressed or whether it is ultimately overturned by a court. Unless this position is taken, the distinction between lawful and unlawful actions is obliterated and the purpose of law, understood in the sense of an aggregate of standards designed to control private and official conduct, is defeated.

The acceptance of this viewpoint does not imply that a legal system exhausts its significance in the promulgation or recognition of rules, regulations, standards, and general principles forming the theoretical and prescriptive structure of the law. The normative side of the legal order is complemented by a factual side.[17] In order to obtain a full grasp of the living law of a society, it is necessary to observe to what extent the normative precepts and value judgments embodied in the law have filtered down into the consciousness of the people, thereby exerting a decisive influence on their conduct. If the law on the books fails to mold the behavior of the large majority of the people, the legal system is merely a poor, sickly copy of its authentic image. It is also necessary to find out how the norms found in constitutions, codes, and other sources have been interpreted and applied by the courts, and whether there are motivations for judicial and other legally relevant action which are not primarily rooted in the society's prescriptive system. Furthermore, a firmly grounded understanding of the legal order requires a study of the enforcement practices engaged in by the non-judicial organs of the law.

What legal officials do in fact is not coterminous with the law; but it is also not possible to understand a legal system simply by studying the norms in the books.[18] In analyzing and evaluating the law, our glance must constantly wander back and forth between the theoretical structure, the

---

[17] This point has been validly and persistently made by Jerome Hall. See particularly his *Living Law of Democratic Society* (Indianapolis, 1949), pp. 56-146. See also the noteworthy comments by Reinhold Zippelius, *Das Wesen des Rechts* (Munich, 1969), pp. 27-31, 174-176.

[18] This position implies a rejection of extreme versions of both legal normativism and legal realism. It has been the great merit of legal realism, however, to call the attention of the legal profession to the factual side of the law and its operation in practice. For some helpful comments see Jones, *supra* n. 3, pp. 3-12.

"rule" part of the legal order, and the practical implementation of this structure. In undertaking this comparison between abstract prescription and concrete execution, one may in some circumstances come to the conclusion that a certain practice in enforcement and application of the law has created a new "living" law contrary to the law on the books. This conclusion might be drawn legitimately, for example, when juries, in personal injuries cases where fault on both sides has been proved, regularly and persistently apply the comparative negligence principle (reducing the amount of damages awarded to the plaintiff in proportion to the degree of his negligence), although the statutory or case law require a judgment for the defendant in this situation. Also, when judges, in a jurisdiction in which collusion between two spouses prevents the granting of a divorce, as a matter of daily routine ignore this old rule without ever overturning it explicitly, a silent modification of the law may be assumed to have taken place. The further possibility of holding that an abrogation of outdated law may under certain circumstances occur through non-invocation by law enforcement officers over extended periods of time has already been discussed.

As has been suggested earlier in connection with the last-mentioned example, we are confronted here, not with arbitrary volitional acts by organs entrusted with the administration of justice, but with responses to decisive shifts in community standards of justice. A sharp distinction must be drawn between these situations and others in which this justification for a *sub rosa* change of the law is lacking. Violations of constitutional provisions, disregard of statutes or regulations, flouting of judicial mandates by policemen, district attorneys, executive or administrative officers, in the absence of special vindicating reasons, bear the stamp of unlawfulness because a comparison of their acts with the norms applicable to their duties reveals a discrepancy between what has actually been done and what ought to have been done in the particular situation.

When lawless practices of certain organs of the State become widespread and continuous in a society, affecting perhaps whole groups of the population, the gap between the normative structure and its factual implementation becomes ominously large. Examples would be refusals by law enforcement officers to prosecute certain types of crimes committed against members of a disfavored group, or the prevalence of illegal searches and seizures in certain sections of the community. As long as there exists at least a probability of redress by the courts, it cannot be said that the legal order has been partially suspended. But when the perversion of legal processes has been carried so far that even this last remedial avenue has been cut off for all practical purposes, then the conclusion should be reached that law, in certain areas of the social order, has given way to lawless, arbitrary power.[19]

SECTION 13
General Conclusions

The investigations pursued in this chapter have shown the existence of a complex and not always easily discernible relation between the inertial and dynamic forces in the evolution of legal systems. It was pointed out that the change-resisting, centripetal forces inherent in the law can be overcome in part or reduced in strength, in decidedly varying degrees, by constitution-makers, legislators, judges, and even to some extent by law enforcement officials. But it is clear that they cannot be wholly eliminated short of an all-out destruction of the legal system and its replacement either by the reign of unchecked, free-flowing power or by the erection of an entirely new legal edifice. Such an eradication of all backward pulls in the social order, resulting in a total break with continuity, has always remained a rare event and temporary condition in the history of the human race. For the most part, the law has yielded slowly and somewhat reluctantly to the dynamic social forces pressing upon it from the outside, with the consequence that a certain state of balance between the conservative and progressive tendencies in societal evolution has been maintained.

The conservative element in the law reveals itself with particular distinctness in primitive forms of society. Customs ingrained in the consciousness and ways of life of people in early times are not easily changed, and necessary improvements in the law often remain hidden behind the veil of fictions designed to simulate constancy and immutability of legal arrangements.[1]

The strings which tie the law to the past become loosened in those societies which are able to overcome social inertia and develop sufficient momentum to carry them towards higher, advanced forms of civilization. When human ingenuity and resourcefulness, combined with increase in knowledge, attempt to improve the conditions of life on this earth in a

---

[19] One of the most conspicuous historical examples was the factual withdrawal of legal protection from the Jews by the Hitler Government in Germany, which extended to crimes of violence committed against them. See Fritz von Hippel, *Die Perversion von Rechtsordnungen* (Tübingen, 1955).

---

[1] See *supra* Sec. 8.

persevering effort, the dynamics of social experimentation do not remain without effect on the processes of the law. Endeavors are made to keep the law abreast of the changing times, and this activity is by no means inconsistent with the function of law to preserve continuity and smooth the transition from the past to the present. A rigid stability applying old, outdated rules to new situations would in effect produce discontinuity rather than continuity because it would open up a bridgeless gap between the normative order and social reality.

We have seen that a large amount of creative freedom to shape the law is possessed by constitution-makers and legislative organs. These bodies change the law from the outside by transforming political power into l.gal norms and legal arrangements. But they are limited in their lawmaking discretion by the psychological facets of human nature, sociological conditions, the state of the productive forces, and strongly-ingrained traditions. The lawmakers may try to erase the heritage of the past by bold social experiments, but it is likely that they will only partially be successful in this endeavor.[2]

When we enter the domain of the law's internal dynamics, the fetters upon forward-looking creation of novel legal patterns become noticeably tighter. It was shown that the agency of law improvement known as equity was to a lesser extent than is commonly believed an offspring of the internal administration of the law by the courts. Equity owed its origin and creative impetus, in Rome as well as in England, largely to the operation of forces external to the judicial process.[3]

In the typical exercise of judicial power, the conservative, past-oriented attitude is prevalent. This is an inevitable corollary of the fact that the subject matter within the contemplation of the judicial decision-maker is a past event or set of events rather than a future desired state of society. It is a command of common sense that under ordinary circumstances legal disputes should be decided on the basis of rules, principles, and judicial pronouncements which were known or ascertainable at the time when the controversy arose. This requirement cannot always be met and is not an absolute postulate of justice. On occasion a court will and should render a trailblazing decision designed to bring some outmoded part of the law into harmony with contemporary standards of justice. But the very nature of the judicial process imposes fairly stringent limitations on the innovative

---

[2] See *supra* Sec. 9. Cf. J. Roland Pennock, "Reason in Legislative Decision", in *Rational Decision* (Nomos Vol. VII), ed. C. J. Friedrich (New York, 1964), pp. 101-102.

[3] See *supra* Sec. 10.

power of judges. For great structural changes in the law, the courts must usually rely on outside assistance.

When the area of enforcement and execution of law is reached, the discretionary scope of official action will normally shrink to even smaller proportions. The mandates of the legal order should be carried out consistently and effectively. But there is no good reason why the dead wood of the past may not sometimes be cast aside by law enforcement officers for the sake of reducing the application of wholly obsolete law. Moreover, limitations of personnel and financial resources may in some instances necessitate or justify selective policies in this area.[5]

Thus, growth and flexibility of the law can to some extent be promoted on all levels of the legal process. The distinction between the external and internal dynamics of the law suggests, however, that the chief responsibility for growth and law reform rests upon constitution-makers and legislative assemblies, while the safeguarding of legal continuity and stability is the primary (though not the sole) concern of courts and law enforcement agencies.

The considerations developed in this chapter reemphasize an important facet in the polarism of power and law. Power is the great instrumentality for accomplishing fundamental social change, although not a proper final goal of such change.[6] Intense power struggles often precede a large-scale remodeling of the social order. When the stage has been set for a major overhauling of the system, constellations and realignments of power are almost invariably transformed into relations and arrangements of law. The new order of things becomes stabilized and consolidated. But this does not mean that the legal order designed to neutralize disruptive tensions and mitigate lesser ones will thereafter remain wholly unaffected by the play of social power forces. In a dynamic society, power constantly tugs at the substance of the law. Radiations in the social field have an impact on the law by penetrating the solid harness with which the law seeks to protect existing interests, relations, and institutions. Some verifications of this phenomenon will be offered in the historical parts of the next chapter.[7]

---

[4] See *supra* Sec. 11.

[5] See *supra* Sec. 12. As pointed out there, other persuasive reasons may exist for non-enforcement of the law in an individual case.

[6] See *infra* Sec. 18.

[7] See *infra* Sec. 16, under VI, and Sec. 17, under VII.

CHAPTER III

EQUALITY AND DOMINATION IN THE LAW

Section 14
Law as a Promoter of Equality

The problem of stability and change in the law, which was the theme of discussion in the preceding chapter, focuses attention on the scope and limitations of the function of law to provide a reasonable measure of security, order, and predictability in human affairs. The question was asked to what extent the stabilizing objective of legal regulation needs to be sacrificed for the purpose of adjusting legal relations to the ever-changing panorama of the social scene, and what are the most suitable institutional means for accomplishing this accommodation of normative arrangements to sociological reality.

There exists a connection between the set of problems dealt with in the last chapter and the principal topic of the present one. As a consequence of significant social developments, a time is likely to arrive in the life of nations when the order of things protected by the legal system is viewed as unsatisfactory, discriminatory, or oppressive by large numbers of people. The feeling will emerge that the legal order has become tarnished by badly drawn lines of differentiation between individuals and groups. If the social equilibrium is seriously disturbed by this condition, the cohesiveness of the social and legal structure is placed in jeopardy. Legal security can be restored only by restructuring the relations that had previously been maintained between the various layers and groups of the population.

The law perennially has had to face the crucial issue of human equality and inequality, and many influential works on political and legal philosophy have recognized this fact. Just law, Aristotle declared, aims at "some sort of equality".[1] This thought has been reiterated many times in ancient, medieval, and modern literature.[2] But little consensus has been

---

[1] Aristotle, *The Politics*, ed. E. Barker (Oxford, 1946), Bk. III, Ch. xii, sec 1.

[2] See Edgar Bodenheimer, *Jurisprudence: The Philosophy and Method of the Law* (Cambridge, Mass., 1962), pp. 179-184. A comprehensive treatment of the history of the equality notion is given by Sanford A. Lakoff, *Equality in Political Philosophy* (Cambridge, Mass., 1964).

reached in legal theory and practice as to what particular "sort of equality" corresponds most adequately to the nature of man and the needs of social organization.

The term equality is one of many meanings. To illustrate the polymorphous character of the notion, five basic kinds of equality configurations will be set forth and discussed, to be denominated as follows: (a) equality of rule classification; (b) commutative equality; (c) equal treatment of equals; (d) equality of fundamental rights; (e) equality of need satisfaction. These five categories by no means exhaust the wide variety of patterns that may be encountered in social attempts to deal with the problem; they merely represent broadly-defined ways of approach to a solution. It will be found in the course of the discussion that certain features of inequality are built into the structure of each of the five equality patterns named above and form a complement to them.

a. Equality of Rule Classification

"To fall under a rule is *pro tanto* to be assimilated to a single pattern. To enforce a rule is to promote equality of behavior or treatment."[3] These words of Isaiah Berlin state the truth that any norm of law, however limited its scope may be, performs an equalizing function by grouping people, things and events into classifications with the expectation that the rule be applied consistently to all situations coming within its purview. A statutory rule to the effect that a father must provide support and education to the children in his custody imposes a uniform obligation on all fathers covered by the provision, although the actual extent of the obligation will vary with the circumstances. A judicial determination that a principal is liable for torts of his agents committed within the scope of their employment sets up an equality of responsibility for all persons qualifying as "principals". A customary rule of international law granting to States the right of innocent passage of their ships through the territorial waters of other States carries with it the recognition of an equality of States, large and small, with respect to the exercise of this right. Since a rule of law never deals with a single case only, but always embraces a number of like or similar occasions described in general terms, the persons and situations included in the rule are made subject to a common standard. In this sense, even a crude system of rules is a sentinel of equality. Inasmuch as all societies are guided by some rules or general standards

---

[3] Isaiah Berlin, "Equality as an Ideal", in *Justice and Social Policy,* ed. F. A. Olafson (Englewood Cliffs, N. J., 1961), p. 132. See also Felix E. Oppenheim, "The Concept of Equality", in *International Encyclopedia of the Social Sciences* (New York, 1968), Vol. V, p. 103.

(whether these be of a predominantly legal, moral or religious character), some modicum of equality can be assumed to be realized everywhere by the very operation of a normative system.

The equalization provided by normative classifications may, under certain circumstances, be little more than a matter of form. It requires that "all those who are alike in the eyes of the law be treated in a fashion determined by law",[4] but it erects no safeguards against the adoption by the legal order of arbitrary or unreasonable differentiations leading to highly inequalitarian results. If a statute declares that left-handed persons are ineligible for public office, it establishes an equality of treatment for all who possess the classifying trait but at the same time creates a condition of inequality between right-handed and left-handed persons. A law which would reserve the right of acquiring citizenship to immigrants of the Caucasian race would have an equalizing effect in relation to Caucasian applicants for naturalization but a decidedly discriminatory impact on persons of non-Caucasian origin.[5]

As long as the differentiations made by the law are accepted as essentially reasonable by the people affected by them, the equality achieved by rule classification must be regarded as more than a mere matter of form. By subjecting groups of persons, defined by some common characteristics, to a preannounced uniform standard of treatment, precautions are taken against the contingency that some individuals may be singled out as victims of irrational whim by a person having power over them and be coerced into doing things which others in a similar position would not be required to do. Thus when the legal custom of the feudal manor determined the duties owed by the serf to his lord, it created barriers against the practice of playing favorites by lords, who without the existence of the custom might have vented their wrath against certain serfs by oppressive forms of treatment. In this sense rule classification, as long as it does not serve distorted or inhuman purposes, provides a safeguard against arbitrary domination even in a hierarchically organized social system.[6]

---

[4] Chaim Perelman, *Justice* (New York, 1967), p. 24. Cf. also Perelman, *The Idea of Justice and the Problem of Argument* (London, 1963), pp. 15-17.

[5] For a more detailed discussion of the implications for a formally-conceived rule of law see Edgar Bodenheimer, "Reflections on the Rule of Law", 8 *Utah Law Review* 1 (1962).

[6] The psychological roots of the law discussed *supra* Sec. 6 thus cover, to some extent, even that form of equality achieved by the law which comes closest to being a merely formal principle. A further discussion of the question is found *infra* Sec. 17 (especially under *a* and *b*) in the context of Anglo-American legal history.

b. Commutative Equality

One of the oldest notions of justice conceived in terms of "some sort of equality" was the doctrine of reciprocity developed by the Pythagoreans in ancient Greece. Their writings have not been preserved but their views were restated in a refined version by Aristotle in his *Nicomachean Ethics.* Aristotle declared that a principle of "reciprocal proportion" should govern in transactions of exchange. There should be a reasonable degree of equivalence between the value of goods sold and the price paid by the buyer, as well as between the labor or services performed by men and the compensation received by them. Aristotle realized that it was neither feasible nor desirable to insist on strict, mathematical equality in determining the fairness of human bargains. He felt, however, that there should be at least an approximation to equality, an absence of unjust disproportionality, in transactions of this kind.[7] They usually involve relations between individuals or groups of individuals, and an equality of bargaining power of these parties is often a precondition to the consummation of a fair deal between them. Where equality of position exists, Aristotle did not seem to object if one party, for subjective reasons and of his own free will, was willing to give more than would objectively correspond to the value of the *quid pro quo.* For he said that the standard of measuring fairness in matters of exchange was individual want or demand.[8]

A different and stricter standard of equality was demanded by Aristotle in cases of wrongful acts calling for reparation or payment of damages. Where a party has sustained a loss by another's breach of contract, commission of a tort, or act of unjustified enrichment, "corrective justice" requires that the parties be restored to a position of "equality". This means that a person who has made an improper gain must return it to the deprived party, and that the person who has caused an injury to another must make full compensation to him. Unlike the merely proportional reciprocity appropriate for the making of bargains, the measure of "equality" held proper by Aristotle for the payment of reparation or compensation was an arithmetically correct computation of gains or losses. "This process will then enable us to ascertain what we ought to take away from the party that has too much and what to add to the one that has too

---

[7] Aristotle, *Nicomachean Ethics,* Loeb Class. Lib. ed. (Cambridge, Mass., 1947), Bk. V. v.

[8] *Id.,* Book V, v. 11.

little."[9] Universal experience with compensation awards has taught the lesson, however, that it is very difficult to accomplish the arithmetic exactness at which Aristotle had aimed.

c. Equal Treatment of Equals

This principle adds a measure of substantive due process to the formal conception of equality discussed under (a). It requires lawmakers to treat men and situations equally or at least similarly if under the prevalent community standards they are considered equal or similar. While the equality inherent in rule classification would form no bar to a law disqualifying all left-handed persons from obtaining drivers' licenses, such a law could not be justified under the equal-treatment axiom unless the community was convinced of a causal connection between left-handedness and diminished driving aptitude. The substantive limitations placed on legal differentiations by the equal-treatment principle are, of course, very imprecise and wholly contingent upon the social philosophy dominant in society at a particular time. The principle can be used to support strictly hierarchical structures as well as essentially equalitarian ones. To what extent are men equal, and in what respects are they unequal? No unanimity of opinion has ever been reached on this question. Nietzsche relied on the equal-treatment postulate in recommending the imposition of a political caste system.[10] The American sociologist Lester Ward invoked it for the purpose of pleading for a far-reaching implementation of egalitarian policies.[11] "Equality to equals, inequality to unequals" has served as a battlecry to both the proponents of racial equality and their adversaries.

d. Equality of Fundamental Rights

A further milepost on the road towards increased equalization is reached when certain basic rights are accorded to the members of a community regardless of their race, sex, religion, national origin, or ideological conviction. Such universal allocation of rights will necessarily remain

[9] Id., Bk. V. iv. It was convincingly shown by James W. Baldwin that Aristotle drew a distinction between a commutative justice involved in the making of consensual agreements and the corrective justice concerned with the rectification of breaches of contract and tortious acts. See Baldwin's "The Medieval Theory of the Just Price", 49 Transactions of the American Philosophical Society (N. S., Philadelphia, 1959), Pt. 4, pp. 10-12.

[10] Nietzsche, "The Twilight of the Idols", in Complete Works, ed. O. Levy (London, 1909-1911), Vol. XVI, pp. 108-109 (9th essay, No. 48); Nietzsche, "The Antichrist", id., pp. 217-219 (No. 57).

[11] Lester F. Ward, Applied Sociology (Boston, 1906), pp. 7, 11-12, 22, 95-103, 281.

confined to fundamental ones, because special types of rights (such as rights of mortgagees, vendors, policemen, stockholders, or persons over 65 years of age) are in their very nature reserved to particular classes of individuals. Under the United States Constitution, the most fundamental rights open to all without respect of person are life, liberty and property. To these may be added, with certain qualifications, the right to vote and the right to hold public office. Constitutions of some other States have increased the scope of fundamental rights by guaranteeing, for example, a right to work, a right to rest, a right to medical care, and a right to education.

A grant of fundamental rights to all members of a political community goes far in eliminating grievous types of discrimination among persons and groups but may still preserve substantial areas of inequality in the social system. Equality of the right to own property, in Oppenheim's words, "is compatible with extreme inequality in the distribution of property".[12] A right to vocational liberty may appear theoretical in the contemplation of people unable to find suitable employment in their chosen field of occupation. A guarantee of the right to work does not insure equal compensation for equal types of labor. A right to education does not, in and of itself, produce uniformity in the quality of instruction offered by different educational institutions.

e. Equality of Need Satisfaction

To overcome some of the limitations inherent in the preceding solution of the equality problem, a society may endeavor to approach this problem from the angle of human needs rather than through the allocation of basic rights. This may be done in two different ways. The first way is to confine the satisfaction of needs by social and legal action to the most urgent ones. The second way, proposed by Marxian economic theory as an objective for the society of the future, is to go beyond the gratification of minimum needs and take care of all needs of men, except perhaps unreasonable and fastidious ones.

The chief aim envisaged by the first alternative is to alleviate poverty and palpable misery. Measures designed to accomplish this end may include the enactment of minimum wage laws, the institution of a system of welfare or the adoption of a guaranteed family income plan. In conjunction perhaps with a system of graduated income taxation, such policies will tend to reduce the gap between wealth and poverty in their most glaring

---

[12] Oppenheim, *supra* n. 3, p. 106.

manifestations but will keep intact the existence of large economic inequalities.

The second alternative is epitomized by the principle which Karl Marx considered the most adequate solution of the social problem: "From each according to his abilities, to each according to his needs".[13] If such a system were put into effect (which would presuppose a degree of economic affluence and abundance not in existence anywhere in the world today), there would again emerge a combination of egalitarian and inegalitarian components. There would be equality in the sense that everybody's needs (at least those deemed to be reasonable) would be considered and fulfilled. There would, on the other hand, be a presence of inequality in two important respects. First, the distribution of goods would be unequal, because the needs of different persons vary greatly. Secondly, the contributions made by individual members of society to the common welfare would be unequal in quantity and quality, although all kinds of work would be rewarded equally by the full satisfaction of needs. It is likely that, in the absence of a radical change in human nature, such equal treatment of persons with unequal achievements would affect social motivation and create a psychological problem of major dimensions.

It is the gist of the foregoing analysis that there exists in all forms of social organization a condominium of equality and inequality. "Some sort of equality" is achieved everywhere by the adoption of social or legal norms bringing certain groups of persons under a more or less uniform regime of rights and obligations. But there is no known society in which the degrees of power and riches are or have been absolutely identical for everybody. Nor does there appear to be any influential political party anywhere in the world today which has inscribed on its banner the propagation of an uncompromising egalitarianism. It is probably recognized by all reasonable men that a certain hierarchy of talent and capability is an indispensable condition for the adequate discharge of social tasks. This fact carries with it the corollary that, regardless of the particular form of political and economic organization of a society, there are bound to be inequalities in decision-making power (especially where the knowledge and judgment of an expert are required) and in the assignment of ranks and rewards based upon merit. The truly critical problem posed to legal and social policy is not to extirpate all forms of inequality, but to segregate irrational and arbitrary categories of differentiation from reasonable and constructive schemes and to eliminate or reduce the former ones. It will

---

[13] Karl Marx, *Critique of the Gotha Program*, ed. C. P. Dutt (New York, 1966), p. 10. For a comment on the meaning of the principle see Ernest Mandel, *Marxist Economic Theory*, transl. B. Pearce (New York, 1968), Vol. II, pp. 663-664.

always be necessary to preserve those inequalities which are indispensable to the effective discharge of social functions.[14]

The historical disquisitions included in this chapter[15] are designed to demonstrate that law, in its socially most significant manifestations, has been a promoter of equality in the sense that it has been helpful in its overall effects to restrict or diminish certain heavy-handed and oppressive uses of power. This has, in fact, been one of its main functions in the evolution of States and other political communities. The efforts of the law relating to the domestication of power have not been confined to the curbing of public power; they have also (and sometimes more successfully) been directed towards private misuses of power. It can be said that whenever the law has succeeded in taming an exercise of power that bore down capriciously or with unreasonable harshness on individuals or groups, it has taken a step (sometimes a major, sometimes a minor one) towards the enhancement of equality in human relations.

This view of the law will be questioned by those interpreters of social and legal history who maintain that the most conspicuous function performed by the law has been to imprint the stamp of legality upon palpable forms of human inequality. These interpreters would say that the law has frequently sanctioned human slavery, a social institution characterized by the conferment of absolute, unfettered powers upon certain privileged classes of men to treat other human beings as chattels rather than persons endowed with rights. The law of feudalism relating to serfs would be referred to in support of the same proposition. It might also be argued that, during the *laissez-faire* period of European and American economic history, employers of labor were given authority by the law to subject their employees to any arrangements of their choosing with respect to wages, working hours, and plant conditions, and that this state of the law amounted to a legalization of exploitation.

It is true that conditions of subjugation and exploitation have existed in the past of many societies and can still be found in many parts of the world today. In order to understand the relation of the law to the creation

---

[14] Rawls takes the position that inequalities are arbitrary unless it is reasonable to expect that they will work out for everyone's advantage. John Rawls, "Justice as Fairness", 67 *Philosophical Review* 164, 165, 167-169 (1958). Rawls does not define the term "advantage" in terms of purely subjective feelings, but in the light of what rational persons could agree on as meaningful limits on equality. This position might seem acceptable if the hypothetical "agreement" is based on a consideration of the common good of the society. See also the comments by Charles Fried, "Justice and Liberty", in *Justice* (Nomos Vol. VI), ed. C. J. Friedrich and J. W. Chapman (New York, 1963), pp. 133-138.

[15] See *infra* Secs. 16 and 17.

and perpetuation of such conditions, some observations on the significance of legally vacuous areas in the social order are called for. A distinguished American judge has expressed the view that the legal order is pervasive and universal; that it blankets all conduct in an organized society; that there is no non-law in the social order because whatever the law does not forbid it allows.

> It is a fallacy of the false negative to believe that because law makes no provision in any described area of human conduct, it does not oversee the area. The very decision not to intrude upon an area is a determination that persons are legally free to act as they wish in that area.[16]

If the law does not prohibit racial discrimination, says Judge Breitel, it permits it; if the law does not compel a debtor to pay his debt after the statute of limitations has run, then it allows him to disregard his obligation after a certain period of time has elapsed. These are arguable propositions, although there remains room for debate whether the law meant to provide a positive authorization for the non-proscribed conduct. The doubts become stronger when the judge suggests that dismissal of a complaint because of lack of an affirmative remedy implies enforcement of a negative judgment on the part of the law as to the existence of a cause of action.[17] If a court, in the absence of statutes or precedents, for the first time allows an action of unjust enrichment or grants a remedy for invasion of privacy, must we assume that the earlier law by its silence condoned unjust enrichment, or that it meant to give the green light to acts of prying into another's private life? There are certainly many judicial decisions according novel remedies which are not based on the premise that the prior law had meant to deny redress by not acting on the matter. It would seem more appropriate to assume that omission to deal with the problem pointed to the existence of a vacancy in the legal system, an area of "non-law".[18]

The problem of vacant areas in the law will not be discussed here in all of its perplexing facets. The analysis will be confined to two historically important refusals by governmental lawmakers to cross the boundary into a wide territory of intersubjective human relations and thereby to open up possibilities for an arbitrary exercise of power. The first example will be the authorization of slavery under the legal system of ancient Rome, the

---

[16] Charles Breitel, "The Lawmakers", 65 *Columbia Law Review* 749, 755 (1965).

[17] *Id.*, p. 749.

[18] Some ramifications of the problem are discussed by Bodenheimer, *supra* n. 2, pp. 293-297.

second one the extreme reluctance of nineteenth-century American law to
enter into the field of employment relations.

During the Roman Republic, the rights of the slave owners were legally
unrestricted. The slave was incapable of having rights, either civil or
political. He could be sold or pledged. He was incapable of marriage. His
owner could kill or cruelly mistreat him without facing penal sanctions. If
a slave murdered his master, all slaves in the household could be executed
without proof of suspicion.[19]

The argument that under these circumstances the Roman law sanctioned and legitimized the arbitrary, uncontrolled, even inhuman exercise
of power by a master over his slaves can be advanced with some degree of
persuasiveness. And yet, it appears to be more plausible to take the
position that Roman law, in the earlier phases of its development, stopped
at the threshold of the Roman household or slave estate, barring its entry
into the field of master-slave relations by an "off limits" sign. Without
authorizing or legalizing any use or abuse of power by the slave owner, the
law simply refrained from extending its sway over this area of social life.

It is useful, in forming one's judgment on this problem, to keep in mind
that a reservation of regulatory immunity by the law is often not due to a
deliberate, purposive policy of conferring unlimited authority upon a social
group, but may be attributable primarily to a weakness of State power, a
governmental inability to subject certain powerful classes of men to its
commands. During the reign of feudalism in the Middle Ages, for example,
the legal arm of the central governments on the European Continent was
not strong enough to reach many significant aspects of the political, social
and economic life; a great deal of leeway was left for the exercise of local
feudal autonomy. The same condition probably prevailed in the earlier
epochs of Roman history. The power of individual landholders was very
substantial, and it was expected that they would lay down the law
themselves for their families as well as for their slaves. Many slave owners
did in fact voluntarily grant certain rights to their slaves, endowed them
with far-reaching authority to conduct a business, and treated them in a
manner not essentially different from that in which at later times many
employers dealt with their servants and employees.[20] Thus, whether or not
the slave was a mere object of oppression, deprived of anything resembling
the right of a human being, depended on the autonomous law of the slave
estate rather than on the general law of the State.

---

[19] See William W. Buckland, *The Roman Law of Slavery* (Cambridge, Eng., 1908), p. 80.
[20] See Rudolph von Jhering, *Geist des Römischen Rechts,* 5th ed. (Basel, 1894), Vol. II,
pp. 179-181; Otto Seeck, *Geschichte des Untergangs der Antiken Welt* (Stuttgart, 1921),
Vol. I, pp. 310-312.

The exercise of a certain moral authority by the State over cruel and inhuman treatment of slaves in the Roman Republic also weakens the contention that the law, by not prohibiting the mishandling of slaves, clothed a sphere of wholly arbitrary domination with the attributes of positive legality. A group of State officials known as the censors had power to affix a black mark to the name of a man on the official citizens' lists who had violated the canons of human decency in his dealings with his slaves. The result of such moral stigmatization, according to the discretion of the censoring officers, might be to reduce the offender to a lower social status.[21] In later times, the moral condemnation of opprobrious conduct on the part of slave owners was supplanted by positive legal regulations and penal decrees.[22] The State had become powerful enough to substitute the stronger sanction of legal prohibition for the weaker expedient of moral censure.

In nineteenth century America, the law interfered almost as little with employment relations as Roman law had touched the working and living conditions of slaves. There were hardly any laws proscribing inhuman conditions in factories, limiting the working day or setting standards of plant safety. As the Roman legal system had remitted matters of concern to the slave owner and his slaves to the autonomous law of the household or estate, so nineteenth-century American law relied for the regulation of conditions in industry and commerce on the law of free contracts. It was assumed that employers and workers, as rational beings, would agree only on such terms as were mutually satisfactory to them, and that the laborer could go elsewhere if his needs were insufficiently met by his employment situation. The law refused to involve itself in economic affairs of men deemed to be within the province of autonomous contract law. We know today that the equality of bargaining power which was presupposed at that time, with its implication of freedom to reject an unfavorable contract, frequently did not exist on the part of workers or employees, and that many of them were forced by the circumstances to work under sweatshop conditions and for minimal wages.

Thus there may be areas of human conduct which the social order regards as largely immune from legal intervention.[23] The question remains

---

[21] Jhering, *supra* n. 20, Vol. II, pp. 177-178; Theodor Mommsen, *Römisches Staatsrecht*, 2d ed. (Leipzig, 1877), Vol. II, p. 367; Herbert F. Jolowicz, *Historical Introduction to the Study of Roman Law*, 2d ed. (Cambridge, Eng., 1952), pp. 50-51. We have insufficient information on the extent to which this right of moral censorship was actually exercised by the authorities.

[22] See *infra* Sec. 16.

[23] This is conceded by Breitel, *supra* n. 16, p. 756.

whether the law, by refusing to correct or limit exercises of power which may take on arbitrary or oppressive forms, authorizes or sanctions such uses of power by its policy of abstention.

The problem is to some extent one of semantics. Let us suppose, for purposes of the argument, that a country adopts a constitution in a legally valid way which contains a provision that the legal relations of the subjects are to be determined and judged according to the free and unfettered discretion of certain judicial organs appointed by the ruler, who are to decide each case on its individual merits without reference to any rules — legal, moral or religious. Let us suppose further that after a short period of operation of the system it becomes evident that the decisions of the judicial magistrates are characterized by randomness, inconsistency and obvious partiality. It might be said under a panlegalist approach that a basic norm of constitutional stature has validated each and every one of these decisions, and that we are confronted here with a legal order just as "pervasive and universal"[24] as one in which the powers of individuals and governmental organs are defined, circumscribed, and limited by articulate prescriptions.

In reality, however, it is clear that the constitutional norm proclaiming complete "anomie" and individuality of decisionmaking, although in form a law, constitutes a full-scale abdication of law. Wherever legal systems have appeared in a developed form on the historical scene, they have been characterized by substantial restrictions on capricious wilfulness. Norms of private law have erected fences barring antisocial forms of conduct by individuals, while prescriptions in the field of public law have subjected official actions to some regulatory control. It is undesirable to designate a state of affairs which in every respect represents the negation of a typical legal system by the same linguistic term. Such an overinclusive use of a word violates the first law of semantics, which requires that dissimilar phenomena should be denominated by different concepts.

The consequence of the approach here suggested is that wholly arbitrary and oppressive systems of domination are held to be outside the realm of the law. They are structures of power rather than law. Furthermore, when a legal system permits the maintenance within its domain of a major enclave of unfettered power, it thereby recognized the existence of a legal vacuum, an area of non-law (which may or may not be filled with autonomous law of a different order). Viewed in this light, the law in its essential character necessarily assumes the role of promoting "some sort of

----

[24] *Id.*, p. 755. Whether Judge Breitel would subscribe to this particular conclusion is not at all certain, since he did not discuss the hypothetical situation dealt with in the text.

equality", even though its equalizing effects may under certain historical conditions be quite limited.[25]

SECTION 15
The Class-Rule Concept of Law

The notion that law strives to promote, as Aristotle put it, "some sort of equality" is not one that can be said to enjoy general recognition and acceptance. At variance with it is another viewpoint which has found repeated expression in the history of human thought on government and law. It has already been referred to in the preceding section and may be summarized in the formulation that law is in its very essence an order of inequality set up for the purpose of solidifying the rule of a dominant group.

In ancient Greece, the sophist philosopher Thrasymachus gave voice to this conception, in Plato's rendering of his thought, by declaring that "justice is nothing else than that which is advantageous to the stronger".[1] It will be noted that Thrasymachus cast the prosposition in terms of a definition of justice rather than of law. In the context of his thesis, the difference between justice and law is, however, without any relevance. The idea he sought to express was that governments are instituted for the benefit of the governors rather than the welfare of the governed, and that it is the natural propensity of those entrusted with power to feather their own nests. We do not know whether or not Thrasymachus actually made his often-quoted statement in the form in which it was attributed to him by Plato: it is not impossible that Plato put the apothegm into his mouth in order to lay the ground for an exciting intellectual argument.[2]

One cannot find any noteworthy protagonist of the "right is might" notion in Roman jurisprudence or in the legal theory of the medieval world. The most eloquent exponent of legal philosophy in the Roman Empire, Cicero, viewed law as an emanation, not of class rule but of

---

[25] Marcic goes a step further by declaring that coordination (as distinguished from subordination) is "the principle of law conceived as a normative system". René Marcic, *Rechtsphilosophie: Eine Einführung* (Freiburg, 1969), p. 215 (My translation). See also Marcic's discussion of the relation between law and equality, *id.*, pp. 205-213.

---

[1] Plato, *The Republic*, Everyman's Lib. ed. (New York, 1950), Bk. I. 338.

[2] This hypothesis has been suggested by Erik Wolf, *Griechisches Rechtsdenken* (Frankfurt, 1952), Vol. II, p. 104.

reason, and he took the position that pernicious enactments totally repugnant to the postulates of civilized decency lacked the quality of law.[3] This
view was received into medieval legal doctrine and formed one of the
cornerstones of the Thomist theory of government.[4] Its effect was the
consummation of a far-reaching identification of law and justice, the latter
being conceived as the promotion of the common good of the subjects and
not, as Thrasymachus had proclaimed, the advantage of the mighty.

After the portals to the modern age had opened, this fusion of law and
justice was gradually abandoned. The growth of the doctrine of State
sovereignty, which began with Machiavelli, caused a separation of law from
social ethics, which became sharper and sharper as the doctrine of natural
law slowly but surely receded into the background. In the opinion of Carl
Friedrich, the view that laws are nothing but commands of a secular power
(to be distinguished from law in the sense of a body of good and equitable
precepts) is apparent already in the writings of Jean Bodin, the sixteenth-
century founder of the doctrine of sovereignty.[5] This conception of law
found its most consistent expression in the nineteenth century, when John
Austin defined law as the command of the sovereign and propounded a
clearcut divorce between law and morality.[6]

It bears emphasis, however, that the command theory of law is not
identical with the view which equates law with class rule. It formed, to be
sure, a stepping stone toward this view because it disavowed the medieval
contention that an enactment unrelated to the general welfare should not
be regarded as law in the genuine sense of the term. But it refused to go so
far as to assert, as Thrasymachus had done, that it was the essence of law
to serve the advantage of dominant groups. The command theory of law
maintained a benevolent neutrality towards the pronouncements of the
sovereign by simply assuming that their thrust might be directed towards

---

[3] Cicero, *De Re Publica and De Legibus*, Loeb Class. Lib. ed. (Cambridge, Mass., 1928),
p. 385.

[4] St. Thomas Aquinas, *Summa Theologica*, transl. Fathers of the English Dominican
Province (London, 1913-1925), Pt. II, 1st pt., Qu. 90, art. 4; Qu. 92, art. 1; Qu. 95, art.
2. See also Walter Ullmann, *The Medieval Idea of Law* (New York, 1946), pp. 4, 35-39.

[5] Carl J. Friedrich, *The Philosophy of Law in Historical Perspective* (Chicago, 1958), pp.
60-64.

[6] John Austin, *The Province of Jurisprudence Determined*, ed. H. L. A. Hart (London,
1954), pp. 22-24, 126. Austin did not extend the separation to the lawmaking stage,
which in his view was governed by principles of utilitarian ethics. *Id.*, pp. 127-128. But
the application and interpretation of enacted law were to be free from the infusion of
moral considerations.

beneficial as well as undesirable objectives. A study of the writings of John Austin, for example, will convey the impression that in his opinion many, and perhaps most, laws are in actuality passed for the utilitarian purpose of promoting the happiness of the greatest number.

The view that all law is an open or disguised expression of ruling-class selfishness is implicit in certain basic presuppositions of the Marxian doctrine. An unbiased exegesis of the relevant texts will disclose, however, that Marx himself never enunciated this thesis in an extremist formulation. "Your jurisprudence," he told the bourgeoisie of his day, "is but the will of your class made into a law for all, a will whose essential character and direction are determined by the economic conditions of existence of your class."[7] It is to be noted that this statement does not include a charge to the effect that such class will is always exercised in a manner detrimental to the interests of the non-dominant classes.

In *The German Ideology,* Marx and Engels deemphasized the "will" element in law and, in accordance with their economic determinism, attributed many phases in the development of law to the operation of social forces which were not of man's own choosing. Law in this view becomes an expression of a "will" shaped by preexisting and objective conditions of social life. The legal system of the bourgeois world, it was stated, allows a great deal of individual self-assertion, but it also demands certain forms of self-denial necessary for social order. The authors made it clear that these characteristics of the system apply not only to the ruling group but to all classes in society.[8]

In spite of these rather cautious references to the institution of law, there is implicit in the Marxian theory of capitalism the assumption of a division of society into two groups of antagonistic economic interests. One of these groups, it is maintained, seeks to maximize its profits by utilizing to the utmost the labor power of the other and larger group. Since law is an important instrumentality in the organization of production relations, it has generally been believed with some degree of justification that Marx regarded the law as a tool of class oppression.

The view that law and the state are machines for upholding the dominance of one class over another received its most radical expression in early Soviet theory. Lenin himself had applied the class-rule concept mainly to State power. The law, he said, maintains some sort of formal equality of rights which carries different meanings for the man of property and the

---

[7] Karl Marx, *The Communist Manifesto,* ed. S. T. Possony (Chicago, 1954), Pt. II, p. 47.

[8] Karl Marx and Frederick Engels, *The German Ideology,* ed. C. J. Arthur (New York, 1970), pp. 106-107.

man without it.[9] But one of his commissars of justice, P.I. Stuchka, bluntly characterized law as "a system (or order) of social relations which corresponds to the interests of the dominant class and is safeguarded by the organized force of that class",[10] and this definition was incorporated into a statute enacted in 1919.[11]

In the course of time, Stuchka's sociological characterization of law as a "system of social relations" (*i.e.* as a mirror of the actual social and economic activities of human beings) was converted in the Soviet Union into the imperative conception of law as a system of State-created norms. According to Yudin, this normative order

> is the actively reflected will of the dominant class, sanctifying and perpetuating the economic and political interests of that class. In bourgeois society, all statutes constitute in their aggregate a legal institution which safeguards the interests of the bourgeoisie and is directed against the worker class.[12]

During the reign of Stalin, the class-rule concept of law received its most authoritative formulation in the writings of his attorney-general, Andrei Vyshinsky. Rejecting Stuchka's sociological approach, Vyshinsky described law as "the totality (a) of the rules of conduct, expressing the will of the dominant class and established in legal order, (b) of customs and rules of community life sanctioned by State authority — their application being guaranteed by the compulsive force of the State in order to guard, secure, and develop social relationships and social orders advantageous and agreeable to the dominant class".[13] This definition, which was published in 1938, assumed an official and authoritative force and was not subjected to criticism until 1961.[14]

---

[9] Vladimir I. Lenin, "The State", in *Soviet Legal Philosophy*, ed. J. N. Hazard (Cambridge, Mass., 1951) [hereinafter referred to as *Soviet Legal Philosophy*], pp. 10-11.

[10] Pavel I. Stuchka, "The Revolutionary Part Played by Law and the State", in *Soviet Legal Philosophy*, p. 20.

[11] R. S. F. S. R. Laws 1919, § 590.

[12] Pavel F. Yudin, "Socialism and Law", in *Soviet Legal Philosophy*, p. 284.

[13] Andrei Y. Vyshinsky, *The Law of the Soviet State*, transl. H. W. Babb (New York, 1948), p. 50.

[14] See Harold J. Berman, *Justice in the U.S.S.R.*, rev. ed. (New York, 1963), p. 92. Since the 1960s, Soviet legal theory has been going through a period of transition and the end result is not as yet in sight. Some developments pointing towards an eventual abandonment of the class-rule theory of law are described by Edgar Bodenheimer, "Antilaw Sentiments and Their Philosophical Foundations", 46 *Indiana Law Journal* 175, 178-181 (1971). A recent valuable article on the subject is Eugene Kamenka and Alice Erh-Soon Tay, "Beyond the French Revolution: Communist Socialism and the Concept of Law", 21 *University of Toronto Law Journal* 109 (1971).

The notion that law means forcible imposition of norms by the dominant class to keep the dominated class in check was for a long time applied by Soviet theorists not only to bourgeois law but also to their own system of law. Vyshinsky, for example, declared that "Soviet law reflects and confirms social orders agreeable to the toiling classes", and he maintained that it was the function of Soviet legal institutions to suppress the activities of groups antagonistic to the interests of the workers.[15] He and other Soviet leaders expressed the conviction, however, that after the victory of socialism had been achieved on a global level, the institution of law, conceived as a system of governmental constraints, was bound to become superfluous.[16]

The class-rule theory of law has not remained the monopoly of Marxian philosophy. It has also been propounded by thinkers of a non-Marxist persuasion. Ludwig Gumplowicz, for example, agreed with the Marxists that in all historically known organized societies a ruling minority has kept an oppressed majority in a state of subjection.[17] In his opinion, the law enacted by this minority (whose passage has sometimes been assured by cleverly enlisting the active assistance of the majority) has always been a law designed to stabilize and protect existing relations of inequality. Although in developing civilizations, Gumplowicz said, there can be observed a strong pressure on the part of the submerged masses of people to secure for themselves an increased share of freedom and equality, this struggle for emancipation will only be partially successful and, if carried too far, will result in a full restoration of the rule of inequality and reaction.[18] The Marxian hope of a classless and stateless society was

---

[15] Vyshinsky, *supra* n. 13, pp. 129-130.

[16] Vyshinsky, "The Fundamental Tasks of the Science of Soviet Socialist Law", in *Soviet Legal Philosophy*, p. 332; Joseph V. Stalin, "Report to the XVIIIth Party Congress", *id.*, pp. 345, 349. The source of the doctrine is Engels's often-quoted statement in *Anti-Dühring*, transl. E. Burns (New York, 1934), p. 309. Marx himself had merely made the comment that in a fully-developed communist society "there will be no more political power properly so called, since political power is precisely the official expression of antagonism in civil society". Karl Marx, *The Poverty of Philosophy* (London, 1956), p. 197. Political power "properly so called" was defined by Marx as "the organized power of one class for suppressing another". Marx, *supra* n. 7, p. 56.

[17] Ludwig Gumplowicz, *Sozialphilosophie im Umriss* (Innsbruck, 1910), pp. 54-55; Gumplowicz, *Die Soziologische Staatsidee* (Innsbruck, 1902), pp. 3-4; Gumplowicz, *Outline of Sociology*, ed. I. L. Horowitz (New York, 1963), pp. 200, 203, 262.

[18] Gumplowics, *Die Soziologische Staatsidee*, pp. 39, 130, 135; Gumplowicz, *Outlines of Sociology*, pp. 23-232; Gumplowicz, *Grundriss der Soziologie* (Innsbruck, 1926), p. 103.

dismissed by Gumplowicz as an utopian dream, and the definition of justice by Thrasymachus was accepted by him as realistic and essentially correct.[19] Similar interpretations of legal and social history can be found in the writings of the modern Neo-Machiavellians, such as Mosca and Pareto.[20]

In any evaluation of the class-rule conception of law, it is necessary at the outset to clarify one's thinking on the concept of "class". In the contemplation of Marx, this concept carries with it a predominantly economic connotation. The truly significant class division in society was for him between the owners of the means of production and the laborers whom they employ to perform work for them.[21] It is somewhat paradoxical that Marx, in spite of his firm belief in the supremacy of social and economic factors and his relegation of law to the status of a "superstructure", viewed the class concept in essentially legalistic terms. The fact which according to him sets capitalists apart as a separate class is their ownership of the means of production. Ownership is not, in his theory, determined by conditions of factual control over an enterprise but is based on the holding of legal title.[22] It is apposite to observe in this connection that, during the lifetime of Marx, industrial firms were normally owned by individual entrepreneurs or groups of partners. But joint-stock companies had already made their first appearance in the economy, and the fact that under their structural setup there occurs a separation of ownership from control made it hard for Marx to fit this phenomenon into his theory of social classes. He attempted to solve the difficulty by pointing out that stock corporations assumed "the form of social enterprises as distinguished from individual enterprises"; that they represented "the abolition of capital as private property within the boundaries of capitalist production itself"; that they accomplished a "transformation of the actually functioning capitalist into a mere manager, an administrator of other people's capital"; and

---

[19] Gumplowicz, *Outlines of Sociology*, p. 265.

[20] See Gaetano Mosca, *The Ruling Class*, ed. A. Livingston (New York, 1939), p. 50; Vilfredo Pareto, *The Mind and Society*, ed. A. Livingston (New York, 1936), Vol. III, p. 1293; Vol. IV, pp. 1512, 1532, 1617-1618. For a discussion and critique of the ideas of Mosca and Pareto see Carl J. Friedrich, *Man and His Government* (New York, 1963), pp. 316-320; Friedrich, *The New Belief in the Common Man* (Boston, 1942), pp. 238-270.

[21] Karl Marx, *Capital*, ed. F. Engels (Chicago, 1909), Vol. III, p. 1031. Besides the owners of capital and the wage laborers, Marx names the landlords as a third class in capitalist society.

[22] This interpretation is convincingly substantiated by Ralf Dahrendorf, *Class and Class Conflict in Industrial Society* (Stanford, 1959), pp. 21-23.

that by virtue of all of these features stock companies constituted "a phase of transition to a new form of production".[23]

Dahrendorf has shown that without this identification of capitalist class power with legal ownership of industrial property Marx would have been unable to link his sociological theory with his philosophy of history.[24] Marx was convinced that the world was traveling from lower to higher forms of social organization, and that the highest stage of social existence would be one in which all traces of class dominance had been eliminated from the relations between men. He assumed that this ideal state of affairs could be brought about only in a society in which the means of production had been converted into public property. If industrial and commercial enterprises were owned by all, he thought, the possibility of exploitation of laborers without property by a minority of private owners would be obviated. A "classless" society would be the inevitable result.

If Marx had defined the "ruling class" in terms of actual control and decision-making power, instead of accentuating the factor of legal owner-ship, it would have been necessary for him to revise his account of social evolution. If control is the crucial element in class supremacy, the national-ization of industrial enterprises would by no means erase relations of domination and subjection between the managerial group and the labor force, unless the decision-making power of the administrative elite was subjected to stringent democratic controls. As the history of socialist States has demonstrated, particularly strong occasions for the exercise of total power will arise in a political and social setting in which the right to determine the uses of collectivized property has been entrusted to those who at the same time wield the political power in the society in question.[25] If there exists in a social order a group of people which is in a position to make authoritative decisions affecting the well-being of the whole population, such a group might be called a "ruling class", even though its

---

[23] Marx, *supra* n. 21, Vol. III, pp. 516-517, 519.

[24] Dahrendorf, *supra* n. 22, pp. 21, 29-32.

[25] This is the thrust of the argument in Milovan Djilas, *The New Class* (New York, 1957). Djilas points out that in socialist countries in which the making of major decisions concerning the use of collectivized property is combined with the exercise of political power, the resulting monopoly of power is apt to create harsh conditions of class rule. Concern about "elitism", producing an aversion on the part of many young people to join the ranks of ordinary workers, was expressed by the director of a Soviet industrial plant in 1971. See *New York Times,* June 20, 1971, p. 3.

power is not tied to the ownership of capital or other forms of property.[26]

Marx may have believed that an economic transformation of society in the direction which he considered desirable would provide a more or less automatic solution of the power problem. He may have assumed that the collectivization of the means of production, after a transitory period of dictatorial reorganization, would *eo ipso* carry in its train a democratization of decision-making processes. If this was his belief, it would have been a logical corollary of his economic determinism, according to which political, social, and ideological problems are epiphenomena wholly dependent on the economic structure. Twentieth-century universal experience would seem to demonstrate, however, that the distribution and control of power is not merely an adjunct of economic relations but a problem of primary and independent significance, which each society has to solve regardless of the particular form of its economic organization.

The preceding discussion has attempted to demonstrate that the Marxian class concept is a narrow one because it links class status to the ownership of private property. It was suggested that the Marxian approach was ideologically induced by the desire to provide plausibility for the contention that a society based on a system of collective ownership would be a society without classes.

The historical sections which follow will raise the question, among others, whether the record compiled from two highly developed legal systems tends to bear out the major contentions of the class-rule theory of law. In pursuing this investigation, the concept of class rule will be applied to all groupings of men which are invested with authoritative decision-making powers, regardless of whether or not their superior position is based on private property or wealth. A governmental hierarchy or private managerial group will thus be deemed a class as long as substantial numbers of people are subject to its authority and command.

---

[26] This is the position of Dahrendorf, *supra* n. 22, pp. 136-141, 166-167. In his essay on "The Eighteenth Brumaire of Louis Bonaparte", Marx stated that the French bureaucracy under Napoleon III seemingly exercised an independent power not directly linked to any economic class. He went on to say, however, that the State during this period actually represented the interests of small landholders and also, by protecting the material power of the bourgeois middle class, assisted in the restoration of its political power. *Marx and Engels: Basic Writings on Politics and Philosophy*, ed. L. S. Feuer (Garden City, 1959), pp. 337-338, 345.

SECTION 16
The Strong and the Weak in Ancient Roman Law

The history of Roman law provides a valuable empirical testing ground for any theory of law or justice because the jurisprudence of the Romans can be surveyed over its entire range from a reasonably early period of its development to the end of what may be called the ancient Roman Empire. The earliest beginnings of the story are shrouded in uncertainty and conjecture: we have no reliable legal or historical records for the regal period preceding the founding of the Roman Republic around 500 B.C. The conclusion of the story represents a terminal point only from the aspect of cultural periodization. Justinian was the last emperor presiding over a unified Roman Empire which, after he had reconquered large parts of it, covered the western as well as eastern countries of the Mediterranean area. After his death in 565 A.D. the western part, including Italy, reverted back to the rule of Germanic tribes which had penetrated into it in the preceding two centuries, while the eastern region governed from Constantinople entered into a new phase of its history usually referred to as the history of the Byzantine Empire. Although the Roman law survived these political events in both the East and the West, its story as the leading legal system of ancient civilization may be said to terminate with the end of Justinian's reign. Its subsequent development coincides with its medieval transformations and its reception after 1500 A.D. as a major source of continental European legal systems and their offshoots overseas.

The story of ancient Roman law will be surveyed here from a single perspective, that of confirming or disproving the opposing views of the law outlined in the preceding two sections. What light does the record of this legal system cast on the hypothesis that law throughout its past history has served the advantage of dominant elites? Can those who have denied this assumption and contended that law has always promoted "some sort of equality" derive any comfort from a study of one thousand years of Roman legal evolution?

In pursuing this theme, attention will be focused in the first part of the inquiry on certain areas of Roman public and private law which bring to light some features of class stratification, privilege, and discrimination in Roman society: the division of the free population into ranks or "orders", the recognition of serfdom and slavery, the treatment of women and children, the position of debtors and other economically inferior persons. The analysis will then turn to some more general aspects of Roman legal development which are relevant to the solution of a question implicit in the subject of the inquiry: Has Roman law, in the main, performed the

function of protecting citizens and subjects from heavy-handed exercises of
authority by the government, or was it, conversely, considered the foremost task of the law to safeguard the State organization and the ruling
groups, by means of repressive measures, against potential challenges and
threats to their power? Thus far, these problems have received scant
attention in the professional literature on Roman law and its history.

a. The Ranks of Free Men

Roman political, social and legal history does not bear out the Marxian
thesis that "the history of all hitherto existing society is the history of
class struggles",[1] but there were two centuries — the fifth century B.C. and
the last century of the Roman Republic (133-27 B.C.) — in which prolonged feuding and warring between antagonistic social and economic
groupings constituted the most characteristic hallmark of the times. In the
early Roman Republic, the orders (*ordines*) which became involved in
political strife are known by the names of "patricians" and "plebeians".
After the expulsion of the last king, control of the Government fell into
the hands of the patrician nobility which organized the popular assembly
on a timocratic basis. The citizens were divided into five classes according
to the amount of their possessions, and the voting was arranged in a way
that made it possible for the wealthier classes to outvote the poorer ones.
This resulted in the monopolization of high governmental offices by the
patricians, whose habit it was to assign the public lands acquired by
military conquest to members of their own class for occupancy and
cultivation. It also became a source of contention that the customary law
administered by the patrician priesthood prohibited intermarriage between
the patricians and plebeians.

The plebeians attempted first to secure an amelioration of their status
through negotiations with the patricians. When this device was unproduct-
ive of results, they left the city in a body and settled somewhere in the
vicinity of Rome. This exodus, known as the "first secession of the plebs",
amounted in fact to a general strike, since the patricians were deprived of
the labor and services of the plebeians. They also lost an important source
of military recruitment.

The plebeians returned to Rome only after considerable concessions had
been made to them. Perhaps the most important one among these concessions was the integration into the State machinery of certain officers who
had previously, it is believed, defended the class interests of the plebeians

---

[1] Karl Marx, *The Communist Manifesto*, ed. S. T. Possony (New York, 1954), p. 13.

in an unofficial capacity. These functionaries were called tribunes of the plebs; their original number was two, but it was soon increased to ten. The tribunes were given the right to protect the plebeians against unjust punishment and other arbitrary acts committed by patrician officials. A little later, they were granted the much more far-reaching power to interdict any act of the patrician magistrates. Thus, when the consuls decided to bring a certain bill before the popular assembly, the tribunes could interpose a veto and thereby prevent a vote on the proposal. By this device, the revolutionary possibilities previously inherent in the activities of the tribunes were transformed into a legally sanctioned right of intercession on behalf of the plebs.

The next step taken by the plebeians was a demand for codification of the law. This request was aimed at a clarification of an obscure and imprecise body of customary law and also had in view the securing of greater legal equality to the members of the plebeian class. The history of this proposal was stormy, and action on it was delayed for a long time. The code finally adopted in 450 B.C. is known as the *Twelve Tables;* it was inscribed on bronze tablets which were set up in the *forum Romanum,* the market square of the city.

The adoption of this legislation represented another success for the plebeians. The law was rendered more certain and definite, some fences were erected against abuses of power by the judicial magistrates, and the law was changed in a number of points in favor of the lower classes. Further concessions obtained by the plebs in the decades following the enactment of the *Twelve Tables* included the right of intermarriage, greater equalization of the right to cultivate the public land, and passage of a statute providing that one of the two chief magistrates (consuls) must be a plebeian. The plebeians also obtained access to other high public offices.[2]

It is clear that in this struggle of the orders the law functioned as a vehicle for improving the position of previously inferior strata of the population. But, as was pointed out earlier,[3] equality of rights does not, in itself, entail equality of political influence or economic status. Although legal discrimination between patricians and plebeians was eliminated, a new aristocracy of prominent and wealthy families (partly of patrician, partly of

---

[2] For other descriptions of the struggle between the orders and the resulting legislation see Herbert F. Jolowicz, *Historical Introduction to the Study of Roman Law,* 2d ed. (Cambridge, Eng., 1952), pp. 7-16; Albert A. Trever, *History of Ancient Civilization* (New York, 1939), Vol. II, pp. 65-74; Max Kaser, *Römische Rechtsgeschichte,* 2d ed. (Göttingen, 1967), pp. 66-73.

[3] See *supra* Sec. 14.

plebeian origin) appeared on the scene which by the use of skillful tactics managed to preempt all or most important governmental posts. Since men who had held high office in the State were more or less automatically appointed to the Roman Senate, this prestigious body developed into a stronghold of political conservatism.

The new aristocracy was successful in strengthening and expanding the Roman State but failed in the long run to find a satisfactory solution for the social problem. Civil strife broke out in the second century B.C. and reached its climax in the first century. The contestants in the struggle were the senatorial party, representing the landed wealth of the country, and the popular party, in which the interests of the lower classes, including the landless masses in the city, had found their political expression. The fortunes of battle shifted back and forth. Under the dictatorship of Sulla the full domination of the senatorial order was temporarily secured. Later, the cause of the popular party found a powerful sponsor in the person of Julius Caesar who, after having been invested with almost unlimited power, started out on a program of social improvement which was cut short by his assassination in 44 B.C.

The class struggle was put to rest for more than two hundred years by the establishment of the Principate (a moderate form of monarchy disguised in republican forms) in 27 B.C. The senatorial nobility, which formed an extract of the upper class, for a time maintained its primacy in terms of wealth and prestige but lost its political influence step by step as the position of the emperors grew stronger and stronger. At the same time, a second estate, known as the knights (*equites*), strengthened its status in the social order. Originating as a purely military institution, the knights developed into a class of traders and businessmen, occupations which by law were closed to members of the senatorial order; they also received certain definite rights in public life, as members of the jury courts, officers in the army, financial agents of the emperors and governors of certain provinces. The third estate consisted of the remainder of the free population. It was the most numerous class and included professional and business men below the two upper ranks, artisans, craftsmen and free laborers.[4]

In spite of the maintenance of social stratification in the Principate, certain legal and economic developments led to a reduction of the gross

---

[4] For a description of the class system under the Principate see Jolowicz, *supra* n. 2, pp. 344, 361-362. Unlike other authors, Jolowicz regards the local governing groups in the municipalities *(curiales)* as a separate class, which he ranks below the knights. On classes in the Empire see also Michael Rostovtzeff, *A History of the Ancient World* (Oxford, 1930), Vol. II, pp. 190-192; Trever, *supra* n. 2, pp. 316-318; Ludwig Friedlaender, *Darstellungen aus der Sittengeschichte Roms,* 8th ed. (Leipzig, 1910), Vol. I, pp. 225-405.

inequalities that had marked the turbulent history of the late Republic. Class lines lost some of their earlier rigidity, transitions from one class to another became facilitated, and attempts were made to mitigate the most extreme disparities between wealth and poverty by various measures of social policy. These included extensive programs of public works designed, among other things, to absorb the unemployed, distribution of grain to the impoverished urban masses, granting of pensions and medical benefits to needy persons, limitations of the profits of middlemen in trade and commerce, the imposition of higher taxes and other public burdens on the wealthier classes, the broadening of educational opportunities for the lower classes.[5] Political persecutions of the senatorial nobility by a number of emperors, beginning with Nero, resulted in the confiscation of many huge agricultural estates. Although title to the expropriated estates was originally vested in the person of the emperor, a gradual fusion of imperial possessions and fiscal properties took place.[6] It would be a mistake, however, to overrate the social effect of these imperial policies, since there were many adverse factors of an economic nature which placed serious obstacles in the path of their success.

When the Roman Empire, in the fourth century A.D., became an autocratic monarchy (customarily referred to as the Dominate), which was free of any traces of a republican or representative facade, the class structure of society was maintained but the importance of the Knights declined due to the growing displacement of private economic activity by state management. The elite group that emerged into undisputed supremacy in the late Empire was the imperial bureaucracy, including its military branch. This bureaucracy was not a "class" in the restricted Marxian sense, because its power was not based on landed wealth or on capital; but it fulfilled the requirements of the broader conception of the term because it was in a position to make incisive and authoritative decisions affecting the lives and well-being of the entire population.[7]

---

[5] See Rostovtzeff, *Social and Economic History of the Roman Empire,* 2d ed. (Oxford, 1957), Vol. I, pp. 344-345, 370, 379-383, 389-390, 405-406, 409, 415-425, 534; Ernst Levy, *West Roman Vulgar Law* (Philadelphia, 1951), pp. 103-110; Solomon Katz, *The Decline of Rome and the Rise of Medieval Europe* (Ithaca, 1955), pp. 11-12; Ernst Kornemann, *Römische Geschichte,* 3rd ed. (Stuttgart, 1954), Vol. II, pp. 263, 269, 311, 365-366.

[6] Rostovtzeff, *supra* n. 4, Vol. II, p. 261; Ulrich von Wilamowitz-Moellendorf, J. Kromayer, and August Heisenberg, *Staat und Gesellschaft der Griechen und Römer,* 2d ed. (Leipzig, 1923), pp. 334-338. The imperial estates were cultivated less by slaves than by free lessees who at a later stage of the development became bound to the soil.

[7] See *supra* Sec. 15, especially notes 25 and 26.

The rule of this imperial bureaucracy brought with it a far-reaching regulation of the economy and of the vocations. There were State-operated enterprises, State-controlled monopolies, and extensive regulations of prices. The private organizations of laborers, artisans, and handicraftsmen were converted into compulsory guilds, whose members were bound to work for the needs of the State. In each branch of industry indispensable to the State, the government required the delivery of a certain amount of products and made the organizations responsible for the execution of the orders. Moreover, the members of the compulsory guilds were not only bound to their jobs but their calling was even made hereditary: the son was forced to do the same kind of work as his father.[8]

When we compare the class structure in the late Republic with that of the late Empire, we shall notice a substantial shift in the relation between political and economic equality. Politically, the members of the free population in the Republic had some share in the formulation of the general will by virtue of their voting rights in the popular assembly, and through the activities of the tribunes of the plebs. There is evidence, however, that in the late Republic the latter not infrequently used the masses for their own political ambitions. Economically, the disparities between the precarious condition of the lower classes and the affluence of the senatorial nobility were so pronounced that protracted civil strife became unavoidable. In the late Empire, political equality had been eliminated by the ascendancy of a governmental elite. On the other hand, a certain leveling on the economic front occurred by means of the disappearance of many large fortunes and the pursuit of policies of social welfare. It is also of interest to note that the Dominate created the position of *defensor civitatis*, an official who as "Ombudsman" for the poorer classes was given the task of protecting them against economic oppression.[9]

b. Clients and Slaves

Rome during the regal and early republican period was a community of farmers with a system of land-holding that bore a certain resemblance to

---

[8] On social and economic conditions in the late Empire see Wolfgang Kunkel, *An Introduction to Roman Legal and Constitutional History*, transl. J. M. Kelly (Oxford, 1966), pp. 127-134; Rostovtzeff, *supra* n. 5, Ch. XII; Tenney Frank, *Social Behavior in Rome* (Baltimore, 1932), pp. 104-105; Herman Gummerus, "Industrie und Handel in Rom", in *Paulys Realenzyklopädie der Classischen Altertumswissenschaften* (Stuttgart, 1916), Vol. IX (2), pp. 1461, 1513-1519; Paul Huvelin, *Etudes de Droit Romain* (Paris, 1929), pp. 62-63.

[9] See Kaser, *supra* n. 2, pp. 216-217; Gerhard Dulckeit and Fritz Schwarz, *Römische Rechtsgeschichte*, 4th ed. (Munich, 1966), p. 232. There is evidence that in the course of time the *defensores* came under the influence of the powers whose activities they were supposed to watch with a critical eye. *Id.*

medieval feudalism. The institution of the *clientela* was based on a bond of personal fidelity between the client and his patron. The client was given a (revocable) concession to cultivate part of the land occupied by his patron. The patron could claim a yearly sum of money or a quota of the products from the client, and the latter was also obliged to render certain personal services to his lord, among them support in war and politics. The patron in turn was obliged to afford his clients protection and help in every necessity. Although, as far as we know, the client was not permitted in the early period of Roman legal history to invoke the jurisdiction of the ordinary courts in suits against his protector, it was possible to institute quasicriminal proceedings against a patron derelict in his duties that might lead to his outlawry.[10]

The part played by slavery in early Roman history was small, but the institution assumed a highly prominent role in the late Republic and early Empire. While in the old times the few slaves owned by a farmer were usually well taken care of and ate at the family table, the treatment of the slaves deteriorated as large numbers of them were brought to Rome as prisoners of war during the age of military conquest. Most of them were employed on estates, in factories, in mines, as porters and oarsmen, and their labor power was used to the utmost. To a conservative politician and landowner like Cato, forcing slaves to work on the soil in chain gangs was the proper, unquestioned system. He viewed the use of slave labor purely from the point of view of economy and lucrative yield, without any regard for human welfare.[11] While his recommendations were perhaps not typical for the attitude exhibited by all or most slave owners, there is no reason to assume that Cato was altogether an exception. The outbreak of numerous slave uprisings, some of them lasting several years, during the period of the late Republic attests to the fact that the kindlier atmosphere of earlier times had given way to harsher forms of treatment.

It was pointed out elsewhere that during the Roman Republic the rights of the slave owner were legally unrestricted; he was permitted to kill or chastise his slaves at will.[12] During the Principate, the growth of humani-

---

[10] On the institution of clientship see Kunkel, *supra* n. 8, pp. 6-9; Kaser, *supra* n. 2, pp. 28-29; Max Weber, "Agrarverhältnisse im Altertum," in *Gesammelte Aufsätze zur Sozial- und Wirtschaftsgeschichte* (Tübingen, 1924), pp. 202-207.

[11] See M. Porcius Cato, *On Agriculture,* Loeb Class. Lib. ed. (Cambridge, Mass., 1934), Ch. II. 3-4; Ch. XXIII. 1; Ch. XXXIX. 1-2. Cato suggests that a slave should not be without work for a single moment, except for necessary periods of sleep; that in case of a slave's illness his meals should be reduced for reasons of economy; that very little money should be spent for the clothing of the slaves; and that senile slaves should be put in the category of worn-out inventory, like old ploughs, and be sold for a cheap price.

[12] *Supra* Sec. 14, n. 19.

tarian ideas (which can in part be attributed to the then prevailing philosophy of Stoicism) caused an improvement in the status of the unfree
population. The Emperor Hadrian forbade masters to kill their slaves
except upon the judgment of a magistrate. An earlier law had stopped the
sale of unfree men and women to purveyors for gladiatorial shows. Other
emperors issued orders decreeing a status of freedom for slaves abandoned
by their masters, granting a right of complaint to the magistrates to slaves
who had been mistreated, and protecting female slaves from abuse by their
owners. Many of these measures, however, were limited to individual cases
of abuse and did not attain a general obligatory force.[13]

This trend toward an improved position of the slave population continued under the Dominate; for example, a limited right to own property
was given to the slaves. During this period, the number of slaves declined
continuously, and slavery gradually lost its economic importance. One of
the reasons for this development, among many others, was the encouragement of emancipation by the authorities of the Christian Church. But,
although Justinian's Code stated that slavery was "contrary to nature", the
institution as such was never abolished in antiquity.[14]

c. Women and Children

While the position of slaves, notwithstanding the gradual amelioration of
their status in the course of Roman history, was always a strictly inferior
one, a definite movement from abject subordination to a farreaching
equality (which never, however, extended to eligibility for public office)
can be discerned in the legal treatment of women. In the early republican
period, the prevailing form of marriage was characterized by *manus,* i.e. the
unlimited power of the husband over his wife's person and property. The
manus included the power to put the wife to death, as well as the right to
chastise or repudiate her. The husband was, however, expected to convene
a domestic court or family council consisting of close relatives, before
taking severe measures against his marital partner. Abuses of his power
were first penalized by the religious sanction of outlawry. Later, the
censors exercised a moral supervision over husbands which might, in their
discretion, result in the infliction of political or economic disadvantages.[15]

---

[13] See William W. Buckland, *The Roman Law of Slavery* (Cambridge, Eng., 1908), pp. 2,
27, 80; Fritz Schulz, *Principles of Roman Law,* transl. M. Wolff (Oxford, 1936), pp.
219-222; Max Kaser, *Das Römische Privatrecht* (Munich, 1955), Vol. I, pp. 244-247.

[14] Inst. 1, 3, 2; Dig. 1, 5, 4. On the status of slavery in the late Empire see Kaser, *supra* n.
13, Vol. II, pp. 73, 84-85; Rostovtzeff, *supra* n. 4, Vol. II, p. 355.

[15] See *supra* Sec. 14, n. 21.

The marriage with *manus* gradually came into disuse in Rome. In the course of time, it gave way to a freer type of marital relationship, and in the third century A.D. it disappeared completely. As a general rule, husband and wife were equal partners in this freer form of marriage. The wife could as easily divorce her husband as he could divorce her. Both owned their property separately and exercised full powers of disposition over it. Even during the Principate, however, the equality of husband and wife did not become complete. A law of Augustus gave the husband a unilateral right to kill his wife if caught by him in an act of adultery. This right was not abrogated until the Roman Empire adopted the Christian religion, and the duty of marital faithfulness was thereafter imposed upon both spouses. There were also changes made at that time in the law of divorce, including a restriction of the right to dissolve a marriage to specified grounds of incompatibility or misbehavior. Furthermore, women acquired the right to become guardians of their children.[16]

While the developmental trend from subjection towards equality was definite and pronounced in the case of women, a somewhat different picture presents itself with respect to the legal position of children. It was the guiding principle of Roman law in this area that the unfettered power of the family father over his descendants (*patria potestas*) did not cease when they reached adulthood; the power also extended to grown-up sons and daughters unless they were emancipated by their father, or unless a daughter contracted a *manus* marriage by which she passed into the power of her husband. This principle of autocratic leadership of the family head exhibited a great tenacity throughout the history of ancient Roman law. It was in fact never abrogated, although it was made subject to many exceptions and qualifications in the course of time. These restrictions often became incorporated into the law long after public opinion and social conditions had made their recognition highly desirable. Thus, the inertial properties of the law made themselves felt with particular force in this branch of the Roman legal order.

Under the early law, the *paterfamilias* held the power of life and death over his children, but before inflicting severe forms of chastisement, he was expected (as in the case of punishment of the wife) to convene a family council. He could expose a newborn child and sell even a grown-up one, at

---

[16]On the Roman Law of marriage see Kaser, *Roman Private Law*, 2d ed., transl. R. Dannenbring (Durban, 1968) [hereinafter referred to as *Roman Private Law*], pp. 238-249; Kaser, *supra* n. 13, Vol. I, pp. 18-19, 44-57, 67-74, Vol. II, pp. 72-75, 111-123; James Bryce, "Marriage and Divorce under Roman and English Law", in *Studies in History and Jurisprudence* (New York, 1901), Vol. II, pp. 782-811.

least for the purpose of performing labor for the buyer. He could, under the early law, force his children to marry a person not of their own choosing, and he could deny permission to them to marry a partner they had selected. He could also, in the early period, compel sons and daughters under his power to divorce their spouses at his pleasure. All property acquired by or given to children under *patria potestas* belonged to the head of the family, who had full powers of disposition over it; it happened frequently, however, that the *paterfamilias* would grant his children some property (called *peculium*), whose income they were permitted to use.

Abuses of the paternal power were dealt with in the early law by sacral law and later by censorial supervision of morals. When the latter institution died out in the late Republic, the dangers of an arbitrary exercise of *patria postestas* were naturally increased. The lawmaking arm of the government finally felt called upon to step into the breach and impose regulations and restrictions.

The right to sell a child (except a newborn baby) did not survive for very long. The power of the father to dissolve the marriage of a son was also abrogated at an early time; but it was not until the reign of Antoninus Pius in the second century A.D. that the father was prohibited from interfering with the marriage of his daughter. The paternal right to put a child to death (which was rarely exercised except in the case of exposing newborn children) came for all practical purposes to an end in the Principate. The right was formally abolished in the fourth century A.D., preserving, however, the right of exposure. The father's duty to support his children was recognized under the Principate. But not even in late antiquity did the descendants (including adult and married ones) acquire full capacity with respect to the ownership of property. In spite of this very slow growth of the offspring's liberation from the onerous incidents of *patria potestas,* it is fair to state that a comparison of the law of the early Republic with that of Justinian's time demonstrates an impressive degree of improvement.[17]

d. Creditors and Debtors

A particularly vivid illustration of the readjustments which took place in the position of the strong *vis-a-vis* the weak during the course of Roman history is offered to us in the law of obligations. Under the legal code of

---

[17] The history of *patria potestas* is discussed in detail by Kaser, *supra* n. 13, Vol. I, pp. 290-299, Vol. II, pp. 141-155. See also Kaser, *Roman Private Law,* pp. 256-264; Schulz, *supra* n. 13, pp. 165-168.

the early Republic, a man who did not pay a sum of money he owed to another on account of a tortious act or breach of contract had to brace himself for subjection to an extremely severe proceeding. Thirty days after he had confessed the debt or suffered judgment against his person, his creditor could seize him and take him before a magistrate. There he laid hands on him in a formal ceremony called *manus iniectio*. Following it, the debtor could not free himself from the creditor's power except by full payment. Only a third person (*vindex*) had the right to dispute on his behalf the creditor's right of seizure; if he was unsuccessful in this endeavor, the amount of the debt was doubled.[18]

If the *manus iniectio* was not challenged, or if the praetor upheld it, the creditor could take the debtor with him and keep him in captivity for sixty days. He was allowed to bind him with fetters not exceeding fifteen pounds in weight but had to feed him unless the debtor preferred to obtain his own provisions. On three consecutive market days, the prisoner had to be produced before the praetor and the amount of the debt had to be publicly announced. If nobody appeared who was willing to redeem the prisoner by paying the debt, the creditor was permitted to kill the debtor or sell him into slavery. If there were several creditors, they could divide the debtor's body; if the cutting-up operation did not result in mathematical proportionality of the pieces to the respective shares of the debt, no liability was to attach to such iniquity according to a special provision of the *Twelve Tables*.[19]

In actual practice, instead of resorting to this gruesome procedure, creditors probably availed themselves of an old rule of customary law, according to which debtors could work off their debts in order to save their lives and freedom from slavery. This particular form of execution into the person of the debtor was never abolished in antiquity, but it was pushed into the background by the introduction and growing use of a procedure *in rem*. The belongings of the debtor could be seized in their entirety to serve as a means for the satisfaction of all claims of his

---

[18] Jhering points out that this regulation is a striking example of the inequality of the rich and poor in early Roman procedure. The creditor was not subjected to any special penalty if his seizure of the debtor was wrongful. Rudolph von Jhering, "Reich und Arm im Römischen Zivilprozess", in *Scherz und Ernst in der Jurisprudenz*, 13th ed. (Leipzig, 1924), pp. 196-197.

[19] See *Twelve Tables*, Ch. III, in *Sources of Ancient and Primitive Law*, ed. A. Kocourek and H. H. Wigmore (Boston, 1915), pp. 465-466; Jolowicz, *supra* n. 2, pp. 190-192; Kaser, *Roman Private Law*, p. 338; Kaser, *Das Römische Zivilprozessrecht* (Munich, 1966), pp. 94-104. Professor Kaser has informed me that no case in which this procedure was actually used in practice is reported in legal and general literature.

creditors. This seizure resulted in the *infamia* of the debtor, which amounted to a loss of certain civil and political rights. The creditors then chose a *magister bonorum* who sold the assets of the debtor in a public sale to the highest bidder, *i.e.* the person offering the creditors the highest percentage of their debts.

From the time of Augustus, a debtor who had become unable to discharge his obligations due to misfortune could avoid execution into his property, as well as the resulting infamy, by making a voluntary cession of the property to his creditors, with the proviso that he could retain what he needed to support himself and his family. Furthermore, special execution into particular pieces of property gradually replaced the harshness of the generalized bankruptcy procedure. The latter was restricted during the Dominate to situations where the debtor had become totally insolvent, and where there were several creditors.[20]

In numerous other ways, too, the imperial period of Roman history starting with Augustus came to the aid of economically disadvantaged groups in society. At various stages of the development, rates of interest were reduced, moratoria granted on the payment of debts during times of economic crisis, penalties introduced for usurious practices, maximum prices set for certain articles of use and consumption. The last-mentioned price control measure was introduced by Diocletian around 300 A.D. but encountered extremely great difficulties with respect to its enforcement.[21]

e. Other Aspects of the Equality Problem

The *Twelve Tables* forbade the granting of *privilegia*, i.e. enactments made in favor or disfavor of particular individuals.[22] This provision did not prohibit the adoption of legislative differentiations according a privileged position to certain groups or classes of the population.[23] It did serve, however, to guarantee a certain amount of formal equality within the

---

[20] On these developments See Jolowicz, *supra* n. 2, pp. 224-226, 411, 463-464; Kaser, *Roman Private Law*, pp. 355-357, 362, 366-367.

[21] See Jhering, *supra* n. 18, pp. 214-224; Ivo Pfaff, *Ueber den Rechtlichen Schutz des Wirtschaftlich Schwächeren in der Römischen Kaisergesetzgebung* (Weimar, 1897) pp. 26, 35-36, 56-58, 66-67.

[22] *Twelve Tables*, Ch. IX. 1. On this provision see Kaser, *Roman Private Law*, p. 28; Hans J. Wolff, *Roman Law* (Norman, Okla., 1951), p. 67.

[23] We have seen earlier under (a) that certain public offices were reserved for members of the senatorial and equestrian classes, and that women were barred from government positions.

boundaries of a legal classification, which could not be set aside by the passage of what today is called a "special act".

It must be asked whether or not this minimum guarantee of equal justice under general laws was watered down or erased by a legal axiom adopted during the Principate and retained in the Dominate, according to which the emperor was absolved from the obligatory force of the laws (*legibus solutus*).[24] Did this mean that the ruler of the State could disregard the statutes for his own advantage, and that he could also order dispensations on behalf of persons favored by him, or to the detriment of those who had incurred his displeasure? In answering this question, it is necessary to distinguish between the period of the Principate, when certain constitutional restraints were still recognized (though unevenly observed by the several emperors) and the time of the Dominate, when the imperial power had become total and illimitable.

It is likely that during the Principate various statutes were passed which exempted the person of the emperor from certain commands of the law.[25] Even in the absence of such specific statutory exemptions, according to the opinion of leading historians, the emperor could grant dispensations for his own benefit or that of another person from any prescription from which dispensation was held legally permissible. While this principle made it possible for the head of the State to decree equitable exceptions from a rule or regulation in cases where the generality of the law might subject an individual to hardship or injustice, it cannot be assumed that the *legibus solutus* axiom conferred authority on the ruler to commit tortious or criminal acts. The immunity from suit or prosecution enjoyed by the *princeps* was limited to his term of office, which at the time of Augustus was not necessarily coincident with the span of his life. Later, however, when the Principate evolved into a lifelong reign, the responsibility of the chief of State was capable of being enforced only in those rare instances when he was deposed by force or abdicated voluntarily.[26]

This state of affairs underwent a change in the Dominate when the emperor became an absolute ruler. Henceforth, all powers of government were formally united in his person, and he was considered the source of all law. And yet, the idea of law was so deeply ingrained in the Romans that a

---

[24] Dig. 1, 3, 31.

[25] An example mentioned in Justinian's *Corpus Iuris* is a statute relieving the emperor from certain formal requirements for legal transactions. Dig. 40, 1, 14, 1.

[26] See Theodor Mommsen, *Römisches Staatsrecht*, 3rd ed. (Leipzig, 1887), Vol. II. Pt. 2, pp. 749-754; Jolowicz, *supra* n. 2, p. 337.

study of this late period does not (with the exception perhaps of certain times of extreme turmoil and trouble) convey to us the impression of a wholly capricious and lawless rule. Although tremors of arbitrary power were felt from time to time throughout the reaches of the Empire, it seems that, for the most part, the norms of the law were respected by the monarchs and applied by them to persons and situations coming within their purview.[27]

This last statement should, however, be made subject to the qualification that much (though not all) of the body of Roman law at this stage of its history had lost the clarity and consistency of the classical system. Roman law had undergone a process of loosening, vulgarization, and destructuralization which, in conjunction with the infusion of unsharp moral reasoning, must have affected the certainty of the law significantly.[28] Thus, although the rule of law was not obliterated in the Dominate, a certain disintegration of the legal system itself, combined with an always present possibility of *ad hoc* sovereign interference in an individual case, posed a threat to legal stability and justice. It is also to be taken into account that the cumbersome and not always reliable bureaucratic apparatus of the Dominate was often not able to administer the legal system effectively, and that the landed nobility, which still enjoyed considerable power (especially in the western part of the Empire), sometimes offered passive resistance to the measures of legal enforcement.[29]

f. General Conclusions

What light does the record of ancient Roman law cast on the hypothesis that law throughout its history has served the advantage of dominant elites? Can those who have denied this assumption and contended that law has always promoted "some sort of equality"[30] derive any comfort from a study of one thousand years of Roman legal evolution? These were the questions posed at the beginning of this section. An attempt will be made to answer them on the basis of the facts already discussed and some

---

[27] See John B. Bury, "The Constitution of the Later Roman Empire", in *Selected Essays*, ed. H. Temperley (Cambridge, Eng., 1930), pp. 114-115; Steven Runciman, *Byzantine Civilization* (London, 1933), pp. 62, 74.

[28] On the vulgarized Roman law see Levy, *supra* n. 5, pp. 1-18; Levy, *Gesammelte Schriften* (Cologne, 1963), Vol. I, pp. 163-247; Kaser, *supra* n. 13, Vol. II, pp. 13-18.

[29] See, for example, Kaser, *Das Römische Zivilprozessrecht*, pp. 412-417.

[30] See *supra* Sec. 14, notes 1 and 2.

additional data to be presented in the course of the concluding observations.

Jhering has said that in Roman private law "the most complete equality was realized, without distinction of city and country, rich and poor, noble and lowly".[31] It is hardly possible to accept his statement in this pointed formulation. A certain formal equality before the law was indeed assured by the fact that, at least in the preclassical and classical Roman law, rules phrased in general terms were applied, without respect of individual persons, to all who came within the purview of the classifications established by these rules. Thus, all persons who were able to own property and enter into contractual agreements could avail themselves of the rules of property and contract law. We have seen, however, that certain groups in society were either incompetent or only very partially competent to own property and to conclude contractual arrangements. Slaves, women under *manus*, persons subject to the *patria potestas* were to a far-reaching extent excluded from the enjoyment of these basic personal rights.

It also needs to be emphasized that many of the detailed and finespun rules of Roman property and contract law were of real significance and value only to the members of the wealthier classes.[32] The masses of free men in the cities usually did not possess the means to acquire property beyond the most indispensable household articles, and they often obtained the necessaries of life not by way of contracts but in the form of public donations or distributions. These facts are attested, among other verifications in the sources, by the almost exclusive preoccupation of the classical Roman jurists with the affairs of the well-to-do, above all their wills and inheritance problems. It is also a fact that the Roman law of lease exhibited a lopsided concern for the interests of the lessor.[33]

It was shown, on the other hand, that when the law of the State began to take an active interest in the position of slaves, women, and persons subject to the paternal power (areas which the early social structure tended to entrust to the autonomous lawmaking power of the family head),[34] its

---

[31] Rudolph von Jhering, *Geist des Römischen Rechts*, 5th ed. (Basel, 1894), Vol. II, p. 97 (My translation).

[32] On some aspects of the impact and non-impact of Roman law upon the "have-nots" see David Daube, *Roman Law: Linguistic, Social and Philosophical Aspects* (Edinburgh, 1969), pp. 71-91.

[33] Kaser, *Roman Private Law*, pp. 184-185.

[34] See *supra* Sec. 14.

intervention usually took the form of reducing the element of domination and subjection in personal relations in favor of enhanced equalization. Various attempts were also made by the law to mitigate the impact of privilege by ameliorating the position of debtors and poor people. It has also been pointed out that in the field of political relationships, the *Twelve Tables* legislation accomplished a great deal in improving the status of previously disadvantaged groups. Furthermore, while during the Republic and Principate public offices were largely reserved to the members of the senatorial and equestrian orders, the bureaucracy of the Dominate was recruited on a less restrictive basis. These changes cannot, however, alter the basic conclusion agreed upon by all general and legal historians that elements of class stratification and class power were preserved through the entire span of Roman history.

Such class power often manifested itself not so much by the concession of positive, legally confirmed advantages but by extra-legal manipulations and practices. First of all, economically and politically powerful groups were often in a better position than the bulk of common men and women to evade the law and sabotage commands felt to be burdensome. For example, it is reported in some ancient sources (but not fully confirmed) that in 367 B.C. a statute was passed to the effect that no citizen should occupy more than 500 jugera of public land and keep more than 100 oxen or 500 sheep on the common pasture. The purpose of these provisions was to obviate large concentrations of landed wealth and to enable the poorer classes to obtain allotments of public lands. Assuming such a law was passed as reported, the senatorial nobility was able to prevent its enforcement for more than 200 years. A similar law (which did, however, increase the acreage of permitted holdings) was put into effect in 133 B.C. during the Gracchan Revolution. Even after this enactment, the poorer sectors of the population, because of lack of capital to pay for the right to cultivate the land, did not profit a great deal from this legislation, and half a century later the *ager publicus* was well-nigh exhausted.[35] It is also reported that, during the imperial period of Roman history, governmental impositions of financial and other burdens were frequently disregarded or evaded by those whose economic power afforded them a certain degree of leverage in political circles.[36]

A second type of extra-legal action designed to preserve the rule of a

---

[35] On the public lands question in the Roman Republic see Jolowicz, *supra* n. 2, pp. 14-16; Max Weber, *Römische Agrargeschichte* (Stuttgart, 1891), pp. 130-131.

[36] See Rostovtzeff, *supra* n. 5, Vol. I, pp. 384-385, 410.

dominant elite or governmental hierarchy is the open use of naked power, which in a true crisis situation may assume the dimensions of terror. To be sure, there were in Rome — as in all organized societies — laws designed to protect the state structure against seditious activities. Such acts as treason, conspiring with the enemy, attempts to overthrow the Government, insubordination and riot were penalized by stringent sanctions.[37] When the state of the Roman nation was healthy and the Government supported by the bulk of the people, such laws served the purpose of safeguarding the public order under formalized legal procedures, and they were probably rarely invoked. In times of social disruption or civil war, on the other hand, these laws were sometimes felt to be insufficient in scope, and in that event the Government and the groups loyal to it tended to resort to strong-hand measures of a nonlegal character to preserve their authority or existence.

Sometimes the men in command of the State contrived the assassination of a public figure felt by them to constitute a threat to their power; the murder of Cicero ordered by the triumvirate consisting of Marc Anthony, Lepidus and Octavian is a well-known historical instance. Another drastic example of substitution of unfettered force for the rule of law is presented by the proscriptions which Lucius Cornelius Sulla decreed during the civil war of the first century B.C. Lists were published in rapid succession which outlawed all persons suspected of being antagonistic to the dictator. A reward was offered for the heads of such persons, and their possessions were confiscated by the State. Inasmuch as there was no inquiry, no trial, no proof of guilt, it is obvious that not even the most elementary procedural prerequisites of legality were observed. It also happened that names were surreptitiously added to the lists by others who found this an inviting opportunity to get rid of rivals and personal enemies. This system of political terrorism did not remain confined to one-time use but served as a precedent for several subsequent repeat performances.[38] Such conditions of pervasive lawlessness were, however, exceptional in Roman political history and usually not of long duration.

The colorful and instructive story of the Roman State thus reveals the existence of antithesis as well as interpenetration between power and law. Relations of domination and subjection manifested themselves in class

---

[37] See Theodor Mommsen, *Römisches Strafrecht* (Leipzig, 1899), pp. 537-555.

[38] See Trever, *supra* n. 2, Vol. II, pp. 186-187, 248-249; Ulrich Kahrstedt, *Geschichte des Griechisch-Römischen Altertums* (Munich, 1948), pp. 299-300; Rostovtzeff, *supra* n. 4, Vol. II, pp. 124, 318.

structures of varying forms, and lawless struggles for control of the State occurred in several stages of the development. Power factors were also operative in the nonpolitical field. The earlier centuries of Roman history were characterized by a far-reaching maintenance of male supremacy. Economic inequality was practiced in a radical form in the institutions of feudalism and slavery; it also was evidenced by the imperious position which creditors enjoyed during the republican period.

The law in many ways counteracted the unscrupulous use of political, economic, and social power. It did a great deal in equalizing the rights of patricians and plebeians, and in securing the gains made by the latter on a lasting basis. It ameliorated the position of women, children, slaves and debtors. It protected the life, bodily integrity and property of at least the free members of the population against acts of violence and spoliation, and later also accorded some rights to the unfree. It sanctioned a far-reaching freedom of transaction for family heads and gradually extended it to other members of the household. Whatever gains were made by the subjects of the Roman Empire in strengthening their liberty, equality, and security were to a large extent due to the guarantees provided by law.[39]

No legal system, however, is free form corruption by powerful interests. Armed violence by political groups in periods of civil strife at times interfered with the regular processes of the law. The rich sometimes bought favors or procured exemptions from civic burdens, and the owners of landed estates in the imperial period often resisted the enforcement of laws by the central administration. The law as laid down in the books was not always congruous with the law as practiced in action.

While irruptions of power caused some disturbances in the administration of Roman justice, the law at the same time penetrated into domains where power was formally unlimited. The absolutism of imperial rule in the late Empire was rarely carried to the extreme of wholesale caprice. The general rules of law in force were ordinarily observed by the authorities until a change was officially promulgated. Although the dispensing power of the emperors posed serious dangers of misuse, the sense of need for the

---

[39] The peak period of Roman law coincided with the first two centuries of the Principate. This period was characterized by an absence of international and class wars. Contrary to the subsequent period of the Dominate, there prevailed, on the whole, some reasonable balance between freedom and authority. Furthermore, under the influence of the Stoic philosophy, more steps toward the realization of some notion of human equality were taken than in the preceding period of the Roman Republic. On the influence of the Stoic notion of equality on the legislation of the Principate see Edgar Bodenheimer, *Jurisprudence: The Philosophy and Method of the Law* (Cambridge, Mass., 1962), pp. 13-20.

rule of law was deeply ingrained in the thinking of the Romans. If the effects of the preferred position accorded to law had not been experienced as mostly beneficial by Roman society, there is doubt that many basic institutions of Roman law would have survived until our own time in a new and different civilization.

Section 17
The Equality Record of Anglo-American Law

Anglo-American law was the product of a civilization which, although it profited a great deal from the accomplishments of the Greco-Roman world, attained a high degree of technical and cultural proficiency. Many social and economic forces whose blossoming in antiquity had been hampered by the predominance of an agricultural economy, operated largely by slaves, burst into full flowering in the civilization of the Western World which was built upon the ruins of the Roman Empire. This had the consequence that the sociological phenomena responsible for the growth of law, including the relation of legal institutions to the political and economic power structures of society, move into sharper focus as attention is shifted from the ancient Roman law to one of the most influential legal systems of the post-Roman world.

In pursuing further the subject which formed the keynote of the preceding section, the method of presentation will be modified. When the problems of domination and equality were discussed in a Roman law setting, the sequence of exposition was marked by a breakdown of the analysis into substantive areas of legal regulation, such as slavery, domestic relations, enforcement of obligations, etc. The pattern of organization to be followed in this section will instead be focused on the five basic types of equality which were previously listed as particularly important concerns of the legal order.[1] These are (a) equality of rule classification, (b) commutative equality, (c) equal treatment of equals, (d) equality of fundamental rights, and (e) equality of need satisfaction. The question will be asked whether and to what extent these forms of equality have been realized in Anglo-American law. This discussion will be followed by an inquiry into the impact which the evolutionary trends operative in this legal system have had on the promotion of human freedom, and by a consideration of the role which forces opposed to equality have played in this development.

---

[1] See *supra* Sec. 14.

a. Equality of Rule Classification

Anglo-American law has performed its political and social functions largely, though not exclusively, through the formulation and enforcement of general norms or commands. These may have originated in constitutional provisions, statutes, administrative regulations or judicial pronouncements. By exercising social control primarily by way of general norms addressed to certain classes and categories of persons, the amount of constraint achieved through executive fiat, *i.e.* special orders addressed to particular individuals in response to concrete exigencies, and of special privileges conferred by one-time acts, has been reduced substantially. Although this facet of the "rule of law" establishes no guaranty against the adoption of general rules which create unfair distinctions between the races, sexes, nationalities or other social groupings, it provides important safeguards against an overallocation of individualizing discretion to public officials, including judges, and thereby promotes "some sort of equality".[2] In making this statement it is presupposed, of course, that the general norms of the law are, in the large majority of cases, applied and enforced without bias and respect of persons.

The history of the famous clause 39 of the *Magna Carta* of 1215 provides an exemplification of the equalizing effects of general classifications. By virtue of this clause, King John promised that "no freeman shall be captured or imprisoned or disseised or outlawed or exiled or in any way destroyed, nor will we go against him or send against him, except by the lawful judgment of his peers or by the law of the land". It may well be true that the original purpose of the clause was self-protection of the small group of feudal magnates who wrested the charter from the King or, differently expressed, "the hardening of the privileges of some hundred petty kings".[3] But it also cannot be overlooked that in the long run the use of the broad term "freeman" resulted in making the benefits of clause 39 available to increasingly large numbers of people. During the Middle Ages, a sizeable class of human beings, the serfs, were barred from invoking the provisions of the charter. When this disadvantaged class became smaller in numbers towards the end of the Middle Ages and finally disappeared from the social scene, the safeguards against arbitrary arrest, lawless deprivation of liberty and executive seizure of property established by clause 39 attained the character of universal rights.

---

[2] See Albert V. Dicey, *Introduction to the Study of the Law of the Constitution,* 10th ed. (London, 1965), pp. 188, 202-203.

[3] Max Radin, "The Myth of Magna Carta", 60 *Harvard Law Review* 1060, 1062 (1947).

It should, of course, not be overlooked that the equalizing effect of broad classifications used by the law may have adverse rather than beneficial consequences for an individual. This is the case when a general definition which brings an individual within the purview of a statute or other legal source subjects him to a deprivation, disability or penal sanction. Let us suppose, for example, that in times of national emergency a law is passed which authorizes the commitment to detention camps of persons "likely to engage in activities detrimental to the national security". The breadth of this classification creates an equality of jeopardy for all persons who by their past political activities have demonstrated an active antagonism to the government in power. The proponents of the class-rule theory of law would contend that provisions of this character reveal the true nature of law, and that the equality created by legal classifications is for the most part an equality of repression.

The answer to this contention should be that legal provisions designed to protect the fabric of government against subversion and sabotage, if they are carefully drawn and sufficiently specific, serve, under certain presuppositions, the benefit of society. If the governmental structure is healthy and rests on a popular basis, such laws may be said to safeguard a going concern from destruction by internal enemies. If the State ceases to be an engine for the promotion of the common good and becomes an institution for the preservation of the privileges of a dominant but uncreative minority,[4] then the body of political criminal law is likely to take on a predominantly repressive character. If this contingency occurs, the function of law to guarantee a reasonable measure of security, liberty and equality to individuals is usually undermined.

It was pointed out in the preceding section that in a deep crisis of the State the rule of law tends to be replaced by the untrammelled rule of power. The fear of being overthrown induces the governing elite to discard the restraints of legality and, as the threats to its preservation grow in force, to move towards the politics of terror. Although the outer forms of the law may be retained, the edicts of the rulers may become so vague and indeterminate in content that one of the chief benefits of the law — to insure calculability of the consequences of individual conduct — is negated. Thus conditions of severe political crisis are frequently accompanied by

---

[4] The distinction between a "creative minority", pushing the inert masses of people forward along the path of progress, and a "dominant minority", holding down a population no longer willing to follow its lead, was elaborated by Arnold J. Toynbee, *A Study of History* (London, 1935-1939), Vol. I, pp. 53-54, Vol. IV, pp. 5-6, 297, Vol. V, pp. 31-33.

perversions of legal processes and thus throw little light on the nature and chief characteristics of law.

There are, of course, other instances of rule classifications in which the generality of the law confers no advantages on those who are subject to its commands. Statutes excluding women from the franchise, for example, although they were enforced scrupulously without respect of persons, did for a long time perpetuate the inequality of the sexes. Tax laws, although urgently needed to make the operations of government possible, may be harsh in their effects on certain groups of people.

b. Commutative Equality

In the Middle Ages, the ideas of Aristotle concerning equality in matters of exchange,[5] in combination with the prevalence of ambivalent feelings towards merchants, produced an antipathy against the making of exorbitant or unfair profits. Purely speculative sales and practices of price discrimination were also frowned upon. Legal equality between the buyer and seller was sought after by requiring a just equivalence between the price of goods and services and their true economic value.[6] In the words of St. Thomas Aquinas, "if the price exceeds the quantity of value of the thing, or conversely, if the thing exceeds the price, the equality of justice is destroyed".[7]

St. Thomas defended this principle by reference to the Golden Rule: since no one wishes to have things sold to him at unfair prices, no one should sell to another at a price greater than the actual value. Even if the buyer is in great need of an article, the seller ought not by virtue of this fact raise the price; but the buyer in that event may "of his own accord pay the seller something over and above".[8] In determining a fair standard of value, not only the subjective factors of want or demand, as proposed by Aristotle, but also the objective elements of labor and expenses were in his opinion to be taken into account.[9]

----

[5] See *supra* Sec. 14.

[6] For a thorough and scholarly study of the medieval theory of the "just price" see James W. Baldwin, "The Medieval Theories of the Just Price", in *Transactions of the American Philosophical Society,* N. S. Vol. 49 (Philadelphia, 1959), Pt. 4, pp. 21-80.

[7] St. Thomas Aquinas, *Summa Theologica,* transl. Fathers of the English Dominican Province *(London, 1913-1925), Pt. II (Second Part), Qu. 77, Art. 1.*

[8] *Id.* See also Edmund Whittaker, *A History of Economic Ideas* (New York, 1940), pp. 410-412.

[9] Difficulties faced in determining the just price and pragmatic expedients to overcome them are discussed by Baldwin, *supra* n. 6, pp. 75-80; Joseph Schumpeter, *History of Economic Analysis* (New York, 1954), pp. 98-99.

The doctrine of the just price prevailed not only on the European continent but also in medieval England.[10] Its foundations were questioned and finally toppled with the coming of economic liberalism. According to the liberal philosophy, it is not the ethical price, but the price on which the contracting parties have actually agreed which should, as a general rule, be the legally sanctioned price. Inadequacy of the *quid pro quo* for a promise is, under this view, not considered a sufficient ground for invalidation of a contract. As early as 1587, an English decision proclaimed the principle that "when a thing is to be done by the plaintiff, be it never so small, this is a sufficient consideration to ground an action".[11] This principle has become generally accepted in modern law. Courts tend to interfere with the making of contracts only if there is fraud, mistake or duress, or if the contract violates a fundamental principle of public policy.

And yet, the idea that justice requires some measure of proportionality in dealings of exchange has not become wholly extinct in modern law. There are a number of cases in which courts of equity have denied specific performance of contracts when they felt that the prices for goods or services, or some other terms of an agreement, were grossly unfair.[12] This result has been reached especially in situations where the bargaining power of the contracting parties was unequal, so that one of them was in a position to take undue advantage of the other. It might also be noted that statutory provisions against usury contain a limited recognition of the "just price" doctrine by outlawing the charging of excessive interest rates. Modern consumers protection legislation seeks, in various ways, to promote a course of fair dealing in credit transactions.[13] The Uniform Commercial Code enjoins upon the parties to a contract an obligation of "good faith" and frowns upon "unconscionable" agreements.[14] In a different economic

[10] See William S. Holdsworth, *A History of English Law*, 3rd ed. (London, 1923-1924), Vol. II, pp. 468-469; Vol. IV, pp. 375-376. We are not well informed about the actual administration of the just price doctrine in the practice of the medieval courts.

[11] *Sturlyn v. Albany*, 78 Eng. Rep. 327, 328 (1587).

[12] See William F. Walsh, *A Treatise on Equity* (Chicago, 1930), pp. 481-483 and cases cited therein; *Campbell Soup Company v. Wentz*, 172 Fed. 2d 80 (1948).

[13] See William J. Pierce, "Address on Consumer Credit Protection Legislation", 2 *Indiana Legal Forum* 106 (1968).

[14] See Uniform Commercial Code Secs. 1-203 and 1-302. Cf. also the statement by Kessler to the effect that "the conviction is gaining ground that the function of warranty law is to establish a 'subjective' equivalence between price and quality". Friedrich Kessler, "The Protection of the Consumer under Modern Sales Law", 74 *Yale Law Journal* 262, 278 (1964).

context, the equality principle in matters of exchange has been protected in the United States by the Robinson-Patman Act of 1936, which prohibits persons engaged in interstate commerce from discriminating in price between different purchasers of commodities of like grade and quality.[15]

c. Equal Treatment of Equals

This principle, as was pointed out earlier,[16] can be used to support strictly hierarchical structures as well as essentially equalitarian ones. In spite of its flexibility and dependence on historically-conditioned conceptions of equality, the principle has served as a handmaiden of justice in the development of Anglo-American law by subjecting social relations to certain uniform norms of rightful conduct and thereby establishing barriers against an unimpeded sway of a chaotic Nietzschean will to power.

Feudal law offers an example of how the principle operates under conditions of a hierarchical social order. English feudal society was a stratified class society organized along the lines of a social pyramid. At the top stood the King. Immediately below him ranked the feudal magnates, who in certain periods of English history were the true rulers of English society. Various layers of feudal vassals and subvassals subordinate in power to the upper aristocracy formed the next stratum of the populace. At the bottom of the social ladder stood the villeins or serfs, who were unfree in the sense that they were bound to the soil and incapable of owning property.

The relations between these various groups were regulated in part by the general law of the realm, in part by feudal contract, in part by the custom of the manor. All of these three sources of normative regulation sought to invest the various groups in the graded structure with certain definite rights and obligations and thereby to insure equal and nonarbitrary treatment of each class by the law. From the point of view of justice, this had the advantage that relations between members of a superior and inferior group depended on objectively-grounded standards of conduct rather than on subjective attitudes of individuals toward their fellowmen, or on the strength of the power impulse of a particular overlord. A disadvantaged group of people may accept hierarchical inequality on the basis of tradition or religious teaching, but it will expect that those who share a common status receive equality of treatment.

----

[15] 15 U.S.C.A. ≠13.

[16] See *supra* Sec. 14, notes 10 and 11.

The general law of the realm protected the villein against serious acts of mistreatment by his master and interferences with his personal and possessory rights by third persons. It afforded the subvassals various types of action against the vassals and magnates, which were designed to safeguard their estates and the incidents of feudal tenure to which they were entitled. The law also permitted the barons and tenants-in-chief to the King recourse against arbitrary acts of imprisonment, banishment and confiscation by the supreme power.

The feudal contract entered into between a lord and his tenant contained certain general and typical stipulations in addition to particularized provisions adapted to the special situation. As a matter of universal practice, the vassal swore fidelity to his lord and agreed to render certain services (often including military obligations). The lord, in return, granted a fief to his tenant and vouchsafed to him safety and protection — two values which the State at that time was not strong enough to guarantee to all men. Thus, the lord was bound to come to the vassal's aid when the latter was wrongfully attacked, and to assist him when he became involved in litigation with a third party.

In the early feudal period, disputes between a lord and one of his vassals were settled in the manorial court. The lord himself presided over this court but decisions were made by all of the litigant's covassals. It is likely that the lord's social power and his superior position in the feudal hierarchy often gave him an advantage in such proceedings. We may assume that situations arose in which the vassals were hesitant to take a position against the man from whom they had received their land, and from whom they also expected protection against their adversaries. This problem was to a considerable extent solved, or at least alleviated, by the gradual transfer of jurisdiction over such disputes to the general courts of the land. The legal records in our possession do not convey the impression that the royal courts in England gave a one-sided protection to the holders of superior power against persons of subordinate rank.

The local custom of the realm provided an additional source of normative restraint on pure power rule. Although it faded soon as a major branch of the law in English feudal development, it remained of considerable importance to the villeins, who were the stepchildren of the national common law. The general law gave the villein no rights in the land which he was bound to cultivate; if ousted by the lord, he was without a remedy in the courts of the King. But he held his land with rights, and subject to duties, which were fixed by the custom of the manor and enforced by the manorial court.[17]

Deference to political, social and economic power resulting in capricious departures from legally sanctioned postulates of equal treatment can be presumed to occur, to a greater or lesser extent, in every legal system. But there can be little doubt that the existence of a normative system defining and circumscribing rights, privileges and duties, and making available certain forms of redress against breaches of the law, constitutes a potent weapon for warding off, by way of argument, moral entreaty, appeal to public sentiment, or actual invocation of legal processes, many indefensible irruptions of power into legally guaranteed spheres of individual or group autonomy. Whatever brake existed in medieval England against a relentless sweep of feudal power dynamics was chiefly provided by the law. In this sense one may agree with the words of the medieval legal philosopher Lucas de Penna, who said that the law was "a helpmate for the weaker, a bridle for the stronger".[18]

In the post-feudal age, the hierarchical theory of a societal order based on unequal status gradually gave way to a conception of social relations which found the following formulation in the French *Declaration of the Rights of Man and Citizen* adopted in 1789: "Men are born and remain free and equal in rights. Social distinctions may be based only on common utility."[19] This version of the egalitarian credo was influenced by a thesis of Jean-Jacques Rousseau which he set forth in his *Discourse on the Origin and Foundation of Inequality Among Men.* One of the key passages helpful to an understanding of this thesis is found at the beginning of the work:[20]

"I conceive of two sorts of inequality in the human species: one, which I call natural or physical, because it is established by nature and consists in the difference of ages, health, bodily strengths, qualities of mind or soul; the other which may be called moral or political inequality, because it depends upon a sort of convention and is established, or

[17] For concise descriptions of English feudal law see Geoffrey R. Y. Radcliffe and Geoffrey Cross, *The English Legal System,* 4th ed. (London, 1964), pp. 13-22; William F. Walsh, *A History of Anglo-American Law,* 2d ed. (Indianapolis, 1932), pp. 31-56; Sidney Painter, *Medieval Society* (Ithaca, 1951), pp. 11-27.

[18] Quoted by Walter Ullmann, *The Medieval Idea of Law* (New York, 1946), p. 44, n. 6.

[19] Georges Lefebvre, *The Coming of the French Revolution* (Princeton, 1947), p. 221.

[20] Jean-Jacques Rousseau, *The First and Second Discourses,* ed. R. D. Masters (New York, 1964), p. 101.

at least authorized, by the consent of men. The latter consists in the different privileges that some men enjoy to the prejudice of others, such as to be richer, more honored, more powerful than they, or even to make themselves obeyed by them."

It was Rousseau's view that any kind of "moral or political inequality" authorized by positive law which was not in a relevant and reasonable manner connected with, and based on, a "natural or physical inequality" should be deemed a violation of natural law.[21] According to this view, a law making physical fitness a determinative criterion for induction or noninduction into the armed services would be proper and justified. A law making physical prowess a precondition for the exercise of voting rights would, on the other hand, not meet his test, because a physically infirm person may possess the mental powers necessary to make a well-considered choice. In contrast, a statute which denies the suffrage to mentally incompetent persons should under this standard of evaluation be recognized as a rational exercise of legislative power. A salary scale awarding a higher amount of remuneration to the managers of an industrial plant than to the janitor would presumably be accepted by Rousseau (subject perhaps to an appraisal of the size of the differential), if managerial positions were customarily entrusted to men of considerable organizational talent and the purpose underlying the differentiation was to attract persons of superior ability to key positions in society. In that event, the distinction would be based, in the language of the French *Declaration of the Rights of Man and Citizen,* on "common utility" rather than the desire to accord advantages to men solely because of membership in a privileged social class.

The attitude toward human equality and inequality indicated by Rousseau's statement slowly and gradually gained ground in England after the Glorious Revolution of 1688 and in the United States after the Declaration of Independence of 1776. The chief initial impact of the new approach was an elimination of legal rights and prerogatives based solely on birth or special class status, although in England this development occurred more haltingly than in the United States. There remained, in both countries, a number of areas in which the controversy as to whether or not certain legally sanctioned inequalities could be justified by the existence of relevant factual inequalities went through a dynamic and sometimes turbulent phase. The equality of the sexes and of the races posed problems of particular gravity.

---

[21]*Id.,* p. 180.

Aristotle was convinced that woman's "faculty of deliberation" was inferior to that of man; the head of the household therefore should rule over both his wife and children.[22] The position of the English common law during the Middle Ages and, in many significant respects, until the nineteenth century, was essentially in accordance with this view. The wife owed absolute obedience to her husband, and he possessed a (moderate) power to chastise her. She had no right to sue or be sued in a court of law, unless she was joined by her spouse, and the latter was fully responsible for her torts.

The husband's patriarchal power extended to the marital property relations. The head of the household enjoyed an estate in his wife's real property which entitled him to its usufruct. During his lifetime, he was the owner of her personal belongings, including earnings from her own labor, and he could dispose of her movable property (with some exceptions, such as necessary clothing) freely and without her consent, by testamentary disposition as well as by transactions *inter vivos*. The wife had no right to make contracts on her own behalf. The husband had sole and exclusive custody of the children and the right to determine their education.[23]

In the United States, the common law disabilities of women were received — with minor modifications in some instances — into the legal systems of the several States. Courts of equity, in England as well as the United States, sometimes granted relief against the harshness of some of the rules. But the basic structure of the common law of domestic relations exhibited an amazing tenacity and longevity.

In the course of the nineteenth century, a great deal of legislation was passed in England and the United States which emancipated married women to a far-reaching extent from the disabilities to which the earlier law had subjected them. They gained the right to enter into contracts, although in some States of the United States this right was qualified by restrictions. Married women were allowed to acquire and dispose of real and personal property, although in a number of States the husband must join with her in making conveyances or leases of real property, while in some others the community property system imposes special requirements for joint action. Women became capable of exercising custody over their

---

[22] Aristotle, *The Politics,* transl. E. Barker (Oxford, 1946), Bk. I. 1259b, 1260a.

[23] On the common-law disabilities of married women see Frederick Pollock and Frederick W. Maitland, *A History of English Law* (Cambridge, Eng., 1895), Vol. II, pp. 401-403; Edward Jenks, *A Short History of English Law* (Boston, 1913), pp. 222-225; Walsh, *supra* n. 17, pp. 144-150, 389-391; Joseph W. Madden, *Handbook of the Law of Persons and Domestic Relations* (St. Paul, 1931), pp. 82-98, 369-370.

children, and in the course of time acquired a superior right to such custody in case of divorce. They also became entitled to pursue, in their own persons, legal remedies for the protection of their rights.[24]

The nineteenth-century emancipatory legislation still left the female sex lagging in the field of political participation and employment. Women were not permitted to vote in political elections and to serve on juries. Discrimination in employment and salary scales was widespread. Few women were entrusted with executive positions, few found their way into the professions. Furthermore, in the codes of several American States, the criminal law and the law of divorce treated women in some respects differently from men.[25]

The law intervened in England as well as in the United States to remove or reduce some of these remaining inequalities. The twentieth century witnessed the general recognition of women's suffrage, and with few exceptions members of the female sex were given the right to serve on juries. Statutes were passed by the Congress of the United States and the legislatures of several of the states prohibiting discrimination in employment on account of sex.[26] The Equal Pay Act of 1963 provided that women must receive a compensation equal to that of men for comparable kinds of work.[27] The law of divorce is putting men and women on an equal footing with respect to the reasons for which a divorce may be granted.

Some of the laws designed to promote greater equality between men and women have not had the full effect intended by their sponsors. Although the representation of women in government, in industry, in business, and in various professions has increased substantially, the large majority of higher positions in the fields are reserved to men. It is also a fact that, in England as well as the United States, women are found less frequently in the medical and legal professions than is true for most countries on the European continent. Furthermore, it will presumably take some time until salary differentiations based on sex will have capitulated fully before the sweep of the "equal pay for equal work" principle.[28]

---

[24] See Jenks, *supra* n. 23, pp. 305-306; Madden, *supra* n. 23, pp. 99-123, 137-142, 156-158, 371-374; Leo Kanowitz, *Women and the Law* (Albuquerque, 1969), pp. 35-69.

[25] Kanowitz, *supra* n. 24, pp. 27-34, 84-99.

[26] *42 U.S.C.A.* § 2000 (e).

[27] 29 U.S.C.A. § 206 (d) (1).

[28] Dominik Lasok, *Equality of the Sexes as a Problem of Law Reform* (Exeter, 1969), pp. 12-13; *American Women: The Report of the President's Commission on the Status of Women* (New York, 1965), pp. 131-132.

Today's Women's Liberation Movement takes the position that factual barriers to women's employment, based on attitudes of prejudice, have resulted in failure to use the services of women in proportion to their talents and capabilities. The leaders of the movement deplore the fact that, while in theory the highest public offices are open to men and women equally, in practice leadership has remained in masculine hands. In some instances, their insistence on complete equality of the sexes has led to demands that all traces of a double standard in sexual morality be eradicated, and that men must share the duties of childcare and housework. Here again the question raised by Rousseau will remain the focus of inquiry: To what extent can "moral or political" inequalities, perpetuated perhaps by the positive law, be justified by reference to "natural or physical inequalities"? If there should be intrinsic differences between the sexes in addition to the obvious ones connected with the process of reproduction,[29] these may very well not be a reasonable basis for legal distinctions.

Rousseau's repudiation of legal inequalities not reasonably related to socially relevant natural inequalities also has a bearing on the problem of racial justice. In nineteenth-century America, inferiority of native endowment was widely believed to be a characteristic trait of the black race. This assumption of a natural inequality of the white and black races gave rise to numerous forms of legal discrimination. In 1954, the United States Supreme Court took issue directly and explicitly with the inferiority of endowment notion by stating that "many Negroes have achieved outstanding success in the arts and sciences as well as in the business and professional world".[30] The decision in which this statement appeared outlawed segregation in the field of public education. Other decisions, in conjunction with State and federal statutes, proceeded to ban discrimination in other fields, such as transportation, employment, housing and political life. As far as the law was concerned, race was no longer considered a material ground for creating differentiations between men

---

[29] William James, it is reported, was convinced that monogamous disposition of women and polygamous disposition of men was "the secret of life." Hans J. Eysenck, *Uses and Abuses of Psychology* (Harmondsworth, Eng., 1953), p. 192. This view, with respect to the general disposition of women, received a somewhat unexpected endorsement from one of the leaders of the women's liberation movement, Simone de Beauvoir, who stated that "the peculiar nature of her eroticism and the difficulties that beset a life of freedom urge woman toward monagamy." Simone de Beauvoir, *The Second Sex*, transl. H. M. Parshley (New York, 1968), p. 694. Many representatives of women's movements would disagree.

[30] *Brown v. Board of Education,* 347 U. S. 483, 490 (1954).

with respect to participation in political and economic life and the availability of public services.

In actual practice, however, the laws designed to establish parity of the races have often been disregarded or circumvented. This had led to charges that, while the law on the books has proclaimed equality, the law in action has tended to preserve inequality. In this formulation, the charge would be justified only if statutory and judicial standards set up to guide the treatment of racial minorities had remained entirely or almost entirely on paper, producing no significant consequences in social reality. This, however, would not be a true description of the actual state of affairs. Although the gap between promise and achievement is still very wide, substantial gains have been made by the previously subdued race against strong and long-continued resistance. A comparison of the political, social and economic status of Negroes today with that of fifty years ago reveals a record of distinct improvement. Members of the black race have been more widely admitted to the educational institutions of the country. Their voting strength has increased, and they have augmented their representation in legislative bodies and executive departments of government. They have also succeeded in playing a greater role in the medical and legal professions, holding, among other leadership positions, a number of judgeships. These accomplishments are in no small measure due to the legal system as a promoter of equality, and cannot be explained in terms of a conception of law which views the institution as an instrumentality for the consolidation of the advantages and privileges of a dominant elite.[31]

The advances made in the reduction of discriminations relating to sex and race are conspicuous instances where law has performed an emancipatory function. Other examples illustrating this bent of the law can be found in the legal history of labor relations. A development starting with the outlawing of workmen's associations as illegal conspiracies has gradually led to a sanctioning and encouragement of the processes of collective bargaining, with the result that powerful labor organizations in England and the United States have sometimes achieved a position of equality or near-equality with associations of manufacturers and other producers.

d. Equality of Fundamental Rights

Above the entrance portals to the United States Supreme Court building in Washington stands the inscription "Equal justice under Law." The meaning of this motto is not free from ambiguity. It is often interpreted to

---

[31] See Max Lerner, *America as a Civilization* (New York, 1957), p. 518.

signify that justice is a blindfolded goddess who metes out benefits and deprivations even-handedly without respect of persons. This interpretation is not, however, fully descriptive of the conception of justice prevalent at the present time in the United States. Few would argue today that in visiting punishment upon a man his personality, character traits, individual disposition and past experiences should not be taken into account. Nor would it be regarded as inappropriate for a judge to probe closely into the conduct of a litigant in relation to a particular transaction or set of circumstances in order to determine by highly individual considerations whether he has come into a court of equity with clean hands. Thus, it is widely believed that there are situations in the life of the law where justice must shed its blindfold and fix its gaze upon the individual person before the court.

The chief import of the "equal justice under law" maxim appears to be a recognition of the fact that the enforcement or non-enforcement of legal rights should not depend on extrinsic factors such as birth, race, sex, religion, national origin or size of income. This principle goes further than the "equal treatment of equals" because it declares various dissimilarities between men to be inadmissible criteria of legal differentation. Of special significance in this connection is the insistence on uniformity of enforcement with respect to the most basic rights granted to the individual in Anglo-American law. These include the right to life, personal liberty, acquisition and ownership of property, freedom to enter a vocation and conclude contracts, liberty of assembly and expression. As far as these rights are concerned, the law in our day refuses to uphold or deny them contingent on whether or not an individual happens to belong to a certain economic, social, racial, religious or ethnic group. If, in actual practice, the enforcement of a basic right depends on the external status or social position of an individual, a conclusive presumption of illegality attaches to such action.

It was widely assumed at one time that uniform recognition of basic legal rights meant the fulfilment of the promise of genuine human equality.[32] This hope was to some extent disappointed when it was discovered that equality of rights was not always accompanied by equality of opportunity to actualize these rights. The economic depression of the 1920's taught the lesson, for example, that realization of the right to enter a chosen vocation requires more than legal entitlement and willingness to work. Economic developments in the twentieth century have also demonstrated that the right to establish a business may find its barrier in

---

[32] Richard H. Tawney, *Equality* (London, 1931), pp. 99-100.

the existence of large-scale enterprises in the same field whose economic power, although it may not amount to monopolistic domination of the market, will decisively reduce the possibilities of profit and success for smaller competing firms. Two parties may have equal rights to enter into contractual agreements, but inequalities in their bargaining power may compel one party to accept terms which are disadvantageous to it. The right to acquire property may be firmly guaranteed by the law, but in case of indigency the means may be lacking to enable a person to purchase needed commodities.

e. Equality of Need Satisfaction

The deficiencies attending a merely formal grant of rights, unaccompanied by opportunities for their actual realization, have caused a shift of social thinking from abstract rights to concrete needs. This change of emphasis has not been accepted universally in the Anglo-American world, but it has gained sufficient momentum so as to engender, during the last half-century, many programs designed to promote the social welfare by satisfying at least the most elementary needs of men. The following survey will be confined to illustrative developments in the United States.

Minimum wage rates and overtime pay for work in excess of a certain number of hours, covering broad categories of laborers and employees, have been fixed by the federal government and in some of the States. Persons over sixty-five years of age receive social security payments and (within certain limits) free medical care; in cases of special need, some supplemental income and other additional services are provided. Monthly cash payments are disbursed to persons who have a disabling physical or mental impairment, and an effort is made to create economic opportunities for the blind and other handicapped people. Financial aid is administered to poor families with dependent children. There are school lunch programs, designed to provide children with healthful food, and some medical and corrective services are offered to crippled youngsters. Some increase in the purchasing power of low-income families or individuals is aimed at through the sale of food stamps at a discount. There are also in operation various devices for helping needy persons solve their housing problems, such as interest supplements on mortgages for low-cost housing, loans for home improvements, rent supplements for some forms of housing, grants for the elimination of urban blight. There are special programs for combatting poverty in rural areas. Veterans enjoy various privileges, including some priority rights in employment. Temporary benefits are provided for the unemployed. Law offices have been established in low-income neighborhoods to supply attorneys for clients who cannot afford legal services.[33]

These programs are often administered on a cooperative basis by the federal government and the several States. At the present time, the financial benefits provided by these programs are often precariously low. But there is little doubt that, in keeping with a trend observable throughout the world, the endeavor to satisfy at least the most basic needs of human beings for food, shelter, and physical and mental health will occupy a prominent place on the political agenda of the coming decades.

It is worthy of note that a significant difference exists between protection of equality through recognition of fundamental rights and the manner in which equality of basic need satisfaction is sought to be achieved. When rights are granted to all without respect of persons, the law abstracts from the actual differences existing between men, whatever their nature may be. An equalization of basic need satisfaction, on the other hand, requires an acknowledgment of material distinctions between various categories of people. The elementary needs of old men and women may vary from those of people in the prime of their lives, those of children from those of adults, those of sick and handicapped persons from those of healthy and normal ones; families in rural areas may face problems different from those of city dwellers. In order to pay equal attention to the special requirements of each group, it is often necessary for the law to provide unequal services and dispense benefits of unequal size.

f. The Relation between Equality and Freedom

The gains in equality achieved by various categories and classes of people in the course of Anglo-American legal history have at the same time tended to increase the freedom of these groups. When medieval serfdom disappeared in England in the sixteenth century, no man could thereafter be compelled by law to stay put like a fixture on a piece of land assigned to him for cultivation. When women obtained the right to vote and secured themselves entrance into the professions, their freedom of self-actualization and political participation was thereby enhanced. The civil rights legislation, fair employment acts and open housing statutes passed in twentieth-century America, to the extent that they were carried out in practice by the authorities, liberated Negroes and other racial minorities from restrictions to which they had

---

[33] A very useful and concise description of the various social welfare services provided by the United States Government, with citations of statutory sources, is found in the *Catalog of Federal Domestic Assistance,* published by the Office of Economic Opportunity (Washington, 1970).

previously been subject. Legal provisions limiting the right of arrest, the power to seize, search and interrogate, and the prerogative to enforce conformity of opinion promoted the liberty of all, provided, of course, that such restraints on governmental power were administered without favor and discrimination.

An advance in freedom and equality secured by one group may in some instances produce a diminution in the liberty of action for another group. A law prohibiting the owners of hotels and restaurants from denying service to individuals on account of their race constitutes a restriction of personal liberty in the interest of furthering racial equality. The same characterization is applicable to fair employment and open housing laws. When labor unions were granted the right of collective bargaining, capital and organized labor moved toward a position of greater equality, but the freedom of entrepreneurs to determine the conditions of employment suffered a diminution. Although such conditions in earlier times were fixed by contract rather than imposed by unilateral fiat, the individual worker entering into an employment agreement often did not possess sufficient bargaining power to avoid acquiescence in unfavorable terms.

There are also situations in which a legal measure designed to insure equal treatment entails a restraint on the freedom of all who are affected by it, and not only of one particular group. Thus a law which abrogates privileges which certain categories of persons had previously enjoyed with respect to compulsory military service equalizes a public duty without at the same time increasing individual freedom. A statute repealing exemptions from tax obligations felt to be discriminatory also does not bring in its train an augmentation of freedom.

For centuries men have debated the question whether freedom and equality are congenial or hostile values. Revolutionaries and liberals have held in their minds the image of a society in which men and women have become truly free and equal at the same time. Thinkers of conservative learnings have attempted to show that inherent contradictions exist between freedom and equality.[34] It should be clear to everybody by this time that no generalization or abstract theory is capable of explaining the complex relation between the two values. Only in the context of a particular legal measure, and in the light of its concrete effects upon social arrangements and human relations, is it possible to determine accurately whether or not a gain in equality can register as its correlate an enhancement of liberty.

---

[34] A worthwhile and informed discussion of the tensions between freedom and equality is found in William S. Sorley, *The Moral Life and Moral Worth* (Cambridge, Eng., 1911), pp. 102-113.

g. The Other Side of the Picture

An evaluation of the role of Anglo-American law as a promoter of equality is not complete unless tendencies counteracting the successful performance of this role are also brought into focus. The fact cannot be ignored that England, the United States, and other countries within the common law orbit cannot be described as egalitarian societies. Particularly in the United States, the differences in income, possessions, and economic power between the various levels of the population are as pronounced today as they ever were.

Since every advanced legal system operates necessarily as a condominium of equality and inequality, it is natural and proper that many differentiations among men are maintained and protected by the law. This is true, for example, for unequal scales of remuneration and reservation of certain professional and leadership positions to persons with special qualifications. Criticism usually sets in only at the point when inequalities which decisively affect the well-being of large numbers of people are felt to be excessive or unreasonable. In that event, charges are likely to be levelled at the legal system that it serves as the handmaiden of privilege.

A study of American law from this perspective will reveal that those inequalities that have become the source of conflict or agitated debate are in many instances not the result of clear-cut and deliberate legal policies. They are often attributable to the fact that economic power has penetrated into the lacunae of the legal system or profited from the shortcomings of law enforcement. It is true that tax laws have sometimes conferred deliberate benefits on wealthy industries; the much-discussed oil depletion allowance is a conspicuous example. On the other hand, it cannot be ignored that one of the guiding notions of the tax structure is the principle of the graduated income tax, whose rationale is reduction of excessive disparities in income distribution. The fact that, notwithstanding this principle, many millionnaires have paid no income tax in recent years,[35] is to be attributed more to loopholes in the taxation laws and manipulation of assets than to positive legal privileges accorded to the wealthy.[36]

In a similar vein, the concentration of capital and rise of industrial combines has progressed in the United States in this century in spite rather

---

[35] This was confirmed by a statement of the United States Commissioner of Internal Revenue reported on television in April 1971.

[36] For example, provisions allowing the deduction of interest on loans also favor the poor, but (in the case of large loans) can be used to their advantage by the wealthy. Deductible financial losses can be purposefully brought about by the purchase of run-down farms. See the comments on the general problem of tax evasion by Harry W. Jones, *The Efficacy of Law* (Evanston, Ill., 1969), pp. 27-28.

than because of legal enactments relating to trusts. The philosophy underlying the antitrust laws is maintenance of competition among firms deprived
of power to influence the free play of market forces significantly by their
actions. Yet neither the courts nor the Antitrust Division of the Department
of Justice have vigorously and consistently enforced this basic policy. Various
federal executive agencies set up to increase the equality of the American
consumer *vis-a-vis* industry and labor by protecting him against the marketing
of dangerous or over-priced articles have been criticized for bending the laws
in favor of the producers whose activities they were charged with overseeing.
Since, according to the United States Constitution, it is the duty of the
executive branch of the Government to "take care that the laws be faithfully
executed",[37] avoidable failures to comply with this mandate must be viewed
as infringements of law rather than examples of legal protection of special
class interests. This distinction is meaningful as long as non-enforcement is
sporadic, uneven or selective, as is usually the case; it loses much of its
significance, of course, if the law has in fact become a dead letter.

The general conclusion to be drawn from the survey presented in this
section is not favorable to the class-rule theory of law. The view that law,
essentially and primarily, serves the advantage of the stronger groups in
society does not find support in the record of Anglo-American law. Many of
the most significant phases in the evolution of this legal system can be
characterized as successful, or at least partly successful, attempts to emancipate previously disfavored groups from conditions of domination or discrimination and thereby to enhance the freedom and equality of these groups.
The serfs were freed, the middle classes deprived the feudal aristocracy of its
privileges, labor secured tremendous advances, Negroes and other racial
minorities improved their status. Furthermore, the protective laws designed
to curb assaults against life, bodily integrity, liberty and possessions have not
only benefited the upper classes of society.

These statements are in no way designed to minimize the grievous
injustices that untold numbers of people have experienced throughout the
course of Anglo-American legal history. Some of these injustices were created
or maintained by positive ordainment of the law, others were perpetrated in
the absence of law or in defiance of it.[38] Political and religious persecutions,

---

[37] United States Constitution, Art. II, Sec. 3. The observation in the text also holds true
for the inadequate execution of laws designed to eliminate racial discrimination in various areas of the social system. Cf. also *supra* Sec. 12.

[38] On certain forms of corruption of the legal process by State legislatures granting
special corporate charters, which were widespread in the mid-nineteenth century, see J.
Willard Hurst, *The Growth of American Law: The Law Makers* (Boston, 1950), pp.
444-445.

for example, have sometimes been carried on with the blessing of repressive laws, while in other circumstances they resulted from the exercise of naked, lawless power in times of social turbulence. Since, with the exception of rare periods of total social disintegration or breakdown, active dissenters from the established order always have formed a relatively small minority, the incidence of such persecutions cannot be said to offset or overbalance the protections which millions of people have derived from laws proscribing antisocial conduct or facilitating the arrangements of life. On balance, and from an overall historical perspective, it would seem safe to conclude that, for the majority of people in the Anglo-American world, the total impact of the law on their lives has been beneficial rather than deleterious.

SECTION 18
Law, Power, and Social Ethics

When King Hammurabi declared in the preface to one of the oldest codes of mankind known to us that it was the purpose of his legislation to make sure that "the strong will not deprive the weak of their rights",[1] he pointed in this statement to one of the essential functions of legal ordering. An attempt has been made in the preceding sections to demonstrate that the rule of law, in two highly developed legal systems of the ancient and modern world, has provided a counterweight against heavy-handed forms of domination and class rule. The story of these legal systems reveals that law has often served as a potent weapon used by disfavored groups in society to improve their status and to secure gains made in a struggle for a greater share of freedom and equality. A study of the history of other legal orders, such as ancient Greek and Jewish law and the modern civil law systems, will disclose many parallels to the developments sketched in the preceding pages. Although the proposition that in the march of human civilization the liberative function of the law has preponderated over its repressive uses cannot be proved by mathematical figures, a thorough immersion into the historical record substantiates it as a probable truth.

There are, to be sure, turbulent epochs in the life of nations when the repressive potential of the law rises strongly to the surface, often with the result that at the height of the crisis law dissolves into naked power or despotism. Prior to the French Revolution, for example, the threatened

---

[1] John H. Wigmore, *A Panorama of the World's Legal Systems* (St. Paul, 1928), Vol. I, p. 86. My translation of the passage is based on the German rendition of the text of the code by Wilhelm Eilers, *Die Gesetzesstele Chammurabis* (Leipzig, 1932), p. 12.

nobility in command of the State authorized its judiciary to punish acts as infractions against the public order which had neither been defined beforehand as criminal offenses nor could have been characterized as palpable violations of generally recognized canons of right conduct.[2] This state of affairs was experienced by the populace as lawlessness practiced under the outward forms of the law, and it was the cause, in conjunction with many other factors, for a swing of the political pendulum to the counter-extreme of revolutionary violence.

An analysis of law in terms of its functions must distinguish between proper and distorted uses of this institution. There is a good reason why history — with the exception of some short periods of lawless interregna — has never gratified Nietzsche's wish that conditions of law should remain "exceptional" in a world of unceasing power struggles.[3] The reason is that the law is as indispensable to the maintenance of social health as medicine is to the promotion of individual health. A legal system which adequately performs its functions will protect man's bodily and mental integrity, his possessions and family relations, his freedom to act responsibly, and that kind of equality which flows from the common humanity of men. In carrying out these objectives, the law will build fences around domains of arbitrary power which constitute a threat to the realization of these values. The position has been taken in this book that failure of the legal system to impose normative restraints upon the irresponsible use of power in certain sectors of social life indicates that, in the areas left untouched by such legal controls, the will to power has triumphed over the will to law.

Understood in this sense, the law is neither a value-neutral instrument of governmental power nor an invidious tool of class domination. There is, however, one realistic ingredient in the class-rule conception of law which should not be ignored. No social order thus far has eliminated the predominant position of some economic or political leadership groups. In each society there are categories of individuals whose peculiar abilities in discharging the tasks that are given priority in the cultural matrix will elevate them to the top of the social edifice. In feudal society these were the men of military valor and those who were able by paternalistic methods to provide physical and spiritual security to the masses of the people. In capitalist society, the carriers

---

[2] See Paul Foriers, "Les Lacunes du Droit," in *Le Problème des Lacunes en Droit,* ed. Ch. Perelman (Brussels, 1968), p. 22. The situation adverted to by Foriers differs substantially from the early common law system of criminal justice in England when the judge sometimes punished acts, in the absence of statute or precedent, which clearly violated generally known canons of right conduct.

[3] See *supra* Sec. 2, n. 26.

of social power are entrepreneurs who are able to operate a business undertaking with organizational acumen and financial success. In a socialist order, the social planners and managers of public enterprise are invested with special prestige. Since the legal order reflects in substantial measure the fundamental social and economic structure, there will in each society exist legal rules and legal institutions favoring the leadership groups and serving their advantage. This is a consequence of the fact that all societies have a vertical as well as a horizontal dimension, and the dominant position of certain groups does not necessarily detract from the basic requirements of justice as long as these groups endeavor to galvanize the productive and creative energies of the people for the purpose of developing the potentialities of the whole society to the optimum extent attainable under the limiting conditions of reality.

It cannot be overlooked, on the other hand, that there are countries in the modern world in which a substantial part of the legal apparatus is employed by a racial minority in control of the State to hold down a native racial majority. In such countries, the purpose of the law to provide a measure of security, liberty and equality to the people is not, or very incompletely, fulfilled. In this situation, the law rests on an unsafe and precarious basis and may, at some point of the development, cease to be considered binding by those who are the victims of its discriminatory impact. As long as the legal order retains some normative effect, although it is weakened by lack of general approval or acts of civil disobedience, it may still be called a "system of law," but perhaps only in the sense in which a key which unlocks the door only in two out of every ten attempts may still be called a key. When law is no longer able to fulfill the needs of large numbers of people, it misses its chief aim and becomes an unhealthy institution.[4]

Although it is likely that every legal system contains provisions and arrangements which benefit the ruling groups at the expense of the majority, it was suggested in the two preceding sections that the infiltration of power into the legal system occurs for the most part through the utilization of legal voids and vacancies and through the manipulation of enforcement processes. This observation is confirmed by a study of the law in certain countries of the Western hemisphere in which extremely sharp class divisions exist, although constitutional democracy is the outward form of their political organization. A reading of the constitution, statutes and published court decisions in these countries will reveal little of the extent of social stratification, and the law found in the books and cited by the courts may differ insignificantly from

---

[4] Some valuable comments on the functions performed by a healthy legal system are found in René Marcic, *Recht, Staat, Verfassung* (Vienna, 1970), Vol. I, pp. 13-43.

that of countries that have achieved a substantial degree of democratic equality. It is in the interstices, the "loopholes" of the law and the frequent lack of integrity in the enforcement practices (especially in the areas of tax laws, land reform measures, and wage and hour legislation) that the roots of deference to power and privilege will be discovered. And yet, the law has preserved some efficacy in these societies by affording to the less privileged groups some basic protections of life, liberty and property.

It has been the chief thrust of the argument in this book that the institution of law has deepseated roots in the human psyche. It derives its justification and intrinsic validity from the fact that human beings require some security of the person, possessions and surrounding conditions of life, and that they resent losing their basic human quality as self-directing persons and becoming mere objects for others. It was also pointed out that these traits of human nature are opposed by countervailing tendencies, such as the adventurous urge to break through protective limits and the will to dominate other human beings, with the result that the authority and stability of the law are always jeopardized by the dynamic and chaotic antilaw forces so vividly portrayed by Nietzsche.

Notwithstanding the fact that the life of the law is always exposed to perils, the strength of the pro-law forces, buttressed by the need for tension-relieving continuity, is sufficiently great so as to make it unlikely that the institution of law will ever "wither away" for more than short periods of precipitous change. An observation of the world around us gives us much reason to believe — although this cannot be proved by scientifically adequate evidence — that the will to law is stronger in most men than the will to power. The will to law gives preference to order over disorder. It also militates against forms of inequality felt to be unreasonable or oppressive.[5] It is difficult to see how these psychological urges, which seem to grow in intensity as civilization develops, can be satisfied without a legal system providing some measure of security, equality, and freedom to men. The pervasive presence of law in organized societies since the beginnings of recorded history, which has its ultimate cause in certain inclinations of human nature, suggests strongly that mankind could not survive without some form of law, however imperfect it may be.

Although it is unlikely that the law will disappear as an instrumentality of social control, it is possible that some of its processes and modes of operation will be substantially revamped in the future. In a highly complex and fluid

---

[5] "It is not unjust that in the struggle between power and power one of the beings involved shows a superior power of being ... But injustice occurs if in this struggle the superior power uses its power for the reduction or destruction of the inferior power." Paul Tillich, *Love, Power, and Justice* (New York, 1954), p. 88.

societal setting offering some resistance to rational management under strict and unvarying rules, the legal order may, for example, tend to yield more ground to what has been called "discretionary justice".[6] Such a development would entail an increased resort to mediational proceedings as a partial substitute for the traditional common-law type of justice, which decrees a result favorable either to the plaintiff or the defendant. Mediational procedures — which have a historical predecessor in equity jurisprudence — would be characterized by endeavors on the part of the judicial personnel to accommodate the positions of both plaintiff and defendant, bridge their differences by informal and flexible adjudications, and reduce future sources of conflict by appropriate recommendations as to desirable modes of conduct and adjustment.[7] Family law and labor law are areas in which recourse to such forms of the judicial process may be of particular helpfulness.

More far-reaching in its potential consequences is the fact that growing areas of political or administrative activity seem to be arising in which, to a greater extent than is true for mediational proceedings, norm becomes supplanted by discretion as the determinative force in the making of decisions. A conspicuous example in the United States today is the conduct of foreign affairs. There is an international law governing the relations of nations, but it is a weakly developed body of law. Its fabric is shot through with many large holes, and it often fails to provide a firm principle of action for the most momentous decisions to be made by nations. The Federal Constitution also is silent on most of the crucial issues facing the executive branch of the Government in the handling of foreign policy. Political leaders and statesmen are therefore in many instances left to their own resources in coping with the recurrent crises in international affairs, and decisions are apt to be made by *ad hoc* decrees and instructions rather than in reliance on general legal principles.

When discretion is wide because limits of law are absent or uncertain, a displacement of law by power has taken place. But under such circumstances

---

[6] See Kenneth C. Davis, *Discretionary Justice* (Baton Rouge, 1969).

[7] On mediational justice see Filmer S. C. Northrop, "The Mediational Approval Theory of Law in American Legal Realism", 44 *Virginia Law Review* 347 (1958). Mazor seems to assume that a recession from forms of adjudication "designed to yield a flat yes-or-no answer to a question" points toward a "withering away" of the law. Lester J. Mazor, "The Fate of the Law", 4 *Center Magazine* 68, 69-70 (1971). This is not necessarily true as long as decisions attempting to adjust conflicting interests by satisfying each side's claim in part are made in consonance with general guidelines and basic principles of the legal order. See in this connection Ralph A. Newman, *Law and Equity* (New York, 1961), pp. 11-20.

demonstration or maximation of power cannot reasonably be viewed as the determinative goal of action. Power is an instrumental value and not a proper end of individual or social effort. Power means the capacity for achieving an objective, a chance for a man or group to realize their will even against the resistance of others. It is needed to protect a society from harm, to operate a legal system, to carry decisions into effect. But in itself it is aimless, without direction, wholly neutral towards value.[8] If it is coveted as a form of self-gratification and ego-enhancement, the striving for it becomes pathological.[9]

Nietzsche was alone among the great philosophers of the past in his insistence on power as the highest form of self-realization. Plato, Aristotle, St. Thomas Aquinas, Descartes, Spinoza, Locke, Kant, even Hobbes and Hegel, did not hypostatize power into an absolute principle or value.[10] In more recent times, two distinguished philosophers and two influential psychiatrists have decried the fallacy of worshipping at the altar of power. Bertrand Russell said that "love of power, if it is to be beneficent, must be bound up with some end other than power". The end pursued by an individual or group, he believed, should not be a purely self-serving one but must be linked to some purpose which is, broadly speaking, in harmony with the desires of other people who will be affected if the purpose is realized.[11] According to Martin Buber, historical greatness includes power as a means of accomplishing desired objectives but excludes a will to power aiming at the exhibition of might as an axiological goal. The aim of social action, in his opinion, must be a responsible striving for the promotion, maintenance, or renewal of cultural

---

[8] The Swiss historian Jakob Burckhardt went one step further by declaring that "power is of its nature evil, whoever wields it. It is not stability but a lust, and *ipso facto* insatiable, therefore unhappy in itself and doomed to make others unhappy". Jakob Burckhardt, *Reflections on History,* transl. M. D. H. (London, 1943), p. 86. While this statement would seem to be overbroad in its application to the exercise of power generally, it carries much conviction as a characterization of power conceived as an end in itself.

[9] See the citations *infra* notes 13 and 14.

[10] To Hobbes, the comfort, prosperity and tranquility of the citizens were the goals of autocratic governmental policies. Thomas Hobbes, *De Cive,* ed. S. P. Lamprecht (New York, 1949), Pt. II, Ch. xiii. 13-16. Hegel has often been criticized as an advocate of the Machiavellian power State. Friedrich has shown that this interpretation rests on a misunderstanding, and that Hegel considered power a means towards the creation of the ethical and cultural State. Carl J. Friedrich, *Constitutional Reason of State* (Providence, 1957), pp. 91-107; Friedrich, *The Philosophy of Law in Historical Perspective,* 2d ed. (Chicago, 1963), pp. 131-132, 136.

[11] Bertrand Russell, *Power: A New Social Analysis* (New York, 1938), p. 264.

values.[12] Alfred Adler stigmatized the yearning for personal superiority as a neurotic phenomenon and declared that the normal individual will aim at attainments which are of benefit to all. "The views of Individual Psychology demand the unconditional reduction of striving for power and the development of social interest."[13] Erich Fromm advanced the view that the will to dominate arises from a paralysis of the capacity to function as a productive member of society. When men do not relate well to the world and their fellowmen, they will sometimes become obsessed by the desire to exert power over others as though they were things.[14] Although these indictments of power as an end in itself merely represent the views of a few individuals, their conclusions are probably supported by the general opinion of mankind. A close study of history tends to reveal the truth that, while men are willing to fight for general ideas like liberty or community, they are apt to desert the man whom they suspect of being devoted exclusively to his own self-aggrandizement.

If power falls short of supplying a meaningful goal of individual and social action, the only viable alternative to law as a guide to discretion and responsible judgment is reason informed by social ethics. Social ethics, in a long tradition not confined to Christian altruistic morality, makes empathy toward human beings rather than love of power the controlling principle of political action. It enjoins those to whom authority has been entrusted to exercise it for the benefit of the governed or mankind as a whole.

The first powerful exposition of this viewpoint is found in Plato's *Republic,* when Socrates sets out to refute the argument of Thrasymachus that might is right.[15] Just as the primary duty of the physician is to seek the advantage of the patient rather than his own, says Plato, and that of the ship captain to take good care of the crew rather than feather his own nest, so the

---

[12] Martin Buber, *Between Man and Man,* transl. R. G. Smith (New York, 1965), pp. 150-153.

[13] *The Individual Psychology of Alfred Adler,* ed. H. L. and R. R. Ansbacher (New York, 1956), p. 114. See also *supra* Sec. 4. Cf. the observations of Harold D. Lasswell, *Power and Personality* (New York, 1948), pp. 39-58, with respect to pure power-seeking as overcompensation for a low estimate of the self.

[14] Erich Fromm, *Man for Himself* (New York, 1947), p. 88.

[15] Plato, *The Republic,* transl. A. D. Lindsay (New York, 1950), Bk. I. 341342.

rulers of society must endeavor to promote the general interest.[16] The arguments advanced by him to support his position are not merely moralistic ones but also include pragmatic considerations. "Injustice and hatred make men quarrel and fight with one another, while justice makes them friendly and of one mind."[17] A city divided in itself because of the narrow selfishness of its ruling class will be an unhappy city and will become a prey of its external enemies, who will receive assistance and cooperation from discontented groups within its borders. Plato suggests that even from the point of view of enlightened self-interest of those who wield power in society, it is imperative that they act on the basis of principles which give priority to the common good.

Such ideas are no mere figments of an idealistic imagination. History offers a number of examples of rulers who, although they were invested with absolute power, for the most part exercised this power in a way that, in the appraisal of their contemporaries as well as subsequent historical observers, was deemed predominantly beneficial for the society whom they served. The Roman emperor Marcus Aurelius, for example, was strongly motivated by a sense of public duty and by genuine devotion to the concerns of the social whole.[18] Although his record was by no means an unblemished one, most leading historians have viewed the main thrust of his policies as enlightened and humanitarian.[19] History has rendered a similar judgment on the Prussian King Frederick II. He wrote a book against Machiavelli in which he expressed

[16] Bertrand de Jouvenel has made the argument that a wholly self-seeking exercise of power might be preferable to a statesmanship aiming at social perfection. The egoistic power holder, he says, will cautiously listen to public opinion in order to safeguard his popularity with the people, while the zealous crusader for an idea may be ready to sacrifice millions of human beings for a cause to which he is committed. Bertrand de Jouvenel, *On Power* (New York, 1948), pp. 117-118, 124-125, 134-135. This may be true in some instances but history also offers examples of men (such as some of the Renaissance tyrants in Italy) whose egoistic lust for power impelled them to establish a dictatorial rule, perhaps with the help of a military group or entrenched minority, in disregard of popular opinion or desire.

[17] Plato, *supra* n. 15, Bk. I. 351.

[18] "Have I done something for the general interest? Well then I have had my reward. Let this always be present to thy mind, and never stop doing such good." Marcus Aurelius, "Meditations" (Bk. XI. 4), in *The Stoic and Epicurean Philosophers*, ed. W. J. Oates (New York, 1940), p. 571.

[19] See Edward Gibbon, *The Decline and Fall of the Roman Empire*, Modern Lib. ed. (New York, 1931), Vol. I, pp. 69-70; Alfred von Domaszewski, *Geschichte der Römischen Kaiser* (Leipzig, 1914), Vol. II, pp. 217-232; Ulrich Kahrstedt, *Geschichte des Griechisch-Römischen Altertums* (Munich, 1948), pp. 467-468, 483-484.

the thought that the prince should be "the first servant of his people" and treat his subjects not merely as his equals, but also in a sense as his masters.[20] He put his own individuality in the background in a dedicated effort to work for the general welfare, and he accomplished a great deal in improving social conditions in his country. However, his reign was also marked by numerous instances of a ruthless use of force and by evidence of shiftiness in his diplomatic relations and loyalties. Furthermore, he involved Prussia in a war with Austria which he terminated by compelling his adversary to cede substantial and valuable portions of territory to Prussia. Thus the anti-Machiavellism which he had advocated in his theoretical writings was not consistently observed by him as a supreme rationale of political action. Being aware of the discrepancies between his preachings and his practices, he defended his departures from political morality by the argument that in a world dominated by the ruthless play of power forces, scrupulous adherence to ethical righteousness by a ruler might lead to the destruction of his State by its ambitious neighbors.[21]

The gap which so often exists between ethical theory and pragmatic politics was made the subject of analysis by Reinhold Niebuhr. The conclusion at which he arrived was that a sharp distinction must be made between the moral and social behavior of individuals and that of collective entities and States. Individual men, he said, have the capacity to be moral in the sense that they are able to consider interests other than their own and, at least on certain occasions, to prefer the advantages of others to their self-interest. Such achievements, Niebuhr declared, are much more difficult, if not impossible, for social groups and organized human societies. Niebuhr attributed the inferiority of collective morality to individual ethics to a lack of self-transcendence on the part of groups, an incapacity to comprehend the needs of other groups, which results in the prevalence of a collective egoism far more unrestrained than the normal degree of self-assertiveness exhibited by an individual.[22]

The chasm which, according to Niebuhr, opens up unavoidably between individual and State morality is a very wide one, and the somber picture presented by him is, one must hope, overdrawn. In a world threatened with

---

[20] Gerhard Ritter, *Frederick the Great,* transl. P. Paret (Berkeley, 1968), p. 68. On Frederick the Great see also Friedrich Meinecke, *Machiavellism,* transl. D. Scott (New Haven, 1957), pp. 272-339.

[21] Meinecke, *supra* n. 20, p. 302.

[22] Reinhold Niebuhr, *Moral Man and Immoral Society* (New York, 1932), pp. xi-xii, 35.

atomic extinction, there would seem to be every reason to domesticate the power impulses of collectivities to the maximum degree possible. It is not power but *responsibility* that needs to be made the focus of concern in dealing with the great political, especially the international, problems of our time.[23] "To wield power that is neither determined by moral responsibility nor curbed by respect of person results in the destruction of all that is human in the wielder himself."[24] In an age of global interdependence, the responsibility for actions that may have far-reaching repercussions beyond the confines of a particular national group is one that ought to be displayed towards mankind as a whole.

Such general considerations do not, however, fully meet the problem posed by Niebuhr. In an insecure and largely anarchic world, unforeseeable events may occur against whose traumatic impact even the strongest resolve to observe the highest maxims of ethics cannot always prevail.[25] The absence of a world law guiding the solution of such problems adds to the decision-maker's predicament. In an emergency engendering great fears and raising the specter of large-scale disaster, the taking of harsh actions not in accordance with the highest requirements of civilized decency may on some occasions become well-nigh inevitable. The doctrine of "reason of State" (*raison d'état*) has served as a device for legitimizing such actions.[26] Reasonable men will agree that the doctrine should be used with utmost care and reluctance in a world in which a rash act in the international sphere may have fatal consequences. But even in its limitation to cases of inexorable necessity, reason of State constitutes a restriction on the universal scope of social ethics.

Neither law nor social ethics have thus far been capable of providing full security for mankind against dangerous and violent forms of individual or

---

[23] See Buber, *supra* n. 12, p. 153.

[24] Romano Guardini, *Power and Responsibility*, transl. E. C. Briefs (Chicago, 1961), p. 63.

[25] In individual ethics, the decision-maker faces a purely personal responsibility. In collective ethics, he exercises responsibility not only for himself but vicariously for an entire group. Unless he is a leader of unusual fortitude and persuasiveness, he will attempt to find some common denominator, acceptable to the group, of principles and rationales by which he can explain and justify his course of action. This group standard (into which fear, distrust, and mass emotions might enter) is prone to be below the level of individual ethical conduct.

[26] On *raison d'etat* see Meinecke, *supra* n. 20, pp. 1-22; Friedrich, *Constitutional Reason of State, pp. 1-14, 108-119; Gerhard Ritter*, The Corrupting Influence of Power, transl. F. W. Pick (Hadleigh, Eng., 1952). See also the observations by Ludwig von Bertalanffy, *Robots, Men, and Minds* (New York, 1967), pp. 48-51.

group assertiveness. These two agencies of social control also have often not been in a position to protect men against a chaotic and destructive roaming of the will to power. As Meinecke has shown in a profound analysis, these shortcomings of human normative control are due to an everpresent hiatus between nature and spirit, passion and reason, actuality and potentiality.[27] Especially in a great crisis when large aggregates of human beings become entangled in a bewildering play of historical forces, the calming of explosive emotions and panic-producing fears requires an almost superhuman effort. But it can hardly be gainsaid that a persistent endeavor to bridge the gap between the rational and irrational sides of human nature was never more urgently needed than in the time in which we live.

---

[27] Meinecke, *supra* n. 20, pp. 423-433. See the review of the book by Friedrich, *supra* n. 26, pp. 120-128.

Power, Law, and Society discusses the role of law in the context of its psychological roots in human nature. Particular emphasis is placed on the relation between the power impulse and law.

The first part of the book contains a discussion and critique of Friedrich Nietzsche's political and legal philosophy—a subject which has received little attention in the literature on law. The second part deals with the problem of stability and growth in law. The third part analyzes and evaluates the historical record of Roman and Anglo-American law in curbing oppressive forms of domination and promoting some measure of human equality.

Professor Bodenheimer in this book seeks to answer the arguments of those contemporary skeptics who view the institution of law as a tool of repression, destined to "wither away" in the society of the future, rather than as a beneficial antidote to an unrestrained reaming of a Nietzschean "will to power."

On the basis of evidence drawn from anthropological, psychological, and historical sources, he shows that there exists a "will to law" rooted in certain basic traits and needs of human beings. This, he says, renders the institution of law a necessary and presumably enduring aspect of human life in society as long as it remains faithful to its social and ethical objectives.

Students of law and legal practitioners will find this book particularly meaningful. The book is also addressed to those studying political science, sociology, and philosophy.